WHEN THE WORLD DIES

WHEN THE WORLD DIES

LIFE AND DEATH IN AN AGE OF INFAMY

D.E. DAVIS

Torchflame Books
Vista, CA

ISBN: 978-1-61153-685-0 (paperback)

ISBN: 978-1-61153-686-7 (ebook)

ISBN: 978-1-61153-687-4 (large print)

Library of Congress Control Number: 2025913522

When the World Dies is published by: Torchflame Books, an imprint of Top Reads Publishing, LLC, 1035 E. Vista Way, Suite 205, Vista, CA 92084, USA

Cover design and interior layout: Jori Hanna

The publisher is not responsible for websites or social media accounts (or their content) that are not owned by the publisher.

Portions of chapters VI and VIII are reprinted by permission of the University of Missouri Press.

Bible quotations are taken from the King James Version (KJV). The KJV is in the public domain.

For Chaz and Peg

CONTENTS

PREFACE

This book tells how and when the twentieth century quickly turned from unrestrained optimism to cautious pessimism, carrying into the twenty-first century. That trajectory began with the Parisian Exhibition Universelle of 1900. The marvels of science and technology were glamorized as transforming the drudgery of daily life into a carefree world of ease and comfort.

World War I suddenly changed all of that promise. Its sheer destructive force in human and material costs gave rise to despair and the desperate hope for quick solutions to misery. Communism and fascism resulted. They promised future utopias. Instead, both created dystopias in an Age of Infamy. Their fictional counterparts, like George

Orwell's *1984*, were nightmares. Fascism brought World War II's even more significant destruction and the possibility of a future atomic Armageddon. It turned our Age of Infamy into our nuclear age, one we might call the Age of Oppenheimer, after the name of the father of the atomic bomb, J. Robert Oppenheimer.

I have tried within this big picture to draw several selective illustrations of the broader movement from despair after World War I to our nuclear madness after World War II. I started by looking at literature's reflections on humanity's growing pessimism in the post–World War I's Lost Generation. Then I gave some samples of infamy in Nanking's rape (1937), Auschwitz's genocide (1941–45), and Tiananmen Square's massacres (1989). Hitler's fascism and Stalin's communism provided specific examples of cruelty, such as the Nazi holocaust and communist collectivization. However, the allies in World War II were not exempt from infamy in their firebombings of German and Japanese cities and nuclear attacks on Hiroshima and Nagasaki.

Faced with real dystopias, writers turned to fictional ones to depict what could be worse than the infamy of Hitler, Stalin, or Mao. Finally, my story of an Age of Infamy details the evolution of nuclear policy and efforts to tame the atomic Frankenstein and its relentless march to Armageddon from 1945 to the present.

After all, on some sunny day, you may wake up in a bunker after a nuclear attack and decide to step outside, only to discover that you are one of the last people on earth. Oppenheimer put it this way immediately after the world's first atomic bomb explosion on July 16, 1945, at 5:30 a.m.:

> "We waited until the blast had passed, walked out of the shelter, and then it was extremely solemn. We knew the world would not be the same. A few people laughed, a few people cried. Most people were silent. I remembered the line from the Hindu scripture, the *Bhagavad Gita*: Vishnu is trying to persuade the prince that he should

do his duty, and to impress him, he takes on his multiarmed form and says, "Now I am become Death, the destroyer of worlds." I suppose we all thought that, one way or another.[1]"

Today, we stand on death's "dangerous precipice," as Richard Rhodes put it. He quoted President Barack Obama: "If we believe that the spread of nuclear weapons is inevitable, then in some way we are admitting to ourselves that the use of nuclear weapons is inevitable." One could and did game out such a suggestion with devasting results.[2]

D. E. Davis
Bloomington, Illinois, 2025

INTRODUCTION

NOW IS THE HOUR

> " Now is the hour when we must say goodbye.
>
> MAORI FAREWELL SONG

We live in a tragic era. I call it the Age of Infamy. Its doomsday arrives when the last century's two cruelest ideas, totalitarianism and total war, join hands in the twenty-first century. Some assumed civilization would end quietly from decadence, as with poet T. S. Eliot's whimpering, hollow men, or, as scientist Carl Sagan put it, "We slide . . . back into superstition and darkness."[1] Instead, it may finish in a fiery nuclear exchange. J. Robert Oppenheimer, the father of the atomic bomb, imagined Armageddon as the one he first witnessed at Alamogordo's Trinity testing range. He reacted by quoting from the Hindu scripture, *Bhagavad Gita*: "Now I am become Death, the destroyer of worlds." Christopher Nolan's film *Oppenheimer* visualizes the first atomic explosion at 5:30 a.m. on July 16, 1945. "Oppenheimer was there," Nolan says, "at the moment when the world irreversibly changed."[2] He had become Death, predicting how and when a civilization dies.

Others may also guess about how and when a civilization dies. For instance, art historian Kenneth Clark worried about "that shadowy companion who is always with us, like an inverted guardian angel, silent, invisible, almost incredible—and yet unquestionably there and ready to assert itself at the touch of a button." I guess that any one of us could become, like Oppenheimer, "Death" and press the nuclear button, fulfilling the *Bhagavad Gita*'s warning: the destroyer of worlds. Or, as one of the film's critics put it, Oppenheimer aspired "to create something great, but whose legacy is warped by the terrible things that followed."[3]

This is why I named our era an Age of Infamy after many years of teaching a course on modern history. On the first day of class, I would ask my students to label the twentieth century as the Age of "Something." Many suggestions followed: Age of Aquarius, or War, or Opportunity, or Ideologies, and more. There were no winners or losers, but the "age" game stimulated us to think. This book is about why I titled it *When the World Dies: Life and Death in an Age of Infamy*, defined as a period of history with "an evil reputation brought about by something grossly criminal, shocking, or brutal."[4]

Infamy comes as many "somethings." Today the last century's twin infamies still threaten civilization: totalitarianism and total war. The primary tasks before us are vigilance against the former and elimination of the latter. There are a couple of other points to consider. The first is that an infamous time often turns otherwise reasonable people into mean ones. The second is that such an infamous past may predict how and when our civilization dies.

I often discussed these labels and points with professional colleagues intrigued by my label game. Naturally, they preferred their designations as much as my students and I did ours. British historian Eric Hobsbawm, in the title of his 1994 book, suggested *The Age of Extremes: The Short Twentieth Century, 1914–1991*. I agree with this idea of a short twentieth century and also casting its shadow over the twenty-first century. He meant by that label fierce wars, world revolutions, complete economic collapses, the most fanatic ideologies, abrupt cultural swings, and the end of empires.[5] Nobel laureate Aleksandr Solzhenitsyn said the last century "has proved to be more cruel than preceding centuries." He labeled it as one with "those same old cave-age emotions."[6] That century was much more than just radical or Neanderthal. It was a century of extreme evil committed by ordinary people. Their infamy may remain the common coin of our era, perhaps ending in an eschaton. That is why I champion my label, an Age of Infamy.

I am not alone in my belief. Political scientist Hannah Arendt considered the iniquities of the twentieth century to be extreme and immense in her book *Eichmann in Jerusalem: A Report on the Banality of Evil*. She believed nobodies like Adolf Eichmann committed Nazi crimes. Arendt referred to them by her concept of the "banality of evil." Banal or not, scholar Daniel Goldhagen, in his book *Hitler's Willing Executioners: Ordinary Germans and the Holocaust,* claimed that by 1941–1942, a German consensus existed that the Jews must be eliminated. In *The Origins of Totalitarianism*, Arendt also wrote that a state's total domination—Hitler's Germany, Stalin's Russia, Mao's China—led to the extreme nature of evil. She thought that totalitarianism brought the essential structure of civilization to the breaking point. A third world war would also bring our civilization crashing down.[7] I am sticking to my label, an Age of Infamy, taking cues from these writers.

I propose that modern civilization has bottomed out because of its misguided uses of power, science, and truth. Our civilization's deepest roots were around 800 CE (Common Era) when antique civilization reached its nadir: Either survive the barbarian hordes or collapse. A hero named Charlemagne and his knights came along and saved the West. The new barbarians seek to control the levers of power, including media outlets for propaganda and the military–industrial complex for access to nuclear weapons. They promise to use them. New Charlemagnes must arrive with their legions, or it's curtains for us. We are overwhelmed by the whimpers of transcendent materialism and threatened by the bang of a nuclear war, both of which could end our civilization.

When I say our civilization's survival is on the line, I'm wondering about many things like the rest of you: I'm thinking about the shaky foundations the twentieth century has established for our ongoing civilization; I'm reflecting on how inept our military–industrial complex and its often moronic leadership have become; I'm also considering the noisy truth-deniers; I see our many Middle Eastern fiascos and failures; I worry about conspiracy theorists on the far right and the illiberalism of the far left; I listen to the irresponsibility of media and web talking heads; I am daily exposed to an institutional unwillingness to do anything except squabble; I read about governments unable to find even simple solutions to contemporary problems; I realize the rest of the world probably hates us because of these things; and now Putin's dictatorship threatens civilization with subversion and nuclear war.

The twentieth century reflected a profound cultural shift. As examples, I look at the radical break from the previous century's art as seen in Georges Seurat's *A Sunday Afternoon on the Island of La Grande Jatte*. I compare it to the sensuous abstractionism of Pablo Picasso's *Les Demoiselles d'Avignon*. Or, I contrast the harmony of Giuseppe Verdi's *Aida* to the dissonance of Alban Berg's *Wozzeck*. I once bathed in the optimism of Walt Whitman's *Leaves of Grass,* and now I drown in the pessimism of T. S. Eliot's *The Waste Land*. I ask myself, when did the confidence of Charles Dickens's *Nicholas Nickleby* give way to the hedonism of Ernest Hemingway's *The Sun Also Rises*? My answer is total war and totalitarianism in the last century drove these transformations, and the resulting political and social rifts overwhelmed my conscience and everyone else's. Now there is the ever-present threat of the mushroom cloud.

Sometimes our imaginations expose the forthcoming cultural dispositions that influence the rise of the new barbarians and the downward course of events. For me, two flights of fancy provided the last century's bookends: Robert Wiene's 1920 film, *The Cabinet of Dr.*

Caligari and Stanley Kubrick's 1964 movie, *Dr. Strangelove or: How I Learned to Stop Worrying and Love the Bomb.* Wiene predicts totalitarianism. Kubrick satirizes the dangerous nuclear arms race. Film critic Siegfried Kracauer pictured Dr. Caligari as a premonition of Hitler. Cesare, a somnambulist, is his submissive subject, and the city of Holstenwall is a fascist-like Berlin. The film sees a twentieth century crowded with Caligaries pursuing infamous acts analogous, according to Kracauer, to Wiene's movie and history. Fiction becomes more real than reality. Writer Gertrude Stein's Lost Generation lives in Caligari's surreal world. It has been grossly distorted by its experiences in the trenches of World War I, and it suffers humiliation and death in the desolate landscape that repeats itself in World War II.

Stanley Kubrick explores the threat of an atomic holocaust in his provocative *Dr. Strangelove.* Strangelove shrugs off nuclear catastrophe by assuring the president that humanity will survive in deep caves. Wiene captured post–World War I and Kubrick post–World War II trends. My chapters illustrate the new barbarian mass movements under Hitler, Stalin, and Mao, their willingness to use weapons of immense destruction on their enemies, and their adversaries' use of them in retaliation.

Like everyone who came into the world during the twentieth century, I saw my times almost die of suicide. In his autobiography *The World of Yesterday,* writer Stefan Zweig says the nineteenth century was an "Age of Security." In his opinion, it had political stability, a secure economy, and people with confidence in their futures.[8] The evils of my century destroyed confidence and drove people to suicide. The fascists doomed writers like Stefan Zweig to tragedy, while others, like the cinematographer Leni Riefenstahl, were granted success. Their contrasting lives reveal Hitler's role in their destinies and that of European Jews. The same was true under Stalin in the lives of poet Osip Mandelstam and novelist Mikhail Sholokhov—prison and death to the former, fame and fortune to the latter. At the same time, Stalin destroyed millions of peasants during collectivization. Ordinary folks during wartime were firebombed, like the civilians of Hamburg,

Dresden, and Tokyo. Those of Hiroshima and Nagasaki were incinerated in nuclear storms.

Numerous other examples further illustrate my title, *When the World Dies:* for example, Amon Goeth, who served as the cruel Nazi commandant of the Kraków-Płaszów concentration camp in German-occupied Poland during the holocaust of World War II; the Japanese rape of Nanking in 1937; allied firebombings and nuclear warfare; Mao's Red Guards during the Cultural Revolution from 1966 through 1972; and the slaughter at Tiananmen Square in 1989 committed by Deng Xiaoping. Plus, the twenty-first century is off to a rocky start in the Near East, Afghanistan, and Ukraine.

Dystopian literature, like George Orwell's novel *1984* or Anthony Burgess's *A Clockwork Orange,* projected even worse world orders than the real ones we inherited in the third millennium. Each new brutality seemed to outdo past historical atrocities. Civilized society grew indifferent even to infamies committed on the grandest scale, such as the Nazi holocaust, the retaliatory allied firebombings of Germany's and Japan's cities, and the Hiroshima and Nagasaki nuclear attacks by American bombers to end the war quickly.

Like President Harry S. Truman, we may be either ignorant or unaware of the stark danger posed by the total infamy of nuclear weapons, even though they still threaten our existence. Oppenheimer failed to explain his atomic Frankenstein and angered the president by saying, "I feel I have blood on my hands." Truman told Under Secretary of State Dean Acheson, "I don't want to see that son of a bitch in this office ever again."[9] Truman had ordered the nuclear bombing of those two Japanese cities. He seemed certain America's atomic monopoly would last indefinitely. But the Union of Soviet Socialist Republics (USSR) exploded an atomic bomb on August 29, 1949. Instead of seeking the internationalization of atomic power, the president rushed to develop the H-bomb, or superbomb. The General Advisory Committee (GAC) on atomic energy reported, "A superbomb might become a weapon of genocide." According to Kai Bird and Martin J. Sherwin, authors of *American Prometheus: The Triumph and*

Tragedy of J. Robert Oppenheimer, "even if it was never used, the mere fact that the United States had such a genocidal weapon in its arsenal would ultimately undermine U.S. security."[10]

We may also be ignorant or unaware of that first frightening awe of the observers who witnessed Trinity, the test detonation of an atomic bomb at 5:30 a.m., July 16, 1945, on the Alamogordo bombing range. Chemist Joseph Hirschfelder, the official measuring radioactive fallout, wrote, "Night turned into day, and it was tremendously bright . . . the fireball gradually turned from white to yellow to red as it grew in size and climbed into the sky." Physicist Bob Serber saw a bright violet column rising twenty-nine thousand or thirty thousand feet. "I could feel the heat on my face a full twenty miles away." Another scientist, Richard Feynman, said it was "a big ball of orange; the center that was so bright becomes a ball of orange that starts to rise and billow a little bit and get a little black around the edges, and then you see it's a big ball of smoke with flashes on the inside of the fire going out, the heat."[11]

Perhaps, like Oppenheimer, for all our hand-wringing, we don't regret the bomb's power.[12] The atomic scientists believed they had, of necessity, created the bomb ahead of Hitler, not generally thinking of its possible use against Japan. But the war with Germany was already over when the atomic bomb was tested at Trinity. When Oppenheimer heard of its planned use on Hiroshima, he muttered, "Those poor little people, those poor little people."[13] He spoke with resignation for the Japanese, not guilt, and his thoughts were of his deadly knowledge of the bomb's power. Nevertheless, he told a journalist just before his death, "I have reaffirmed my sense that, with all the black and white, that was something I did not regret." We may have already forgotten about the bomb's power and the possibility of World War III.[14]

Can we neutralize the new barbarians of the twenty-first century, beat down their totalitarianism, and put the nuclear genie back in its bottle? The chances are quickly growing fewer. Perhaps we can—if we can find new meaning in ourselves, our social fabric, and our institutions. The way forward may be by expanding learning and the arts while confronting the barbarians' grunts, insults, and wars, as Charlemagne did in the ninth century. These efforts will require encouragement and patronage at all levels while fighting Neanderthalism in the marketplaces of ideas and the fields of action. The new Charlemagnes might bring about a fresh confidence in ourselves by instituting a modern Renaissance—a recivilization—of intellectual, moral, and cultural courage to combat a whirlwind of lies and destructive activities. That's a tall order.

How are we to distinguish the new Charlemagnes from their impostors? In his 1969 book *Civilisation*, Kenneth Clark characterized Charlemagne and his associates as those who valued learning, patronized the arts, secured the monasteries, and reestablished a connection with the Greco-Roman world. They created the Carolingian Renaissance. These new Charlemagnes, if we may also quote the Roman poet Virgil, would "know the pathos of life, and mortal things would touch their hearts."[15] Then, an Age of Infamy would be replaced by another "Age of Security." This recivilization would restore our moral sense and ideas of reason, beauty, and justice. Unprejudiced people of intelligence would have renewed confidence in their works and institutions. Charlemagne and his heirs took a couple of centuries to accomplish this restoration. Our burning question is: Do we have a couple of centuries left to find ourselves and restore civilization while avoiding more infamy, especially genocide and a nuclear Armageddon? Or maybe we try to escape civilization in some Rousseauan retreat?

We may learn from the infamies of the last century, as I will illustrate in the following chapters. In doing so, we may reinvigorate our institutions to make modern society work. That requires, I repeat, a renewed belief in our society, its values and laws, and our mental abilities. That faith was challenged in World War I and exploded in World War II and the Cold War. It has not yet been restored. Now is the hour to begin a restoration or face the *Bhagavad Gita*'s prophesy.

ONE
WARNINGS OF INFAMY

> Morality was dethroned, the old codes of ethics hung out to dry, replaced with a disillusioned sense of freedom, and the pursuit of this led only to emptiness and futility.
>
> FREDERICK LEWIS ALLEN, *ONLY YESTERDAY: AN INFORMAL HISTORY OF THE 1920S*

Back in the 1950s, when I went to college, the Campanile bells at the University of California, Berkeley campus rang for a moment, commemorating the end of World War I on the eleventh hour of the eleventh day of the eleventh month in 1918. Estimates had the dead at ten million men, the wounded at twenty million, and the total cost at $180.5 billion, with indirect costs at $151.6 billion.[1] British Prime Minister Neville Chamberlain reflected on that day in an appeasement speech of 1938: "Seven million men . . . were cut off in their prime . . . thirteen million . . . were maimed and mutilated, [along with] the misery and suffering of the fathers and mothers."[2] My great-grandmother Anna Urbanscheck and her daughter Annie wept each Armistice Day, remembering a son and brother's death as one of General John J. "Black Jack" Pershing's doughboys.[3] Our culture reflects World War I's miseries, as they left deep emotional wounds and a threatening atmosphere depicted in the Lost Generation.

1. DR. CALIGARI'S GHOST

Critics assessed those miseries and sensed their premonitions of infamy in post-war culture, for instance, in the 1920 film *The Cabinet of Dr. Caligari*. It revealed a German national character susceptible to political agitators like Adolf Hitler. The film's outstanding critic, Siegfried Kracauer, thought that director Robert Wiene had betrayed Hans Janowitz and Carl Mayer's original script by framing it. The scriptwriters raged against Wiene's framing and believed "it perverted, if not reversed, their intrinsic intentions."[4]

Wiene's framing glorified Dr. Caligari's authority over his medium, Cesare, and the madness of the film's young lover, Francis, instead of the reverse. Kracauer wrote, "A revolutionary film was thus turned into a conformist one—following the much-used pattern of declaring some normal but troublesome individual insane and sending him to a lunatic asylum." Kracauer excused this inversion by citing the necessity of selling a commercial product to the masses. The film then came into line with a typical German acceptance of traditional authority. He realized, "The film reflects this double aspect of German life by coupling a reality in which Caligari's authority triumphs with a hallucination in which the same authority is overthrown."[5]

Decla-Bioscop films released this German expressionist masterpiece featuring murder and mayhem. Viewers immediately confront bizarre landscapes of painted sets. They zoom in and out with radical distortions of everything from tilted walls to uneven staircases. The film's crazy gyrations and ghost-like atmosphere defy reality. Wiene intentionally made the story of a madman and harbinger of evil, Dr. Caligari, turn into the delusions of one of his inmates,

Francis. First, Wiene depicts Caligari as a bespectacled carnival vendor with a tall top hat pulled over his head of straggly hair. Then Caligari becomes the well-groomed, respected director of an insane asylum. Film critic Roger Ebert describes Caligari's universe as "at right angles to reality."[6] Three surrealist artists—Hermann Warm, Walter Roehrig, and Walter Reimann—painted the sets.

Janowitz and Mayer's scenario occurs in the fictional town of Holstenwall. It hosts a traveling fair with merry-go-rounds, sideshows, an organ grinder with his monkey, and Caligari's tent containing the curious, coffin-like cabinet of twenty-five-year-old Cesare. He is a somnambulist from birth, whom the doctor hand-feeds. Caligari claims Cesare can answer any question about the future. At the town hall, a pompous city official first turns down the doctor's license for this strange feature. That civil servant is soon found murdered, and the following days feature other killings.

Francis, his friend Alan, and their romantic interest, Jane, wander into Caligari's tent. Fairgoers flock to Caligari's sideshow, drawn by his handbell ringing. Francis, the film's narrator, seems normal. Through the story's framing, he is revealed to be a madman. His narration is delusional. The hypnotized, clairvoyant Cesare opens his eyes and slowly exits his upright, coffin-like cabinet. Alan boldly asks Cesare how long he has to live. Under his master's spell, Cesare answers, "Until dawn."

At dawn, Alan is found stabbed to death, just like the arrogant city official. Suspicious of Caligari, Francis persuades Jane's father, Dr. Olsen, to investigate. With a search warrant, they force their way into Caligari's wagon. Suspecting Cesare of these murders, they demand an end to his trance. However, the police call them away to question a criminal suspect who may have killed an elderly lady.

Francis returns to spy on Caligari through the wagon's window. He thinks he sees Cesare, but it's only a dummy sleeping in his cabinet. Outside, Cesare breaks into Jane's bedroom, planning to kill her with his raised dagger. She screams. He carries her off over wildly slanted roofs, curiously curved and painted walls, and sharply twisting roads.

Chased by her father's mob and exhausted, he drops the soon-rescued girl. According to Francis's delusional tale, Cesare flees, falls, and dies. Or does he?

Meanwhile, the supposedly sane Francis follows the carnival vendor, Mr. Caligari, from his wagon at the fair to the respected Dr. Caligari's sanatorium, where the fair's vendor becomes the director. But Caligari escapes while Francis, the asylum staff, and the police search the doctor's office. They supposedly discover evidence that links Caligari to Cesare. Under the doctor's spell, Francis maintains, Cesare has committed serial murders. Francis insists Dr. Caligari's obsession with Cesare has led him to follow an old medieval tale of an Italian showman who had committed similar crimes under the same name and with a somnambulist. Later, when Francis finally confronts Caligari with Cesare's corpse, the doctor goes raving mad, and attendants force him into a straitjacket and padded cell.

So much for the original story of Janowitz and Mayer. Now comes the framing. Over their objections, producer Fritz Lang suggested a story within a story. Wiene puts that original story into a twisted ending, or frame, that introduces Francis as the madman at the film's start. The first episode begins again, but Francis sits on a bench in the insane asylum's garden and babbles with other inmates. A dazed Jane roams about aimlessly. She passes by them while Francis tells these mentally touched companions about his painful experiences with his fiancée. The scene fades to the flashback of the original story in Holstenwall. Francis and his companions proceed to Caligari's tent, Alan's murder, Cesare's abduction of Jane, and Francis's spying on Caligari. It ends, as before, with Caligari as the madman, screaming while forced into a straitjacket.

That scene fades. There is a final episode or frame. The framing story starts with Francis returning to the mental hospital and mingling with its inmates, including Cesare, looking mournfully at a flower. The director, now a respected Dr. Caligari and his staff join the crazies. Francis mistakes the director for Mr. Caligari, the carnival fiend, and screams. He fights the staff, but they subdue him and jam him into a straitjacket. Dr. Caligari examines the exhausted Francis and tells his staff of Francis's hallucinations of the evil Mr. Caligari. Now that the director understands his patient's nightmares, he can cure him. The film ends with Wiene's framing.[7]

The set designs of Caligari's world remind the moviegoer of gothic patterns. As film critic Roger Ebert put it, they are angular, jagged, and sharp-edged with "spiky leaves, grass that looks like knives." The film's expressionism denies normality and turns reality over to emotional dimensions. Ebert continued by remarking that the town of Holstenwall resembled "houses like shrieks climbing a steep hill."[8] Zigzagged and curved lines adorn the walls, and even the characters and their movements blend into the film's texture. The phantom-like Cesare stalks the city's winding paths and streets. Rather than real people, souls inhabit Holstenwall. The French coined the word "Caligarisme" to characterize this upside-down universe.

Kracauer insisted that tyranny, the film's obsession, pervades the screen to its ending. It is symbolized in the height of chairs and bedsteads or the asylum's three parallel flights of stairs that mark Caligari's position atop the hierarchy. Caligari is a tyrant, controlling Cesare through hypnotism, and he rules the mental hospital's inmates. The director inhabits a world filled with evil people dominating helpless patients. Kracauer sees Caligari as a precursor of Hitler, with Cesare as his submissive subject and Holstenwall as a fascist-like Berlin. Kracauer's analogies between the movie and history have the film predicting a century crowded with Caligaries pursuing infamous acts.

Fiction becomes more real than reality. The post-war world began with a dazed and depressed generation. Francis symbolized it, living in Dr. Caligari's surreal asylum and shaped by experiences of World War I with its haunting landscapes of trench warfare.

The film gives us two sides of Caligari, a Dr. Jekyll and Mr. Hyde character. Caligari is framed as an established director of a mental institution. He will put everything right and cure the insane Francis. In this role, Caligari is the all-knowing master. But what about poor

Francis? No one denies there was a fair with a villainous sideshow huckster. There were several killings. Even the poor somnambulist Cesare, supposedly dead, turns up holding a flower in the final scene. Could he still be the victim of the good doctor? The bespectacled doctor now appears as the well-groomed tyrant of the asylum, not the huckster.

The doctor's curious ambiguity is purposeful on the director's part. Rather than two persons with different personalities, there is a single schizophrenic individual like Dr. Jekyll/Mr. Hyde. Caligari's dual personality suggests Hitler as the split personality in Wiene's framing of the film. This interpretation lends reality to Cesare, the somnambulist. He is not imagined but represents the obedient subjects of Nazi Germany—ready and willing to follow Hitler, believing it is proper and necessary to destroy Jews and carry out his military designs.

Real infamies soon took over. *The Cabinet of Dr. Caligari* symbolizes twentieth-century infamy. Caligari is the artistic product of World War I, the greatest ungluing event of the Age of Infamy.

2. GRAVES'S WAR

Historians prefer starting the twentieth century on June 28, 1914, when Archduke Franz Ferdinand, heir to the Austro-Hungarian throne, and his wife Sophie, Duchess of Hohenberg, were assassinated in Sarajevo. Austria and its German ally blamed Serbia, protected by Russia, an ally of France and Britain. Thus, on August 3, 1914, Germany preemptively attacked France as secretly proposed in 1905 by General Alfred von Schlieffen. Britain came to France's aid while Germany defended against Russia.[9] National animosities, culminating in diplomatic intrigues, brought about World War I. The European state structure, along with its colonial world, collapsed. Modern technology, applied to war, let loose the Industrial Revolution's destructive power on the battlefield.

The symbols of the technological stalemate were the battles of

Verdun and the Somme in 1916, the pivotal year of the war. The Battle of Verdun, fought from February to December, was distinguished by its length and the enormous number of men lost on each side, about 350,000 per side. At the Battle of the Somme, tanks were first deployed but were not enough to determine the outcome. In this battle, from July to November, four hundred thousand British and two hundred thousand French were lost, while the Germans lost between four hundred thousand and five hundred thousand men. Such staggering losses gained nothing in seizing strategic land but only moved the trenches a few miles one way or another. Besides the effectiveness of the machine gun and the use of the tank, gas warfare, submarines, airplanes, and zeppelins made their first appearances. The new quality of fortresses made them able to withstand thunderous artillery barrages. Finally, on November 11, 1918, an armistice was agreed upon after the input of American forces helped turn the tide. (The US entered the war on April 6, 1917.) Russia dropped out of the war at the Treaty of Brest-Litovsk on March 3, 1918. The treaty was made by the communists who had come to power under Lenin (1870–1924) on November 7, 1917, in the Bolshevik Revolution. German Kaiser Wilhelm II abdicated on November 9, 1918, just two days before the Armistice. No war, before or after, has been so costly in human and natural resources. The costs, of course, led to the astonishing political results of the war. The four great empires of Eastern Europe collapsed: Austria, Germany, Russia, and Turkey. Five treaties were signed in the area of Paris by the thirty-two victor states to punish the five losers: Saint-Germain with Austria; Trianon with Hungary; Neuilly with Bulgaria; Sèvres (and later Lausanne) with Turkey; Versailles with Germany. Article 231 of the Treaty of Versailles made Germany responsible for the war, with total reparations set at about one trillion francs. Germany also lost its colonies, divided in two, with East Prussia separated from the fatherland by the Polish Corridor.

In 1929 English poet and novelist Robert von Ranke Graves published his memoir of World War I, *Good-Bye to All That*. The book was "an impressionistic and candid documentary record about a war that Graves was not alone in believing should never have happened."[10] At its core was his rendezvous with death on July 19, 1916, at Bois de Fourneaux. Graves had close German connections to the famous historian Leopold von Ranke's family, and he often visited their Bavarian estate before 1914.[11] His soldiering account provided a path for him to terminate his world of yesterday and announce a new post-war age.

Graves volunteered in the Royal Welch Fusiliers in July 1914. He took officer training, was commissioned as a second lieutenant, and was posted to France in May 1915. By July, he participated in the Battle of Loos and, in September-October, was promoted to captain. In April 1916, Graves was wounded and required an operation in London. He returned to France for the Somme Offensive in July, when he was again injured in a shell explosion, and assumed dead. Found and hospitalized in Oxford, he once more returned to France in 1917 but was repatriated due to bronchitis and nervous exhaustion in February 1918. Graves instructed trainees at Oxford, convalesced on the Isle of Wight, rejoined his regiment at Rhyl, and was demobilized in February 1919.

Graves's wartime account, *Good-Bye to All That*, left the same bitter memories as the rest of the Lost Generation, those born between 1880 and 1900.[12] His biographer noted that it was not the first such book. There were C. E. Montague's *Disenchantment*, H. Read's *In Retreat*, E. Blunden's *Undertones of War*, S. Sassoon's *Memoirs of a Fox-Hunting Man*, and R. Aldington's *Death of a Hero* as well. Graves's book showed the "contrast between an idyllic, pre-war world and the savagery of war [as had been explored by Sassoon] in his semi-autobiographical trilogy." Graves also uncovered and rejected his past by purging himself of superficiality.[13]

The war, these writers insisted, was an unmitigated disaster. Graves summed it up: Soldiers shot their superiors, were falsely court-martialed, and executed. He saw indescribable scenes of warfare: soldiers' brains and disembodied parts gobbled up by rats; whole battalions slaughtered in a single encounter; recruits quickly lost; British soldiers hunting dead Germans for warm clothing; fields covered with dead horses, mules, and human corpses; comrades executed for cowardice and desertion; suicides; the slaughter of prisoners by both sides. He recounts the last dead man he saw in France: "The chaplain was gabbling the burial service over a corpse lying on the ground covered with a waterproof sheet—the miserable weather and fear of the impending attack were responsible for his death. This fatality, as it turned out, was the last dead man I saw in France and, like the first, he had shot himself."[14]

When Graves tried to tell his young son about the time before World War I, the boy looked oddly at his father. "I was born in the reign of Prince Charles's great-great-great-grandmother before airplanes flew, when it was wicked for women to wear trousers or use lipstick, when practically nobody had electric light, and when a man with a red flag was required by law to walk in front of every motorcar."[15] All that was finished by World War I's tragedy. "So, I went abroad, resolved never to make England my home again, which explains the 'Good-Bye to All That' of this title."[16]

Many Lost Generation artists and intellectuals of the twenties and thirties agreed and criticized the middle class for sacrificing its thoughts and feelings for victory. Some artists dreamed of escaping from the corruption of middle-class life. Much of European cultural life centered on finding a new path. German historian and philosopher Oswald Spengler's *The Decline of the West* repudiated Europe. He speculated on civilization's doom. Cultures, he declared, passed through ages. Europe seemed a dated, urban, technical society composed of overly indulged masses. Energy was being drained away from the countryside and concentrated in metropolises that lacked tradition and were unfruitful. Spengler became a precursor of Naziism, though the Nazis rejected him: "But for the official propagandists of the regime, the watchword was total silence."[17]

Other writers also fought against urban life and thought. For instance, Franz Kafka, a Jewish-Bohemian novelist and author of *The

Trial, felt frustrated at bureaucratic irrationality. His alienated heroes came from a world in which power absorbed love. They consented to their destruction by nobodies who used technology to impose authority and execution.[18]

Like the works of Graves, Spengler, and Kafka, James Joyce's 1922 novel *Ulysses* symbolized a cultural break in literature. Joyce substituted the novel's old narrative form for the new and innovative stream of consciousness. He reduced his story's action to a single day in Dublin: "Bloomsday," June 16, 1904. That segmented day is a dizzy array of physical and mental movements.

Novelist Virginia Woolf focused on Ulysses's graveyard scene in. Part II, Chapter 6 ("Hades") at 11:00 a.m. when Patrick Dignam's funeral occurs. She wrote that Joyce lays out not only the nature of death as perceived by the attendees but also makes it the occasion for his own first appearance in the novel, disguised as the "man in the brown macintosh." Leopold Bloom, the novel's main character, meets his creator, Joyce. Woven throughout is the interplay of twelve guests plus this uninvited guy.

The scene consists of an Irish custom of taking the body by a horse-drawn hearse through Irish Town and Tritonville Road, north on Serpentine Avenue, and across River Liffey to Glasnevin (née Prospect) Cemetery. Four mourners seated in the back of the carriage chat about suicides, racism, Bloom's Jewishness, his wife Molly's lovers, and that "lanky looking galoot over there in the macintosh." Nobody knows who he is, and his appearance is sudden and unexpected. Bloom keeps dwelling on him. A reporter wants to know that man's name as the extra beyond the mourners. He bears the dreaded number thirteen, symbolic of death. The speeding hearse, so Bloom imagines, could overturn and send poor Paddy Dignam's coffin spilling and the corpse bouncing out. The attendees witness the burial ceremony with the digging, lowering, and prayers. Afterward, the guests retire to a local pub for more thoughts on birth, life, death, and the afterlife. The new stylistic conversations are between themselves and their thoughts, all jumbled together.[19]

Joyce's modernism arrived as a flash on the heels of the Great War's savagery, mechanization, and colossal deaths. He uses extensive stream of consciousness, where the vocabulary of technology becomes a part of his fiction. Joyce mirrors families, traditions, and society breaking down. His tone of language illustrates the new brutality. Sparse dialogue often replaces former pages dense with words. Now nothing mattered, Joyce suggested. All was futile.

The poet T. S. Eliot told novelist Virginia Woolf that James Joyce's *Ulysses* destroyed the whole of nineteenth-century literature.[20] Likewise, Woolf said about Eliot's *The Waste Land*, "It has great beauty and force of phrase: symmetry; and tensity." She continued, "What connects it together, I'm not so sure. One is left, however, with some strong emotion."[21] More experimentation followed.

Eliot's and novelist Ernest Hemingway's lives were distinctive: Eliot's was conservative and private, while Hemingway's was extroverted and public. Yet, there are many commonalities between them. Although Eliot's sophisticated poetry and Hemingway's stark prose differ, not to be confused with simple-minded ideas, both took a dim view of the post-war Roaring Twenties. Eliot's *The Waste Land* and Hemingway's *The Sun Also Rises* found a Lost Generation floundering in a meaningless universe.

Eliot had a sense of defeat in a civilization he disliked and thought of as destructive, similar to Spengler. Although Eliot himself is often considered conservative and traditional, his poetry is highly innovative. There are paintings by Salvador Dali of timeless, bent clockfaces placed against waste desert spaces that remind one of Eliot's principal symbols—time merging with the past and present, creating a world that is a wasteland. His technique, like James Joyce's, uses stream of consciousness as a problem of time.

Eliot prims pessimism and disillusionment in *The Waste Land*, much like Graves and Hemingway in their own works. In the first section, Eliot meditates on the seasons, with remarks on the barren state of existence. In the second part, he invites us to journey into a desert waste, showing us the reader's fear in a handful of dust. The poem is filled with an air of threatening tones. The third part is an imaginative tarot reading featuring adultery and loss. Eliot accuses us, the readers, of sharing the poet's sins. The final section shows a surrealistic walk through a ghostly London, almost as Orwellian as *1984*, where the reader confronts the corpse of a person who died in World War I. We are trapped in a crowd of dead people, stopped as if in a battlefield trench, and confronted with a maze of foreign languages like Europe.[22]

To Eliot, World War I ravaged Europe and left a degraded mess. Its culture decayed and withered. From his readings, especially of Jessie Weston's *From Ritual to Romance* and Sir James Frazer's *The Golden Bough*, Eliot picked up on the Fisher King legend, whose wounded genitals compare with those of Jake Barnes in Hemingway's *The Sun Also Rises*. Whereas the Fisher King is healed, that is impossible in Eliot and Hemingway's worlds.[23] The Fisher King is Eliot's wasteland. As in the tale, it becomes a description of twentieth-century society.

3. THE LOST GENERATION

Literary critic W. J. Stuckey wrote in the 1970s, "It is widely held that *The Sun Also Rises* is a prose version of *The Waste Land*: its theme, the sterility of life in the modern world. Jake Barnes, Hemingway's version of Eliot's protagonist, is a representative victim of this world. His famous wound, received in the Great War, symbolizes the general impotence of the times." But Stuckey sharply disagreed with this typical interpretation. Indeed, he claimed that Jake Barnes is anything but a victim of this world, nor is his wound a symbol of the general impotence of the times. Instead, Jake and his chums represent the "obvious pleasure Hemingway's characters take in being 'good and lost.'" Only Robert Cohn and perhaps a few minor characters, Hemingway judges, are, as in his case, romantic fools. The others accept that everything is gone. They don't take life that seriously because it's a hell of a world, so let's eat, drink, and be merry.

Stuckey would have us think that's Hemingway's view. Only Cohn believes there's something worth fighting for in life. Even that can't be regained unless imagined. Jake's world is merely a narrative tool, allowing Hemingway to make an objective presentation. Jake can then describe lovely Brett coolly and dispassionately.

Hemingway has us blame the war: "Without it, he would be simply a monster. With it, he is the victim of an atrocious war for whom any allowances can be made." According to this version, Hemingway wants to tell Brett's story of taking over men, taking over the fiesta itself. It's not Jake's story. "Love does not last. *Fiestas* do not last. Generations do not last, not only this generation but any generation." Only the earth abides. What Hemingway offers us, according to Stuckey, is "controlled happiness" or "disciplined enjoyment."[24]

I find it strange to turn the story over to Brett, her affairs, and all the destructiveness they entail. That makes the *fiesta* a symbol of Hemingway's hedonism and pessimism, ending in disaster. They aren't even Hemingway's lifestyle, as Stuckey would have us believe, or Hemingway would never have achieved such success as a hardworking author who was a tireless craftsman. Hemingway projected that persona as if rum and cola were all it took to write masterpieces. Contrary to thinking that the emotional hollowness Hemingway portrayed was done inadvertently and unintentionally, as Stuckey believes, it follows an overarching sense of the age's catastrophic existence due to the Great War. Writer Gertrude Stein had it right: "You are a lost generation." Here, Hemingway shows us what can become infamy, not romance as is generally accepted, but unbridled promiscuity.

Hemingway repeats his reaction of horror at Catherine's death in *A Farewell to Arms*. That is not so-called ironic detachment but a keen sense of what inhumanity has in store for us. As Brett and Jake memorably put it at the end of *The Sun Also Rises*,

> "Oh, Jake," Brett said, "We could have had such a damned good time together." Ahead was a mounted policeman in khaki directing traffic. He raised his baton.

The car slowed suddenly, pressing Brett against me.
"Yes," I said. "Isn't it pretty to think so?"

I see bitterness, not ironic detachment.[25]

What would the new world of the twentieth century be like after
Graves's depiction of the world of yesterday, the one shattered for his
generation by World War I? Hemingway looked back at that new
world of the post-war late in his own life. He reminisced over the
Roaring Twenties by seeing a special relationship between Graves's
experiences in *Good-Bye to All That* and his own in *A Moveable Feast*.
Both were reminiscing about the Lost Generation, a popular term
Hemingway used but did not necessarily believe.[26]

The title of *The Sun Also Rises*, Hemingway's first published novel
and an autobiographical roman à clef, happened as an accident. As
Hemingway put it, the expatriate poet Gertrude Stein and her Parisian
salon of avant-garde artists and writers befriended him. He recalled
how Stein remarked about a garage owner who referred to his inept
mechanic fixing her Ford Model T, "You are all a generation *perdue*."
Stein then used that phrase to label Hemingway's expatriate friends.
"That's what you are. That's what you all are," Miss Stein said. "All of
your young people who served in the war. You are a lost generation."
She elaborated, "You are," further insisting, "You have no respect for
anything. You drink yourselves to death . . ." When Hemingway
objected, she reprimanded him. "Don't argue with me, Hemingway. It
does no good at all. You're all a lost generation, exactly as the garage
keeper said."[27]

Later, he balanced Stein's remark as an epitaph to that first novel
with verses from Ecclesiastes 1:4-7:

> One generation passeth away, and another generation
> cometh; but the earth abideth forever. / The sun also
> ariseth, and the sun goeth down, and hasteth to the
> place where he arose. / The wind goeth toward the
> south, and turneth about unto the north; it whirleth

about continually, and the wind returneth again according to his circuits. / All the rivers run into the sea, yet the sea is not full; unto the place from whence the rivers come, thither they return again.

Hemingway wrote, "When I published my first novel, I tried to balance Miss Stein's quotation from the garage keeper with one from Ecclesiastes." He had thought repeatedly about that one by Stein. Hemingway wondered who was calling whom a lost generation. He would do his best for Stein, but he emphasized, "The hell with her lost generation talk and all the dirty, easy labels." Hemingway's authorized biographer, Carlos Baker, noted the author had toyed with that title and other choices, especially the possibility of "the Lost Generation," before settling on the biblical quote. Carlos thought he believed in his generation, those born between 1880–1900, who came of age during World War I.[28]

While reading *The Sun Also Rises* and *A Moveable Feast*, I once more feel sadness and a tinge of nostalgia for the Lost Generation. I suppose it's because I come down on the side of Gertrude Stein but without her bitterness. Though Hemingway rejected her criticism, the novel again reminds me that those lonely, empty characters surround and suffocate Jake and Brett and their hopeless love affair. It leaves me still wondering where they ended up as they drove off. I don't see the sun ever rising on their Lost Generation. That world is closing in and smothering them. What am I left with to feel about their futures? Not much hope. The standards of yesterday had gone up in the smoke of World War I. It left a dark pale over them. Their sun never rose again.

The darkest moments came between 1930–1945. The Lost Generation, even those angry Germans reaching middle age and voting for Hitler, lived through one of the rarest historical moments when the chips were down. How do people behave when all of their choices are only bad ones?

Then there's Lesley M. M. Blume's recent book, *Everybody Behaves Badly: The True Story Behind Hemingway's Masterpiece, The Sun Also Rises*.

She believes Hemingway gave a voice to the Lost Generation. He eclipses, Blume suggests, F. Scott Fitzgerald as the oracle of the Jazz Age by being the voice of the Lost Generation. As Blume convincingly shows, Hemingway drew his characters directly from companions on Pamplona's real trip. Jake's love interest, Brett, Hemingway modeled after the actual Lady Duff Twysden, who had "something feral" about her and "exuded an air of unattainability." She was a "successful siren."

When Hemingway invited friends to the fiesta, no one could turn down his enthusiasm. With these hard-living lost souls, the trip looked like a powder keg. The Cohn incident with Brett had played out with Hemingway's tennis friend, Harold Loeb, as did the squabbles with Duff's paramour, Patrick Guthrie. The running of the bulls and the bull ring incidents almost followed form, but Loeb was getting the better of Hemingway as "king of the ring." Cayetano Ordóñez, a real-life matador, gave the bull's ear to Hemingway's wife, Hadley. Hemingway and Loeb almost came to blows as the author teased his friend for "running to a woman." They made up but were never friends again.

Out of these events, as Blume puts it, "A story began to shape itself in Hemingway's mind—the intense, poignant story that, in short order, would become *The Sun Also Rises*." Loeb was the "insufferable" Robert Cohn. Lady Duff got branded as an "alcoholic nymphomaniac." Hemingway, of course, was Jake Barnes. Blume concludes, "With the publication of *The Sun Also Rises*, Hemingway's generation—the generation Fitzgerald had written about in *The Great Gatsby* the year before—found that it was not giddy after all. And the label, 'the Lost Generation,' stuck."[29]

A Farewell to Arms tells a simple but tragic love story. While working with the Italian ambulance service during the Great War, an American volunteer, Lt. Frederic Henry, meets English nurse Catherine Barkley. She still mourns the death of her fiancé, who was killed in the war. Catherine encourages Henry. After Henry is wounded, he recoups in a hospital in Milan, where Catherine joins him and tends to his recovery. He falls in love with her. Catherine becomes pregnant but refuses to marry him. After the hospital superintendent, Miss Van Campen, discovers Henry hiding alcohol in his hospital room, she sends him back to the front. Morale on the front worsens. During the Italian retreat from the Battle of Caporetto, Henry deserts the army, barely escaping an Italian military police execution.

Back in Milan, he discovers Catherine's whereabouts. She has returned to Stresa, some ninety-five miles away. Henry journeys there to reunite with Catherine. The couple flees Italy, and Swiss border authorities arrest them. However, they allow them to stay. The couple pass happy months near Montreux. Late one night, Catherine goes into labor. She and Henry taxi to the hospital. Prolonged and painful labor ensues, and Henry wonders if Catherine will survive. Sadly, their son is stillborn. Soon after, Catherine hemorrhages and dies with Henry by her side. He tries to say goodbye but cannot. He returns to their hotel alone in the rain.

Although Hemingway referred to this novel as his *Romeo and Juliet*, the tone is lyrical and pathetic. Hemingway's depiction of Henry reflects the Lost Generation's pathos. The novel's conclusion, in which Catherine and the baby die, leaves Henry desolate, becoming the Lost Generation's emblem.

A Farewell to Arms moved me deeper into the Lost Generation. Graves, Joyce, Eliot, and Hemingway illustrated a break with the past and showed their post-war attempts to start fresh. They expanded on a failed century and initiated discussions of other twentieth-century issues in a literary way. One writer suffered more than just atmospherics. His race and books cost him his life. Let's linger a little longer on fiction turning tragically into real life.

4. A FAREWELL TO EUROPE

The Austrian-Jewish author Stefan Zweig, writing in 1940, compared his two centuries: the one of his birth in 1881 and the other just before his suicide in 1942. He praised the former as the Age of Security for its social stability and scientific progress. He condemned the latter for its sheer destructiveness. Zweig believed that "we know from experience that it is a thousand times easier to reconstruct the facts of an era than its spiritual atmosphere. Its traces are not to be found in official events, but rather in the small, personal episodes . . ."[30] His episodes were first fame, then exile, and finally suicide.

His life unfolded like one of his stories. Readers, intrigued by Zweig's psychological thrillers, found that the Zweigs, Stefan and Lotte, were the subjects of their own tragedy. They committed a double suicide in Brazil's tropical paradise of Petrópolis, just sixty miles north of Rio.

George Gedye, a British journalist and foreign correspondent, alerted Great Britain to the Nazi violence in Zweig's homeland, Austria, and Central Europe. Even Winston Churchill would call *The Daily Telegraph*'s night desk to find out "what Gedye has written." Gedye also attacked Prime Minister Neville Chamberlain in his book *Fallen Bastions: The Central European Tragedy*.[31] He noted the frantic exodus of anti-fascist Austrians, who were often refused entry into neighboring states. Returning, these would-be emigrants were treated harshly, arrested, and their homes and businesses were often plundered by Nazi gangs.

Even before the Anschluss, during Hitler's seizure of Austria on March 12, 1938, suspects, mostly Jews, were sent to the Dachau concentration camp. Nazi sympathizers had quotas to round up cleaning squads, who were forced to scrub off anti-fascist slogans painted on walls and streets during the Engelbert Dollfuss (1932–1934) and Kurt Schuschnigg (1934–1938) regimes. As Gedye put it, "It is impossible for you to conceive of the diseased and degenerate mentality which lies behind the pathological anti-Semitism of the Nazis."[32]

Zweig left after his home was searched, looted, and sold ridiculously cheap. "The sweep of the Nazi scythe continued to cut down ruthlessly the flower of the intellectual and professional life of Vienna, impatient to destroy the last traces of the cultured civilization which for five years had marked the distinction between Austria and the barbarous Germany of Adolf Hitler."[33]

Zweig wrote a biography, covertly used as a primer for Nazi bureaucrats, titled *Joseph Fouché: Portrait of a Politician*. Fouché was the outstanding and most villainous scoundrel of the French Revolution and Napoleonic Age. He betrayed and survived each succeeding regime, finally double-crossing Napoleon to favor Louis XVIII.

Fouché started as a rural school teacher, became a ruthless Jacobin, then the multimillionaire Duke of Otranto. His most famous role was as minister of police during the Directory, where he became a super-spy, the one who knew everyone's secrets while his own remained hidden. His real vocation was as a master political intriguer whose passion was holding power itself. He was the archenemy of Robespierre and played a significant role in engineering "the Incorruptible's" execution on the Ninth of Thermidor (July 27, 1794). Zweig called Fouché the "gambler-in-chief." Hitler's followers shared many of these traits.[34]

Zweig's autobiography, *The World of Yesterday*, reveals an insightful contrast between his youth's nineteenth century and the twentieth century of his maturity. His problem is more than one of Jewish identity or being a spoiled brat of wealthy parents. He could be filled with "portents of destiny" and "detached from daily life," wrote his first wife, Friderike Zweig. He came to prefer silent, efficient women to protect his freedom and privacy for intense work. And that resulted in his excessive fatigue, depression, even fierce and "strange reflexes and fluctuations of mood." It was not without cause that he believed the new generation reveled in sport, not books, in an age of growing materialism.[35]

His generation's optimism and trust were heirs to Europe's rapid progress, great cities, and increased wealth. He said, "Never had Europe been stronger, richer, more beautiful, or more confident of an even better future." This achievement belonged to his parents' generation. Zweig later reflected that "all since have been retrogression and gloom."

Power agitated Europe, setting peoples and nations against each other. Yet, he inquired, "If one asks why Europe went to war in 1914, neither reasonable ground nor even provocation can be found." This well-practiced historian concluded that neither ideas nor frontiers were responsible. It was a "surplus of force and internal dynamics that required a violent release." States wanted more and would not draw back from a game of bluff. There was an unquestioning belief that reason would balk at this madness on the edge of war.

Finally, Sarajevo was the shot that, in a single second, shattered what Zweig believed was the nineteenth century's world of security and reason, the one of his youth. Friderike said, "War was and ever remained the decisive phenomenon shattering his secure and lucid world."[36]

Zweig called the entrance into World War I a "rapturous impetus" and "dreadful hysteria" to the "greatest crime of our time." Its "childish naivety" soon gave way to a "bath of steel" with the "soulless mechanization" of war.[37] Zweig believed the "word" had power and had not yet been overturned by propaganda. He opposed the war and sought Europe's common unity and destiny as a pacifist, even though he was recruited into the Austrian military as an officer in the Vienna War Archives.

By Hitler's time, words had been washed out by lies. Individuals found themselves in the isolation of spiritual despair. People became spiritually numb, and Europe began a long journey into dangerous subterranean currents. When visiting Venice's Piazza San Marco, Zweig saw Mussolini's quick-stepped fascists on the march. Then there started the big lie that the Germans, defeated in World War I, had not lost but were betrayed, especially by Jews. The madness of such a gigantic claim brought the assassination of his friend and Weimar's foreign minister, Walther Rathenau.

In Germany, General Erich Ludendorff was already aiding Hitler's counterrevolution in the Beer Hall Putsch in 1923. Inflation was the key to the German angst, making conditions ripe for Hitler. Weimar Germany felt "soiled, cheated, and humiliated." Germans never forgot or forgave the Weimar Republic. World War I marked the beginning of the end of Austria.[38]

In a chapter of *The World of Yesterday* titled "Incipit Hitler," Zweig recalls when he first heard of Hitler around 1930. And to think, Zweig writes, that this was "the man who brought more evil to the world than any other through the ages."[39] Zweig lived a few hours from Munich by train. Brownshirts (Sturmabteilung or SA) were on the move in nearby Reichenhall and Berchtesgaden, which Zweig often visited. Even Hitler's Munich Putsch of 1923 passed Zweig by, as did the tide of German dissatisfaction in the Weimar years. He overlooked the danger in Hitler's bombastic book, *Mein Kampf*. For Zweig and many others, it seemed unthinkable that "a man who had not even finished high school, to say nothing of college, who had lodged in flophouses and whose mode of life for years is a mystery to this day should even make a pass toward a position once held by a Bismarck, a Baron von Stein, a Prince Bulow." Yet, how foolish it was to think of Hitler as only a "beer hall agitator."

Even when Hitler attained power, the masses regarded him as a "temporary incumbent and the National Socialist's mastery as an episode." Zweig and the rest discovered, "Then it was that the technique of Hitler's cynical genius revealed itself for the first time on a grand scale. Even on the day of his coming to power, there was jubilation in the most diverse camps." They all regarded Hitler as their man, even Social Democrats. "They flattered themselves that a *ministre Jacobin* was no longer a Jacobin; an anti-Semitic agitator become chancellor would, as a matter of course, throw off such vulgarities." With the Reichstag fire, parliament disappeared, and the Nazi hordes smashed German justice in one fatal blow, creating concentration camps and death chambers. The startled world refused to believe. When refugees passed into Salzburg, Zweig still did not think that "my own life and that we all would become victims of the lust for power of this man."[40]

Even in 1933 and 1934, no one imagined the descent into barbarity or that book burnings and pillorying would begin, though concealed from an unconcerned world. "Blood and Soil" writers replaced Germany's literary existence, including Zweig's. "My books had already enjoyed the honor of being widely read by the National Socialists. It had been Fouché in particular which as an example of political unscrupulousness they had studied and discussed repeatedly."

Zweig left Austria in October. His home in Salzburg was searched, then sold for pennies, and his books burned in the Residenzplatz.[41]

By the time of Zweig's fiftieth birthday, November 28, 1931, he had reached the height of his popularity. He could not guess his fate as a wandering refugee and that Hitler would extinguish his achievements. Even though his friends begged him to speak out, Zweig refrained from public condemnation. He refused to criticize Hitler because he believed an exiled writer should not judge events inside Germany.

On Zweig's sixtieth birthday, his race to escape fascism found him and his second wife, Lotte, in faraway Petrópolis, Brazil's former imperial capital. Brazil had granted the Zweigs permanent refugee status. Nevertheless, by November 1941, they had come to a final decision to end their lives there. On February 22, 1942, their bodies were found in a simple, rented bungalow, now the Casa Stefan Zweig Museum. The police described their bodies: "He was lying on his back; she on the right side with her left arm around him."

Life as an exile was a solitary affair, as the acclaimed film starring Josef Hader, *Stefan Zweig: Farewell to Europe* (2016), sensitively captures. Here was the "sophisticated poet-playwright-biographer Stefan Zweig [and] one of the best-known and most widely translated writers" living in a remote tropical outpost. Stefan and Lotte's last "Address Book" of friends, as their Brazilian biographer Alberto Dines named it, helps explain their utter loneliness and hopeless despair.

Their small "Address Book" shows they had abandoned most of their former friends. Only a few remained on the ledger. Dines relates that even Zweig's "guru, tutor, spiritual father, inspiration, and idol for almost three decades [Romain Rolland] simply evaporated." Rolland had "rewarded him with the nickname 'hunter of souls.'" Dines interpreted Rolland's absence as a "tragic element which goes far beyond the mere putting together of an address book."

Dines concluded that the "Address Book," along with Stefan's autobiography, a small telephone book, and a bedside list, represented "the same oppression and sensation of irreparable loss." For Dines, they were "remnants of the shipwreck Zweig depicted in *The World of Yesterday.*" Zweig wrote, "For the most part, I have stopped corresponding and hardly see anyone: I prefer to be alone, which regrettably means with my thoughts."[42]

The nineteenth century of Zweig's birth held all the virtues he saw shattered in the twentieth century of his adulthood. He admired the former century's stability, tolerance, civility, and positive progress for humanity. Those virtues made a productive life possible, even for an "accidental" Jew, as he called himself. He considered himself a citizen of that earlier century's world, which had been thrown into chaos by some overwhelming and unlucky chance and tossed into a mess that it might not be able to emerge from successfully. In Zweig's opinion, positive progress was so wounded that it would wobble and die. It was this destructive spirit that disturbed and destroyed these misfits.[43] The twenty-first century must still resolve that overwhelming and unlucky chance or face its doom.

TWO
CELEBRATED INFAMIES

> Whoever saves one life, saves the world entire.

OSKAR SCHINDLER (TAKEN FROM THE TALMUD)

On December 8, 1941—one day after the Japanese assault on Pearl Harbor, President Franklin D. Roosevelt (FDR) spoke before the joint session of Congress. He began with a memorable phrase: "Yesterday, December 7, 1941—a date which will live in infamy—the United States of America was suddenly and deliberately attacked by naval and air forces of the empire of Japan." He elaborated on infamy because Japan had attacked in peacetime without a threat of war or armed attack. The empire had decided on a premeditated and deliberate deception to gain surprise. This treachery aimed at America's "very life and safety." FDR called Japan's action "unprovoked and dastardly." It posed a "grave danger" by aiming at America's destruction. "I assert," he continued, "that we will not only defend ourselves to the uttermost but will make it very certain that this form of treachery shall never again endanger us."[1]

FDR characterized Japan's action as a state's infamy: It was "sudden," "deliberate," "premeditated," and a "deception" meant to "annihilate." But what of an individual's infamy? Heinrich Himmler, Hitler's Reichsfuehrer of the Schutzstaffel (the Protection Squadron, also known as the SS), explained personal infamy to his SS audience in German-occupied Poland: "Most of you will know what it is like when a hundred corpses lie together, when there are five hundred, or when there are a thousand. And to have seen this through, and—apart from exceptional cases of human weakness—to have remained decent, has made you hard and is a page of glory never mentioned and never to be mentioned."

In her book, *War: How Conflict Shaped Us*, Margaret MacMillan took this quote of Himmler's and commented that what "he was talking about was the extermination of Europe's Jews." Some soldiers, she continued, "come to enjoy the sadistic pleasure of torturing and killing the helpless, and others simply treat it as a job to be done."[2]

MacMillan also refers to Christopher Browning's book *Ordinary Men: Reserve Police Battalion 101 and the Final Solution in Poland*. In his study of a battalion of five hundred men, some were anti-Semites; however, the rest obeyed orders. When given the option to transfer out, fewer than a dozen left, and more uncomfortable for us, MacMillan emphasizes, is that "even the military from good democratic regimes with strong liberal values are capable of committing atrocities. One of the perennial challenges facing even those societies that deplore such wanton violence is to make their military into killers but controlled ones."[3]

In his book *Hitler's Willing Executioners: Ordinary Germans and the Holocaust*, Daniel Goldhagen takes strong exception to all such excuses as "obeying orders." Instead, he writes, "Simply put, the perpetrators, having consulted their own convictions and morality and having judged the mass annihilation of Jews to be right, did not *want* to say 'no.'"[4]

The following are infamous examples of not wanting to say no. They are found in a world like Dr. Caligari's insane asylum, turned criminal, shocking, and brutal.

1. NANKING'S RAPE

In 1931 Japan occupied Manchuria, a Chinese province, and transformed it into the Japanese puppet state of Manchukuo. It was the first step in its drive to control all of China. Six years elapsed before the Japanese took the next step in their conquest. In July 1937 Japanese and Chinese troops clashed in Peking in an incident at the Marco Polo Bridge. Using this excuse, Japan launched an assault on the city at the end of the month, utilizing massed infantry, tanks, and airstrikes. Soon the town and the surrounding area fell to the Japanese. They adopted a policy in northern China of the Three-All: "Loot all; Kill all; Burn all."

In her book, *The Rape of Nanking*, Iris Chang remarks, "While there was no Japanese equivalent of a 'final solution' for the Chinese people, the imperial government endorsed policies that would wipe out everyone in certain regions in China." The Three-All policy was one of the deadliest.[5]

In August the fighting moved to the south when the Japanese attacked Shanghai and pursued the retreating Chinese army up the Yangtze Valley to the nationalist capital at Nanking. They began their Nanking attack in December, forcing its surrender on December 13, 1937.

The Japanese subjected Nanking to a slaughter called the "Rape of Nanking." Residents were shot, stabbed, and tortured as the Japanese army occupied Nanking. Thousands of Chinese soldiers, shedding uniforms, were caught, executed, and dumped into mass graves. Thousands of others were buried alive. Women were raped and murdered. The atrocities lasted for six weeks and took 260,000 lives. Some experts place the number at 350,000.[6]

John Rabe, a German businessman, kept a diary: "There is not a single shop outside our zone that has not been looted, and now pillaging, rape, murder, and mayhem are occurring inside the zone as well. There is no vacant house, whether with or without a foreign flag, that has not been broken into and looted. There are executions everywhere."[7]

General Matsui Iwane promised amnesty to the captured, but Prince Yasuhiko Asaka turned the Japanese army into a terror machine. The occupation army was encouraged to plunder savagely, torture, kill, and practice rape on the 350,000 remaining residents. Iris Chang details the terror and shows how soldiers changed from innocent youths to blood-thirsty murderers through militarization and propaganda. They "began an orgy of cruelty seldom if ever matched in world history. Tens of thousands of young men were rounded up and herded to the outer areas of the city, where they were mowed down by machine guns, used for bayonet practice, or soaked with gasoline and burned alive."[8]

Chang exposes the ferocity of the sexual attacks. The Japanese raped about twenty to eighty thousand women. Japanese soldiers disemboweled women, sliced off their breasts, and nailed them alive to walls. Fathers had to rape their daughters and sons of their mothers. Families had to watch. Not only were there live burials, castrations, and the carving of organs, but the roasting of people alive became routine.[9]

She also noted that although Hitler killed six million and Stalin twenty million, these deaths occurred over some years. The Nanking terror happened within "six weeks of horror," which she calculated in a summary table: Her totals were estimated at 260,000, perhaps in the three hundred thousand or four hundred thousand range.[10]

Chang concluded by insisting that Japan carried the legal burden and moral obligation to acknowledge the evil it perpetuated and, at a minimum, make full restitution. Her parting sentence offers a path to reconciliation: "These long-overdue steps are crucial for Japan if it expects to deserve respect from the international community and to achieve closure on a dark chapter that stained its history."[11]

2. MICE

The SS killings began slowly and, like gathering clouds, lightning soon struck, following the German army's (Wehrmacht) overrunning of Poland in 1939. By the summer of 1942, the world knew something of the SS slaughter of Jews and other misfits, if only from rumors. After Hitler attacked Russia on June 22, 1941, the Wehrmacht steamrolled deep into Russia, though it halted before Leningrad and Moscow. After conquering Kyiv, it went farther south to attack Stalingrad from August 23, 1942, until February 2, 1943, when it sustained its first significant loss. Again, the SS's systematic extermination of the Jews trailed behind the Nazi army. Stories of this genocide are representative.

Oskar Schindler of Plaszow Deutsche Emailwarenfabrik (DEF) near Krakow, while celebrating his thirty-fourth birthday on April 28, shook a Jewish employee's hand and kissed one of his daughters. Two Gestapo men (Nazi secret police, a branch of the SS) arrested him as a "Jew kisser." Unceremoniously, they threw him into Montelupich Prison. A cellmate named Philip asked Oskar, "What are you in for?" Oskar replied, "I kissed a Jewish girl." Philip hooted, "Oh! Oh! Did your prick fall off?" SS Standartenfuehrer (Paramilitary Colonel) Philip then criticized his fellow SS as thieves, orgiasts, and killers. That shocked Oskar, a provincial Sudetendeutsche who seemed to have forgotten himself and caressed a Jewess. At the cell's Judas window, Oskar handed a noncommissioned officer (NCO) some notes and asked for vodka. The guard returned with a bottle, clean clothes, and books. Finally, claiming status as an essential war producer to his buddy Obersturm-bannfuehrer (Lt. Colonel) Rolf Czurda, head of the Krakow SD (district), he freed him with a parting comment: "[Oskar], [w]e give you those Jewish girls at five marks a day. You should kiss *us*, not them." He added, "Of course, it would be ridiculous to keep you from your work just because you felt up some Jewess."[12]

Certain rumors from diverse sources worried Schindler, along with his curious arrest, that significant changes were coming to Krakow, where his DEF factory was located: Ghetto procedures tightened, tougher Sonderkommandos (Nazi death camp work-prisoners) transferred from Lublin to Krakow, and authorities suggested he establish camp beds for night shifts and procure more Blauschein (workers' permits) for his civilian employees. Most unsettling for Oskar, he saw an invitation for bids on the SS Bulletin Board of Budget and Construction to build some crematoria of extraordinary cubic capacity. Cartoonist Art Spiegelman's father described them: "I came to one of the four cremo buildings. It looked like a big bakery." The son furnished a diagram and drawings of the setup from showers to furnaces to pits. "To such places," Spiegelman's dad noted, "my father, my sisters, my brothers, so many."[13]

Then came an unusual incident that cinematographer Steven Spielberg captured in his film *Schindler's List*. At the Prokocim train depot, Schindler noticed a curious string of twenty or more cattle cars on the siding with people waiting to board, and they had already filled many of these Ostbahn wagons. "Had anyone," he asked, "seen Abraham Bankier?" He was Oskar's office manager, missing along with others of his essential staff. Oskar walked down the line, calling Bankier's name. A young SS Oberscharfuehrer (senior squad leader) held a long list of names. When Oskar spotted some of his workers' names on it, he demanded that they get off that train.

"You can't have them back," said the squad leader. Oskar called out the idiocy and threatened the officer by having his friend by the same name, General Schindler of the Armaments Inspectorate, send the lad to the southern Russian front in a week. The kid stopped the steaming locomotive, called out the names, opened boxcar doors, and out popped the DEF workers. Schindler initialed each name and saved more than a dozen who had forgotten their blue-stickered Blauschein cards.[14]

More rumors circulated about the SS emptying the inhabitants of the Krakow ghetto in an Aktion and their removal to Auschwitz. One story suggested children would go to various places to be shot, operated on, or drowned. Much of this hearsay reached Schindler.

By June, recounts historian Thomas Keneally, they were no longer rumors. He and his secretary, Ingrid, rode horseback to see for themselves from the hills high above the ant heap of the ghetto below. There, they viewed crowds of people around the hospital corner and, closer, a squad of SS working with dogs and entering houses. Families poured forth into the streets, putting on coats despite the heat. OD men (concentration camp guards) with truncheons and Jewish police helped the SS for fear their families would follow. Two lines formed, one stable and the other moving. Evaders composing the first line were shot.

"But worst of all," Oskar concluded about the German treatment, "if there was no shame, it meant there was an official sanction. No one could find refuge anymore behind German culture, nor behind those pronouncements uttered by leaders to exempt anonymous men from stepping beyond their gardens, from looking out of their office windows at the realities of the sidewalk."

Schindler had seen his government's policy on these statements, and it was not a temporary aberration. The SS fulfilled its orders. Any child could watch, even that toddler in red seen in Spielberg's film. Witnesses would soon perish. The corpses littering the streets, those fresh from executions against the wall, were loaded onto the trucks. The SS rank and file strolled among the living and advised them to label their luggage. Schindler had never witnessed such dispassionate horror. From behind his playboy demeanor, he laid particular weight on this day: "No thinking person could fail to see what would happen. I was now resolved to do everything in my power to defeat the system." Schindler understood that Hitler, his entourage, and their willing executioners had turned to the darkest side. They had decided on the industrial means for the immediate mass extermination of an entire race of people. Art Spiegelman, in his Pulitzer Prize–winning book *Maus*, quoted his dad: "Abraham I didn't see again . . . I think he came out the chimney."[15]

Shortly after these Ostbahn transportations and the summer massacres of 1942, when the world still knew little or nothing of Nazi slave labor and genocide, Captain Amon Goeth first entered Schindler's life. Goeth, born in Vienna in 1908, joined the Nazi youth organization in 1925. He climbed the party's ladder in Silesia, administering Nazi efforts to isolate, relocate, and exterminate Eastern European Jews. He transferred to Lublin in 1942 and participated in Operation Reinhard, the code name for establishing three camps: Belgic, Sobibor, and Treblinka. "Goeth was responsible for rounding up and transporting victims to these camps (Verichtungslager) to be murdered."[16] As a member of the Death's Head unit (SS- Totenkkopfverbande), his first assignment started in February 1943, overseeing the construction and command of the Kraków-Płaszów concentration camp. He liquidated the Jewish ghettos of Krakow and Tarnow that spring.

Thomas Keneally, the author of *Schindler's List* (or *Schindler's Ark* in its first edition), mentions that Goeth "arrived smiling fraternally" and toured his two-hundred-acre Kraków-Płaszów concentration camp. He dined with local officials, including Schindler, and visited many construction sites the following day. Amon performed his first of many—between thirty and ninety—summary executions, a symbolic warning of his rule: "I am your god."[17]

On this occasion, Goeth noticed a woman walking around a half-finished building. She was speaking to teams of men, pointing and directing. Goeth asked who was claiming insufficient foundations. "Bring me the girl."

When asked, she reported, "The entire foundations at that end must be redug." She explained that it could collapse. Keneally wrote that it was Goeth's first principle that you never listen to a Jewish specialist. They were, he thought, all in the mold of Marx and Freud. She threatened his integrity. Instead of talking to her, he commanded his NCO to shoot her.

The NCO took her away. "Here!" cried Goeth. "Shoot her here!" Shoving her forward, the NCO took out his Mauser and shot her in the back of the neck. The stunned bystanders got the message: Prompt and anonymous labor was the only chance for the others.[18]

The views of that woman's death strengthened Oskar's determination to keep his factory outside Goeth's camp. Oskar's abhorrence for Goeth grew of him as a man who went about the work of murder as calmly as a clerk goes to his office. Even though they were both grifters, Oskar knew that "the Commandant's being lay beyond the normal rational processes of humans." Even so, explains Keneally, Oskar was "somehow and despite himself fascinated by the evil of the man." They both understood that gratitude meant a payoff in liquor and diamonds. There soon followed the destruction of the ghetto, so terrifyingly depicted in Spielberg's film.[19]

This destruction, according to Goeth, was the greatest gift of the party to the SS. That was the corrupting nature of absolute power. As Keneally put it, "they made death in the same manner in which Henry Ford made cars." The SS plundered and killed with impunity, and survivors went to Auschwitz. Stragglers, taken to nearby woods, were shot. By early 1944, Goeth's labor camp became a permanent concentration camp.[20] It was one of thirteen such camps in Poland.

Goeth's random morning killings often punctuated life as he stepped out on his balcony for fresh air and rifle practice.[21] A host of other stories and rumors floated around the camp and its adjoining factories. Oskar even momentarily convinced Amon to forgive a laggard and, by so doing, become, as the Roman Emperor Caligula once did, an immortal.[22]

Helen Hirsch, Goeth's housekeeper, manicured Goeth's fingernails and watched as he shot his shoeshine boy for faulty work. He hanged his fifteen-year-old orderly at another time because he found a flea on one of his hounds. Goeth executed a servant for lending a horse and carriage without first checking with him. When he ordered the bodies from mass executions exhumed and cremated on pyres, heavy ashes fell like snow on the living.

It bemused Oskar to see his factory personnel take the ashes as if they were grit in the air from some honest and inevitable industrial fallout. Then there was the water incident when Oskar demanded hosing railcars filled with victims headed to Auschwitz, only sixty kilometers away. Goeth and his sidekicks found this sidesplitting, as those Jews would be gassed anyway. Schindler saved Helen's life by a lucky turn of the cards with Goeth and added her name to his now famous "Schindler's List" in a space he had reserved for her.[23]

When Goeth's operation finally closed, Schindler moved DEF and his list of workers to Brinnlitz, near his hometown of Zwittau in Sudetenland. Goeth paid Oskar a brief and very unwanted visit.[24]

The Kraków-Płaszów concentration camp in Poland comprised a group of about a dozen. A survivor testified to Goeth's cruelty and random killings. When Adolf Eichmann sent ten thousand Hungarian Jews there in May 1944, Goeth removed the children to Auschwitz and exterminated them to accommodate the new arrivals. The camp had housed two thousand initially but expanded to twenty-five thousand.

Simultaneously, it acted as a transit facility for another 150,000. Goeth commandeered a villa, cars, and horses for his personal use. If a worker escaped, his whole unit was executed. Furthermore, he had his guards randomly murder between eight to twelve thousand. After the war, he was tried and hanged for these atrocities.[25]

3. THE LITTLE DEVILS

Two of the People's Republic of China's (PRC) infamies deserve telling as historical illustrations of Dr. Caligari's fictional insane asylum: Mao's Cultural Revolution (1966–1976) and the massacres at Tiananmen Square and beyond (June 3–4, 1989).

The first began at Beijing's Tsinghua University, the birthplace of the Red Guards of Mao's Cultural Revolution. On May 29, 1966, students of the university's secondary school first called themselves Red Guards. Though repressed by the university's management, Mao rescued them in a letter on August 1, 1966: "I now give you my enthusiastic support." By June the students and faculty were in violent disagreement over the educational system, methods of study, rights of students, the content of courses, attitudes of professors, and the whole aim and objective of education.

The students were opposed by work teams of about five hundred senior party members, headed by Wang Guangmei, the wife of the chairman of the PRC, Liu Shaoqi. Their Red Guard opponents did not quietly strife at the university. They were noisily victorious in cleansing "wrong" ways of thought at Tsinghua University, and their movement spread to other universities. They sent faculty and administrators to May 7 Cadre Schools, labor camps founded by Mao for remolding thought in two-year terms, living a peasant's life, and studying Mao's Marxism-Leninism. Those who sided with President Liu Shaoqi's revisionist line were called "capitalist roaders."[26]

Liu Shaoqi and his supporters swung hard to the right, reversing the collectivist agricultural policy by returning to reliance on private farming. Internationally, Liu favored reconciliation with the Soviet Union. Liu's group of sixty were branded traitors. Mao attacked their publications.

On May 16, 1966, the Cultural Revolution began with the first "big-character" wall posters of hand-lettered ideographs, exposing Liu as a reactionary capitalist roader. Mao's August 5, 1966, poster read, "Bombard the Headquarters." His enemies were those in power who took the capitalist line. On August 18, 1966, Mao appeared on Tiananmen Square wearing a red armband inscribed "soldier" and received the Red Guards, wishing them well. He repeated appearances five more times as thirteen million Red Guards came to Beijing. They also swarmed over the countryside. Ultra-leftists like Defense Minister Lin Biao joined Mao's crusade, as did Foreign Minister Zhou Enlai.[27]

From May 1966, peaking that summer and into 1968, the Cultural Revolution rolled along, teaching the roaders to learn from the people. By this time, most of the senior leadership had retired. Revolutionary committees, in which the army played a significant role, were set up. People were going to the newly formed May 7 Cadre Schools, which were established after a directive from Chairman Mao on May 7, 1966. Enrollees were sent to work with their hands, cleanse their thoughts, and return to Marxist-Maoist basics. It was, one official said, a "wonderful experience—the great experience of my life." He lived and worked for others by learning from peasants and workers.[28]

China's most bizarre political movement, the Cultural Revolution, would gather momentum, ultimately encompassing the country and its people. At the center of the Great Proletarian Cultural Revolution's inner circle stood Mao's head of the secret police, Kang Sheng, his associate Chen Boda, and Marshal Lin Biao. More visible was the Gang of Four—Mao's estranged wife, Jiang Qing, and three veteran party workers: Zhang Chunqiao, Yao Wenyuan, and Wang Hongwen. All three entered the Politburo, and two served on its Standing Committee.

Why did Mao unleash the Red Guards? There were three possible reasons: first, to recapture the power he believed was sliding away from him; second, to overcome the wrong course for China initiated by his revisionist associates; and third, to set a different path for China than Russia intended.

By 1966 Mao was determined to clear away the Four Olds: ideas, culture, habits, and customs. He told his secret police chief, Kang Sheng, "We must overthrow the king of hell and liberate the little devils. We need more monkeys to disrupt the royal palace." The Red Guards, armed with lists of enemies of the people provided by Kang's secret police, forced their victims to their knees, their hands twisted behind their backs sideways and pointed upwards, in airplane mode, slashed off their hair from side to side in a yin-yang style, beat them unmercifully with brass-buckled belts over their heads and faces, and kicked them savagely.

Mao unleashed these little devils and was freed to wreak his vengeance on the society he ruled. Their formula for extracting a confession was identical to that employed by Stalin's secret police chief Lavrentiy Beria against the old Bolsheviks: no secret psychology, no truth drugs, just beat and then beat again. They severely threatened Zhou Enlai and Deng Xiaoping and dragged Liu Shaoqi off to torture airplane-style. Jiang Qing cried out at a mass meeting on

September 18, 1968, "I'm in charge of the most important case in China. He deserves a slow death by a thousand cuts, ten thousand cuts. Flog the cur that had fallen in the water."

Although Marshal Lin Biao originated the little red book, *Quotations from Chairman Mao Tse-Tung*, it did not save him from Mao's wrath. He received an official anointment as Mao's successor at the Ninth National Congress in 1969 and was made vice chairman and official heir. He suggested that Mao become a super-president: a living god, a philosopher-emperor. Such a scheme would turn over to Lin the actual levers of power; Mao had to remove Lin.

As one of the leading backers of the Soviet alliance, Lin saw Mao's move toward the US in 1971 as his end. He planned a revolt, but word leaked out. He fled to Mongolia, where his plane crashed with no survivors. That left Foreign Minister Zhou Enlai in a powerful position, as Mao embraced the Americans, inviting National Security Advisor Henry Kissinger to Beijing (1971). President Richard Nixon would soon follow (1972). It also weakened the Gang of Four. After Mao and Zhou's deaths, Deng Xiaoping relaxed Mao's Marxism. The Chinese were demanding more freedom.[29]

The second infamy was the Tiananmen Square massacre of June 1989 that ended *New York Times* reporter Harrison Salisbury's long love affair with China. It left him saddened, even perplexed. He abandoned his optimistic outlook and became critical of the PRC in his last book about China, *The New Emperors: China in the Era of Mao and Deng*. As he put it in *Tiananmen Square: Thirteen Days in June,* the communist world disappeared before his eyes. He wrote this with the assurance of an insider: "I think I know China as well as, if not better than, any member of the Standing Committee of the Politburo."

He provided eyewitness testimony from his apartment, room 735 in the Beijing Hotel, to the People's Liberation Army's (PLA's) atrocities when it was all over. He had promoted and sometimes defended Deng's government. He now soured on "men I have regarded favorably and known so long [who] have played a cowardly and despicable role." Deng had blown it and thrown away his outstanding reputation in a mighty carnage. Mao's mad monkeys returned in tanks.

The demonstrations originated in 1986 with a campaign against party secretary Hu Yaobang's liberalism. He resigned on January 16, 1987, and was replaced by Zhao Ziyang. On April 15, 1989, Hu's death touched off immediate demonstrations at Beijing's and other universities, rapidly snowballing into student marches on Tiananmen Square.

As early as April 26, 1989, in Plan A, Deng's government employed military force against the demonstrators, but only after Soviet General Secretary Mikhail Gorbachev's visit from May 1–7. Zhao remonstrated, even complaining to Gorbachev. The party elders and Deng secured the PLA's support.

Party elders drove Zhao from office in the bloody aftermath and compelled Deng to abandon his reforms of opening up China's Marxist policies to Westernization. Salisbury had no suspicion of this. He did not imagine that April's student movement for greater democracy or its escalation in May and June presaged disaster. Viewed against the government's inability to cope with economic problems, it seemed inescapable that a tough decision was inevitable. It would solve nothing essential but terrorize the population and give the party a chance to impose absolute control on an unruly citizenry. That, he thought, accounted for the massacre with its extraordinary firepower and randomness.

The party halted at nothing to retain its power. The thousands of students mowed down on Tiananmen Square were only a fraction of the public liquidated elsewhere in the country. The government's line, broadcast over national television, was that almost nothing had happened except by what it called "bad men" and "bandits." Deng's speech of June 9, 1989, Salisbury believed, betrayed a "baffled, almost bewildered old man, painfully clutching at his vision of a new, open, and reformed China, a China that will go forward to economic vigor and meet his goals for the year 2050." Who needed democracy?

Salisbury came to Beijing on June 2, 1989, traveling from Tokyo.

He saw no troops and found the Beijing Hotel, just off the square, almost empty. From his seventh-floor windows, Salisbury looked out directly on Tiananmen Square. He and his Japanese TV crew went out to look around that evening, but they could take only stills, as no taping was allowed. They saw clusters of youth, a tent colony, and the "Goddess of Freedom" statue in the center of the square—the students' symbol of liberty looming high, stark, and white.

"I had a good look at the 'Goddess of Freedom,' still standing, made of plastic and not very beautiful," Salisbury said. It had been put up three days before, and its placement in the square's center further irritated officials. On TV, they called it outrageous. The students were asking for more democracy over the loudspeakers, haranguing passersby.

When returning to his hotel, Salisbury paused at roadblocks, encountering students at the Martyrs' Column. A bulletin board had notices and posters. One student recognized Salisbury from his face in his best-selling book, *The Long March: The Untold Story*. He promised these students to tell the truth when writing about the demonstrations. They would not live to read it.

Back in his hotel room, he tuned into the British Broadcasting Corporation (BBC), and then he went to bed. At about 2:00 a.m. on the third, he awakened to heavy gunfire on the square, then silence. The BBC and Voice of America (VOA) reported twenty-three dead and hundreds wounded.

By 4:00 a.m. Salisbury noticed large, armored vehicles moving onto the square, bursts of artillery fire, and rounds of automatic shots. By 5:00 a.m. the BBC reported casualties all over the city and enormous carnage in Tiananmen. Tanks were mowing down protesters as they pleaded for dialogue.

By 6:00 p.m. BBC News announced thousands had been killed and reported tanks crushing people sleeping in their tents. Hundreds had linked arms and been shot. Salisbury wrote in his diary, "The impression grows that they are bungling again, bungling the end of Tiananmen just as they have bungled everything about the square since the students first turned out to mark the passing of Hu Yaobang." By midnight he collapsed from exhaustion on his bed.

At 3:10 a.m. on June 4, Salisbury awoke to massive firepower and large deployments of troop carriers revving nearby. Column after iron column went by his balcony. Bullets ricocheted or pockmarked the hotel's sides.

By 7:00 a.m. on June 5, closed-circuit television (CCTV) ordered him to the Beijing airport to catch a plane for Wuhan. BBC claimed the death toll was in the thousands. Salisbury telephoned his wife, Charlotte, who told him she "had seen incredible footage of the PLA mowing down the kids on Tiananmen." He packed his gear and by 8:00 a.m. met a van for the airport. He saw tanks occupying the hotel's courtyard and soldiers shooting at anyone on the street. His minibus made its way through the complex of hutongs (alleys formed by lines of siheyuan, traditional courtyard residences) rather than the highways.

By 8:00 p.m. Salisbury's plane reached Wuhan. There, on his trusty 1942 Remington portable, he typed his op-ed piece for *The New York Times*. "I proclaimed the end of the Deng Xiaoping era of enlightenment and opening a new regime that would be run by the doctrine of 'authoritarianism,'" he wrote.

From there, he wandered from Jiujiang to Lushan, Nanchang, Canton, and a plane home. He was eager to leave because he feared being a hostage in exchange for Fang Lizhi, the famous dissident holed up in the US Embassy.

Meanwhile, Chinese TV chattered about the bravery of the soldiers and showed endless visits of dignitaries to the hospitals to honor them. It characterized students as "bad men" and "bandits" by reversing the order of events. According to TV moderators, demonstrators attacked troops, who reluctantly opened fire, and innocents died in the melee. Salisbury reluctantly ended on the note that Deng was responsible, with Yang Shangkun as his chief of staff. The party elders cheered while Zhao Ziyang fell from power. Salisbury lamented, "To think I know the men who did this."[30]

In the aftermath, the title of his *New Long March* book, which intended to praise Deng Xiaoping, changed significantly to *The New Emperors*. This title reflected Salisbury's realization that China remained authoritarian, perhaps forever. In a letter to his sister Jan, he wrote, "I am just back from China having quite by accident stumbled in on Tiananmen, at the Beijing Hotel when it all went up in the god damndest spate of bullets I've ever seen and that includes a good many wars." He saw no better direction for China. Deng, he wrote, ". . . just at the edge of dotage Yang Shangkun is running the army. There is a council of geriatrics and a few younger (sixtyish men) and a slain generation of wonderful young people and fine intellectuals."

Salisbury could not foretell China's future. He spoke with Professor John K. Fairbank of Harvard, who called him a worm for suggesting the Chinese could be educated and enlightened. He talked with diplomat George F. Kennan, who sympathized with China and added that no one understood Russia. Salisbury wrote to Harvard's Yao Wei, "I cannot tell you how appalled I am at the way things have gone beginning with Tiananmen."

Yet, until the end of his life, he remained cautiously hopeful about China. "I think it will get back to the Deng Xiaoping path. Don't see any other. I could be very wrong." He was right only in the sense that China is a fantastic story of modernization. He did not mention anything about China remaining a communist totalitarian state.

These singular incidents—the killing fields in Asia and Europe—reflected the onset of the total wars and totalitarianisms that would characterize the twentieth century and threaten the twenty-first century.

THREE
HITLER'S INFAMY

> The Jews are undoubtedly a race, but they are not human.

ADOLF HITLER, AS QUOTED BY ART SPIEGELMAN,
THE COMPLETE MAUS: A SURVIVOR'S TALE

"Each activity and each need of the individual," Hitler wrote, "will be regulated by the Party as the representative of the general good. There will be no license, no free space in which the individual belongs to himself. The decisive factor is that the State, through the Party, is supreme."[1]

Mussolini defined totalitarianism as "all within the state, none outside the state, none against the state."[2] Its three essential ingredients are the state's one-party ideology of its one-party, the one party reinforced by its secret police, and the one party's state monopolizing an industrialized, mass society. A universal totalitarian state might be established and maintained by exploiting these characteristics.

This new form of government first arose in Italy out of the chaos of

World War I. Its mass appeal lies in ideologically answering all questions, however true or false those answers may be. Such an all-embracing ideology as fascism provides the inner dynamic to remake everything. "Reconstituting" is necessary because the new elite considers former values and institutions decadent. The leader promises a glorious future when totalitarianism's values have been achieved by racial, class, and military means.

One of Hitler's new elite, Albert Speer, joined the Nazi Party in 1931. After spending twenty years in prison for his war crimes, Speer revealed the inner dynamics of totalitarianism through a close personal relationship with Hitler in his 1969 book *Inside the Third Reich*.

1. SPEER'S DEVIL

Only a fourteen-foot-high, heavy, load-bearing cement object remains complete for a man who dreamed of titanic buildings. Albert Speer used it for measuring ground subsidence in feasibility studies for Hitler's proposed Triumphal Arch. Many planned buildings would be placed along Welthauptstadt Boulevard, Germania's (Berlin's) equivalent of the Champs-Élysées. Speer's cylinder is now a protected landmark for all that's left of Germania. His other bombed-out residuals are scattered about Germany, most impressively the partially standing tribune at Zeppelin Field's stadium in Nuremberg, once the place for annual Nazi Party rallies.[3]

Albert Speer, alone among the twenty-one highest-ranking Nazi war criminals tried at Nuremberg in 1946, declared, "They were," in their final speeches, "our last chance to address our people, but also our last chance, by admitting our guilt, by facing the crimes of the past squarely, to show the nation that we had led astray a way out of its quandary." A few, like Speer, regretted the terrible crimes. Even Hermann Goering condemned them, as did Field Marshal Wilhelm Keitel. Hans Frank took Hitler to task, as did Julius Streicher. Walther Funk felt shame, and Hjalmar Schacht was shaken to the depths of his soul. So was Fritz Sauckel. For Franz von Papen, evil proved more decisive than good. Finally, Hans Fritzsche said the destruction of five million Jews was a gruesome warning. Every defendant, except Speer, denied any guilt.

Speer also pointed out a new feature of modern society besides human depravity: technology. Its instruments, everything from the telephone to the teletype, gave totalitarian dictators unmeasured, direct, and indirect control of the masses. "Hitler," he said, "was the first to be able to employ the implements of technology to multiply crime." For his own complicity, Speer was sentenced to twenty years imprisonment at Spandau in West Berlin.[4]

Twelve defendants were sentenced to death, Martin Bormann in absentia, and the others given prison sentences ranging from ten years to life behind bars. Ten of the condemned were hanged on October 16, 1946. These were prominent members of the political and military leadership of Nazi Germany: Hans Frank, Wilhelm Frick, Alfred Jodl, Ernst Kaltenbrunner, Wilhelm Keitel, Joachim von Ribbentrop, Alfred Rosenberg, Fritz Sauckel, Arthur Seyss-Inquart, and Julius Streicher. Hermann Goering, scheduled to hang, died by suicide using a hidden potassium cyanide capsule. Bormann was also sentenced to death in absentia but reportedly had died by suicide while attempting to escape Berlin on May 2, 1945.[5]

Speer, during his imprisonment, secretly wrote *Inside the Third Reich*. He had joined the Nazi Party as number 474,481 in January 1931. His book depicts Hitler from then until the dictator's suicide on April 30, 1945. Throughout, Speer renders a remarkable portrait of Hitler, much as Nazi filmmaker Leni Riefenstahl's *Triumph of the Will* and *Olympia* had done. Speer and Riefenstahl both lived through Germany's Age of Infamy.

Speer was a product of Mannheim's middle class. His grandfather and father had established a successful architectural firm, and Speer followed. The firm espoused a Neo-Renaissance, or neoclassical style, and it featured popular Biedermeier interiors. These styles, along with the romantic landscapes of Heidelberg's painters, Stefan George's poetry, the music of Johannes Brahms and Gustav Mahler, and Max

Reinhardt's theater, comprised Speer's cultural background. His training took place at the nearby Institute of Technology under Heinrich Tessenow.

With Weimar Germany's growing failure, Speer shared historian Oswald Spengler's pessimism in his *The Decline of the West* and the cult of heroes in Ernst Kantorowicz's *Frederick the Second: 1194–1250*. "In a similar vein," Speer noted, "Hitler cried out against the erosion of morals in the big cities, and he warned against the ill effects of civilization which, he said, damaged the biological substance of the people."

Given this background, Speer was coaxed by his students to attend a Hitler rally. Speer described the audience's wild enthusiasm and the speaker's hypnotic persuasiveness. Speer was carried along with the crowd's emotions. He saw hope and fresh ideas in the coming of a new Caesar. Communism could be checked, and economic recovery would begin. Hitler only mentioned the Jews peripherally. But, repeatedly at Hitler's rallies, the crowd's frenzy demanded victims, and Hitler verbally threw them the Jews: "The Jews are undoubtedly a race," Hitler reiterated, "but they are not human."[6]

The following day, after Speer's first attendance at Hitler's rally, he applied for membership in the National Socialist German Workers' Party (NSDAP). Although he knew nothing about the party's program, Hitler had "taken hold of [him] before [he] had grasped what was happening." Speer had done so uncritically, even though Hitler proclaimed an expansion of Germany eastward, called for authoritarian rule, and denounced the influence of undesirables.[7]

This first connection with Hitler was as exceptional as it was fateful for Speer. In anticipation of the July 1932 elections, Speer came to Berlin and was assigned to be a courier with his roadster. When Hitler had made his third speech, a Berlin district leader asked to see Speer. The leader told him to renovate the party's new district headquarters. This task was, he later believed, "the luckiest turning point in my life. I had reached the junction."[8]

Speer finished the renovations by the next election on November 6,

1932. The cost was not an issue, as the party needed to make the right impression. Hitler inspected the building named after him. He liked what he saw.

Speer returned to his Mannheim office. He read in the local papers that President Paul von Hindenburg had appointed Hitler as chancellor on January 30, 1933. That March, Speer received a call to Berlin to see the "doctor," Joseph Goebbels, minister of propaganda, who immediately commissioned him to rebuild and refurnish his ministry's headquarters.

On May 1, 1933, a rally was to be held on the Tempelhof Field in Berlin. Speer saw the party's rifle-club-type sketches for decorations and called them appalling. Asked to do better, with a stroke of genius, he came up with what was to become the superior design for such rallies: "I sketched a large platform and behind it, three mighty banners, each of them taller than a ten-story building, stretched between two wooden struts. Two of them would be black-white-red with the swastika banner between them. They were to be illuminated by powerful searchlights." Hitler enthusiastically accepted Speer's drawing.[9]

Although claiming the idea, Goebbels still gave Speer a commission to redo his ministerial house, add a large hall, and do it in a record two months. Speer selected Emil Nolde's watercolors for decoration, but Hitler rejected them as degenerate art.

After Speer finished Goebbels's assignment, Hitler summoned him to Nuremberg in July 1933. Preparations were underway for the first party rally since coming to power. To accompany his early sketch, Speer added a gigantic eagle with a wingspan stretched more than one hundred feet in length. Along with these enormous swastika banners and a giant eagle, there were 130 air-raid searchlights spaced at twelve-meter intervals, with more at later rallies. They would be turned straight upward to crown the Zeppelin Field as a Cathedral of Light (Lichtdom). Speer brought his drawings before Hitler. "Agreed," Hitler said. Speer left the room. As Speer later noted, few realized architecture was Hitler's obsessive hobby.

Suddenly, Hitler wanted the chancellor's residence redone quickly. Hitler remembered Speer's drawings and the young architect who had completed Goebbels's remodeling in record time. He assigned Speer as an aid to Paul Troost, his Munich designer.

Speer accompanied his supervisor and Hitler on twenty to thirty inspection tours. At one of these, Hitler invited Speer to dinner with his intimate group. He even gave Speer one of his clean jackets to wear instead of Speer's plaster-spattered one and placed the boyish architect beside himself at the table. The others noticed a fuehrer's badge on that jacket, but before Speer could answer how he got it, Hitler said, "No, it's mine." Speer recollected, "Evidently, he had taken a liking to me." Once again, Hitler discovered Speer had designed the three ten-story-high banners, using giant searchlights turned vertically and a colossal eagle behind the rostrum to decorate the Zeppelin Field for the party's rally.[10]

In 1969, three years after Speer's release from Spandau Prison at age sixty-four, his memoir, *Inside the Third Reich,* was published. At the time of publication, an American reporter, James O'Donnell, interviewed him. At the outset, O'Donnell remarked that Speer asserted that the Nuremberg war crimes trial was, whatever its faults, a "necessary step on the path toward re-civilization."

That word, "re-civilization," haunted Speer. How could he—a young, singularly rational and intelligent person among the Nazi rabble—have fallen victim to Hitler's megalomania? "Am I," he asked, "that same man today?" He answered, "I don't honestly know." That remained very troubling for him, even after writing a six-hundred-page personal exposé of the Third Reich, his 450-page prison memoir, *Spandau: The Secret Diaries,* and searching for clues for his behavior in the theology of Karl Barth.

Speer had created an image of himself as one who deeply regretted not having discovered Nazi war crimes at the time and who kept a blind eye to them throughout the war. This has since been disproved.[11] He perpetuated the "Speer Myth" as the one who revolutionized the Nazi armament's production while remaining a mere technician or technocratic bystander. This picture was Leni Riefenstahl's argument or the "Riefenstahl Myth." She produced Nazi documentary masterpieces, *Triumph of the Will* and *Olympia*, while remaining a mere cinematographer, she claimed, an artistic bystander. Speer and Riefenstahl argued that they had not participated in or could be blamed for the holocaust. That was Hitler's doing, with this singular exception: Speer accepted his "collective" guilt as part of the Nazi gang. Riefenstahl steadfastly refused responsibility because she had never been a party member.

While Riefenstahl's two Faustian temptations were her films, *Triumph of the Will* and *Olympia*, Speer's architectural attraction was Hitler's dream of the new German capital, Germania, meant to renew Berlin. On its north-south axis would be the Prachstrasse (Street of Splendor). In its reconstruction, the Nazi imperial city of Germania would be dominated by the Volkshalle (People's Hall). As O'Donnell recounts in his conversation with Speer, two new, colossal railroad stations, three times the size of Manhattan's Grand Central Terminal, would be placed near the Tempelhof Field. Farther along the four-hundred-foot-wide and three-mile-long Prachstrasse, there would be Adolf-Hitler-Platz at the city's center. Even beyond all of that, there stood the Fuehrepalast, or Chancellery, seventy times the size of Bismarck's, and a new Reichstag four times the old one's size.

Alongside them, there were the SS Elite Guard's great barracks, a general staff headquarters, embassies, and other state buildings, such as the Soldiers' Hall, to contain Germany's field marshals' remains. At the south end of this axis, there stood the nearly four-hundred-foot great Triumphal Arch that could fit the Arc de Triomphe into its opening. Finally, at the northern end of the three-mile-long boulevard, there stood the Volkshalle, modeled on Hadrian's Pantheon. Its copper dome was to be seven times that size, and atop it perched a German imperial eagle reaching fifty feet into the air, with a vast wingspread and clasping a golden swastika in its talons, although Speer later substituted a globe.

O'Donnell quoted Speer's cryptic remarks on Germania.

Architecture was a "pregnant clue to this strange man [Hitler because] it was not his hobby. It was his obsession. And long before the end, I knew that Hitler was not destroying to build; he was building to destroy. I and others, caught in the act, were helping him." After conquering the world, Hitler's new order would arise with Speer's buildings as its precursor.

What were the origins of Hitler's architectural views? His artistic taste remained in the late nineteenth century. Specific examples were the Paris Opera (Charles Garnier, 1861–1874) and the Vienna State Opera (August Sicard von Sicardsburg and Eduard van der Nüll, 1861–1869). In Munich, Hitler befriended Paul Troost (Fuehrebau and Haus der Kunst, 1933–1937), whose spare designs were neoclassical. Hitler tended toward the gaudy. He was fond of Late Baroque but liked stricter architecture, such as Gottfried Semper's works in Dresden and his Hofburg in Vienna. He even had Speer make a memorable trip to Brussels to view the Palace of Justice (Joseph Poelaert, 1866).

But Hitler was always drawn back to an inflated Neo-Baroque. He liked romantic landscapes for their naturalism but stopped before Impressionism. As Speer put it, Hitler was full of contradictions. "There was no 'Fuehrer's style' for all that the party press expatiated on this subject. What branded onto the official architecture of the Reich was only its neoclassicism as transmitted by Troost." It was multiplied, altered, exaggerated, and sometimes distorted by Nazi architecture to ludicrousness. Hitler believed he lived in one of the most significant cultural epochs in human history and all of a very middle-class genre.[12]

Two events in 1934 changed things for Hitler and, therefore, Speer: Troost died on January 21 and von Hindenburg died on August 2. Troost's death meant Speer became Hitler's number one architect as head of the Chief Office for Construction. And President von Hindenburg's death opened the way for Hitler to take over Germany.

In June Hitler carried out the Blood Purge of his paramilitary Sturmabteilung (SA) chief, Ernst Roehm, his followers, and General Kurt von Schleicher, Weimar's last chancellor. Hitler claimed that even von Hindenburg and the political right approved these actions, supposedly to prevent an SA coup. Hitler asked Speer to rebuild the Borough Palace to transfer Roehm's SA from Munich to Berlin. He replaced Roehm with Viktor Lutze.

Speer took over the funeral arrangements for von Hindenburg at the Tannenberg Memorial and built a wooden podium for the speakers. He added a black crepe banner to hang inside the courtyard. After the funeral, Hitler surprised Speer with a new assignment to construct a permanent stone installation on Nuremberg's Zeppelin Field for Nazi Party rallies. In one inspired moment, the idea came to Speer: a mighty flight of stairs with an enclosed, long colonnade flanked on both ends by stone abutments topped with Nazi eagles. He had been influenced by the Pergamon Altar, with a platform for guests midway in the stairs' flight. But it was huge—a length of thirteen hundred feet and a height of eighty feet.

Hitler had a way of changing his mind several times, but Speer proceeded without interference. Speer speculated that for Hitler a building's purpose was to transmit his time and spirit to posterity. Monumental architecture reminded humanity of great epochs. In the distant future, such monuments, even in a state of decay, would have, as Speer put it, "ruin value." He meant that in a thousand years, such structures would still be admired. Hitler appointed Speer as Abteilungsleiter (Head of Department) on Goebbels's staff. He invited the Speers to an official reception and told Speer's wife, Margarete, "Your husband will erect buildings for me, such as have not been created for four thousand years."

Speer considered the architectural setting for the 1934 Nazi Party rally in Nuremberg as "for me not only my most beautiful architectural concept but also, after its fashion, the only one that has survived the passage of time. The effect, which was both solemn and beautiful, was like being in a cathedral of ice." The "ice cathedral" comment was originally by British Ambassador Sir Nevile Henderson. Speer assembled 130 air-raid searchlights, blazing vertically skyward to thirty-five thousand feet. They merged into a general glow, as if in a vast auditorium with light pillars forming an outer wall of luminescence. So impressed was Hitler that he interrupted a cornerstone ceremony to shake Speer's hand as his chief decorator and architect.

Speer also used gigantic swastika flags and three-striped ones to introduce colors into the rally and as decorative effects throughout the city and at speeches and marches. He designed the stadium in a horseshoe form for future party rallies. It won the Grand Prix at the Paris World's Fair of 1937. Speer shared a gold medal for the German pavilion with Russian Boris Iofan for the Soviet one. Much later, Speer reflected, "The love for vast proportions was not only tied up with the totalitarian cast of Hitler's regime. They demonstrated strength and wealth. They glorified his works and claim to world dominion."[13] After World War II, all that remained of the Zeppelin Field were the fuehrer's rostrum ruins.[14]

But in 1936 Hitler was at the height of his popularity and power. He had gambled on remilitarizing the Rhineland and occupied it on March 7, 1936. The 1936 Olympic Games, with some remodeling of the stadium by Speer, modified Werner March's design by adding a stone exterior. The Olympic Games became an international sensation, and Germany won the most medals.

Even the former King of England, Edward VIII, and his consort, the Duchess of Windsor, paid their respects by visiting Hitler at Obersalzberg on October 22, 1937. From this pinnacle of success, Hitler told Speer, "I have one more building assignment to give out. The greatest of all." It was Hitler's plan for rebuilding Berlin. It contained a grand new avenue at the city's center, 139 yards wide and three miles long on a north-south axis. Instead of giving Berlin's municipal government the task, which had rejected the avenue's size, he "tersely gave me the assignment." Hitler said, "There's nothing to be done with the Berlin city government. From now on, you make plans. When you have something ready, show it to me."

Hitler always had time for architecture and gave his sketches to Speer. They shifted two railway stations, Anhalter and Potsdam, south of Tempelhof Field, releasing old trackage for buildings lining the grand boulevard. Hitler's monstrous "gigantomania" buildings would dwarf the remainder of the city: primarily a vast domed structure of 825 feet, the Volkshalle, encompassing an area of 410,000 square feet, that could hold 150,000 persons.

Hitler dreamed of his Triumphal Arch, four hundred feet high, with the names of Germany's World War I dead chiseled into its granite. Hitler gave Speer sketches of each and every project. He dreamed of imperial glory won by war. As Speer put it, "What is startling is less the grandiosity of the projects than the obsessiveness with which he had been planning triumph-monumental buildings when there was not a shred of hope that they could even be built."[15] Speer fatefully concluded that it was sinister of Hitler to hold such fantastic dreams during peacetime. That was because the new Berlin, or Germania, implied empire, suggesting war on a vast scale.

Speer made detailed plans of a neoclassical building for Hitler's new Chancellery to be completed by January 1939. He finished the shell the year before. The Marble Gallery in Speer's new Reich Chancellery was twice the Hall of Mirrors' length at Versailles, and it had imposing doors to Hitler's office at the end of its highly polished marble floors. Speer designed Hitler's study as a throne room measuring 4,214 square feet. The Chancellery became Speer's major completed work, built in the Troost style of spare and restrained but monumental to exemplify power and grandeur and to overawe and intimidate.[16]

In a famous phrase Speer attributed to Goethe's *Faust*, he wrote, "One seldom recognizes the devil when he is putting his hand on your shoulder."[17] Speer meant that Hitler's entourage would sue for his favor by every means possible and that their servility, including his own, was endemic in their show of devotion. That obeisance also corrupted Hitler, who vainly believed only he could carry out his dreams. This pomposity revealed itself in Hitler's daily indulgence in endless monologues full of banality and triviality. Hitler was superficial, and his conversations at the table did not go beyond a very narrow range of subjects and limited viewpoints.[18]

Hitler lacked technical knowledge and was ignorant of logistics.[19] Although he was a brilliant amateur, his decisions were often made in a vacuum. But, like so many others, Speer found him a lunatic and a demagogue with a bad temper. In his megalomania, he only worshipped himself and believed his lies. The extent of Hitler's lunacy and megalomania became evident in his making of war with its attendant totality of destruction and genocide.

Hitler's intimate circle considered Speer the "son" the dictator never had. Yet, the portrait Speer paints leaves out much that his boss provides us in his autobiography, *Mein Kampf*.[20]

We should evaluate Hitler's book on two levels. One reviewer called the first "creepy" rather than diabolical or sinister. This critic meant that instead of doing the usual and presenting himself in a positive light to win supporters, Hitler gave us a picture of someone who is an "embittered, envious, traumatized loser."[21] Not only is he a victim, but he pathologically fears impurity while simultaneously admiring strength. His book brims with resentments, especially his rejection by Vienna's Academy of Fine Arts.

Hitler's worldview retains his lower-middle-class origins. He resents Jews as lying competitors who look down and laugh at the Germans. Hitler combined his resentment with his radical racial theory, which "resonated with a big chunk of an entire social class in Germany after war and inflation."[22]

There is a bewildering sense of Hitler's intense will to power in overcoming his misery. He shares modernity in exposing the crisis of German culture following defeat in World War I with others like T. S. Eliot, who resented nineteenth-century values as decadent and believed a Fisher King–like strong man could overcome the past. That belief led Hitler to his political program.

For the second level in understanding *Mein Kampf*, we must recognize that Hitler laid out a political program in its pages: The Jews were racially inferior to Germans and threatened their Aryan purity;

Jews stabbed Germany in the back by subverting the kaiser and losing the Great War; the Jewish plot to control the world justified their destruction (genocide), along with the sick and weak; the need for living space (lebensraum) to the east was Germany's historic destiny, while Germans must stop their failed expansion south and west; in Germany's resurgence to greatness, all German lands and peoples must be united into a New Order; in the struggle for survival of the fittest, there is endless conflict to attain life, and so it is with nations; individualism must be crushed; and the Weimar Republic's democratic failure and decadence must be stopped.[23] Hitler never tired of repeating these political points.

I can't help wondering why Hitler continues to fascinate and captivate humanity. It is, I think, his total grasp of sheer, brutal power in all of its aspects. Further, he betrayed a willingness to use it in any way he pleased, without restraints or constraints. This phenomenon represents one of the most complete leviathans known in history. Very few ever reached power's commanding heights of absolute force over so many for so long and who lived in a country of the highest technological development. It is that totality I term "totalitarianism." Neither Stalin nor Mao exercised that same totality of power.

2. "FASCINATING FASCISM"

Leni Riefenstahl's films gave Hitler an artistic dimension as a superhero. "Fascinating fascism" is how critic Susan Sontag termed Hitler's current attraction. Ben Mankiewicz and his hosts at Turner Classic Movies (TCM) dared to cast the "indomitable priestess of the beautiful" out of their Golden Ten Olympics Film Festival. They honored Tokyo's Games of the XXXII Olympiad in 2021 without Leni Riefenstahl, the Nazi darling or Little Red Riding Hood of Hitler's failed and fractured fairy tale. Her film, *Olympia,* of the 1936 games, fell victim to TCM's probable howls: "Hitler's girlfriend!" "Goebbels's propagandist!" "Himmler's helper!"[24]

I'm echoing Susan Sontag: Why make "fascinating fascism"

fashionable again? She had warned about legitimizing "fascist longings in our midst."[25] TCM heeded her alarm despite enduring the cinema connoisseurs' criticisms. TCM realized Riefenstahl's *Olympia* presented problems: Is it an independent documentary or another Nazi propaganda film? Was it self-financed or the Nazi state's work? Did she control the production, or was Joseph Goebbels in command? Can *Olympia* be treated as an art film, or was it a creature of its fascist environment?

Cooper Graham, the film's outstanding student, concluded that both Hitler and Goebbels supported *Olympia*: "The resources of the Third Reich were at Riefenstahl's disposal." Graham also quotes Goebbels's diary: "Fraulein Riefenstahl has her contract [and] 11½ million transactions. She is entirely happy." Graham remarks that she should have been happy.

When Graham confronted Riefenstahl with his research results, she objected and contended that she would consult the Bundesarchiv (German Federal Archives) herself. She also claimed otherwise in her memoir: The government granted monies to her film corporation, Olympia Film, Inc. They were "to avoid paying enormous taxes." All her company's shares were the property of the state's Ministry of Propaganda "until all the loans and accrued interest had been completely paid off." It was only a "fiscal formality," according to Riefenstahl. Beyond this amount, Riefenstahl received a personal remuneration of another quarter of a million Reichsmarks as project director, with complete artistic and organizational control. Though a masterpiece, this film remains under the swastika's shadow.[26]

Olympia was a prodigious production, divided into two full-length films: *Festival of the Nations* (3,289 meters, 126 minutes) and *Festival of Beauty* (2,712 meters, 100 minutes). The first mainly dealt with track and field events, and the second with water sports. A small camera crew filmed 136 competitions. Only six cameramen were allowed into the arena's field. Another ten could mix into the crowd and get fan reactions from the hundred thousand spectators, including Nazi bigwigs. Film critic David Hinton praised her work as "one of the great moments of world cinema."[27]

Before the games started, Riefenstahl and her crew went to Greece to film a "Prologue." Riefenstahl turned to ancient Greece and the games' origins. Her cameras montaged temples and sculptures, then settled on the Myron statue of the discus thrower. The scene is in various gray tones, lending it a dreamlike quality. It dissolves into a modern, live German decathlon champion.

Riefenstahl shows other classical sports, and they melt into a dance with women. Their dance evolves into their uplifted arms, becoming a flame that turns into the Olympic torch. Torchbearers carried the Olympic flame to Hitler's Berlin, a first for the sport. Riefenstahl's crew filmed the torch bearers' route across the Balkans. She noted their progress on the screen by a moving line, accompanied by Riefenstahl's trademark shots of low angles and clouded skies.

At the games, she used close-ups of the athletes taken from pits and sidetracks, with overhead views from towers. She tried balloons, a traveling crane, and strapped-on and underwater cameras. Some scenes had to be staged and refilmed later to avoid interfering with the athletes.[28]

Riefenstahl's concern focused more on the participants rather than the event itself. "It is both an aesthetic study of the performance of the human body," as David Hinton claimed, and a psychological study of the participants' emotions. She was not interested in making a newsreel of a historic event but rather a cultural and cinematic study of sport. Riefenstahl recorded significant award ceremonies but varied them using close-ups, long shots, and angles to avoid repetition and viewer boredom.

Riefenstahl's film editing developed into what Hinton calls "peaks and valleys"—the concept of high and low levels of emotion. She extended this concept to other aspects of the film, such as music, tone, and form. Theatrical events are edited, so humorous ones follow to relieve tension. She used montage and sound mixing to balance noise and music.[29]

By the time she began editing, Riefenstahl had four hundred thousand meters of the film done by her crew and confiscated newsreels Goebbels had seized. She spent ten weeks reviewing it all. Then she cataloged each section to find things quickly. The whole process of editing took eighteen months, and it was most notable by her emphasis on the marathon, which ends Part I, *Festival of the Nations*. Part II, *Festival of Beauty*, focuses on the swimming and diving sections.

Trumpets announce the marathoners as they approach the finish line to the crowd's roar as Part I ends. She worked on the loneliness of the marathon runners by showing their pounding feet and the lengthening of their shadows. In Part II, the athletes' movements are beautiful, with camera angles pointed skyward to capture the divers' bodies against the sky and clouds. In some of these camera shots, she even has them purposely dive in reverse.[30]

The stadium's great Olympic flame flared as events finished, and the choir sang Richard Strauss's new "Olympic Hymn" in a rising crescendo. On Sunday, August 15, 1936, the Berlin Olympics ended. A bell's tolling faded away to country flags. Giant searchlights aimed skyward, as in Albert Speer's style of the Nazi Party rallies.

Germany almost swept the horse-riding competitions and won the most medals overall. With a great deal of pomp and circumstance, the stadium lit up. Flag bearers entered. The host, Germany, came first, and Greece last. Count Henri de Baillet-Latour, chair of the International Olympic Committee (IOC), made the closing speech, the nations' flags dipped, and a wreath was placed on each. The tremendous Olympic flag was presented to Hitler; he then handed it to the honorees. It ended with Berlin's mayor, Dr. Julius Lippert. He was to pass it to Tokyo in 1940, but that event never happened.[31] The whole spectacle became another Nazi Party rally.

As I'm sure TCM would agree, Sontag conceded that Riefenstahl became "campy" by 1975. If still alive, Sontag would probably have extended her judgment while being alert to racial or social discrimination and injustice. "Without historical perspective, the current film critics' connoisseurship prepares the way for a curiously absentminded acceptance of propaganda for all sorts of destructive feelings—feelings whose implications people are refusing to take seriously." Sontag continued, "And so people hedge their bets— admiring this kind of art, for its undoubted beauty, and patronizing it, for its sanctimonious promotion of the beautiful."

This acceptance she notoriously called "camp," or as *Merriam-Webster* defines it: "absurdly exaggerated, artificial, or affected in a usually humorous way."[32] As Sontag put it, "Indeed, the essence of camp is its love of the unnatural: of artifice and exaggeration." It opens us to various propaganda, from fascist Goebbels to communist Lenin. Sontag argued that a taste for "fashionable fascism" becomes corrupt when it moves from an innocuous ethical issue of an elite minority of film critics to mass culture. She reminded us, "Taste is context, and the context has changed."[33]

TCM was right to omit Riefenstahl from its golden ten. Sontag's comments warn the twenty-first century: Beware of the Nazi's totalitarian myth of Hitler as the superhero.

Celebrated film critic Richard M. Barsam, expert on another of Leni Riefenstahl's films, *Triumph of the Will*, noted, "The modern audience is stunned by the film's artistic power and by its political content." He analyzed its twelve scenes, beginning with the film's short prologue and titles, "Introduction," and closing with its "Finale" and Hitler's speech to the Nazi delegates in the Luitpold Hall, Nuremberg.

Barsam saw the inner reality of Riefenstahl's work as an effort to portray Hitler as a Teutonic god descending to earth, restoring Germany's domestic health, and raising its geopolitical stature. Through the film's slow and stately rhythm, Riefenstahl deified Hitler as if the Sixth Party Congress (September 5–10, 1934) was an "imperial" or "religious procession." Barsam called Riefenstahl's moving montages "cinematic poetry."[34]

Riefenstahl transformed Nazi reality into art. She was a consummate cinematic poet. Nevertheless, the paradox of *Triumph of the Will* and *Olympia* is that they can repel and attract us.[35] Riefenstahl and Speer were more than Hitler's fellow travelers. They were true believers.

3. BANALITY: ADOLF EICHMANN

There were multitudes of Eichmanns. Hitler's deepening lunacy descended on the Lost Generation, as political scientist Hannah Arendt notes in her book, *Eichmann in Jerusalem: A Report on the Banality of Evil*. Arendt claims that Adolf Eichmann, the German Austrian Nazi SS Obersturmbannfuehrer (Lt. Colonel), illustrated the twentieth century's greatest evil in her book's subtitle. Evil reached a new dimension. It made the perpetrators not necessarily monsters but unthinking cogs in a juggernaut of destruction.

Arendt maintained that their evil was more than the work of little demons set free by a Prince of Hell. It was the gigantic evil of Satan himself, the Lord of Hell. History blew millions of people with humdrum lives, nobodies, onto the world's stage. They were predisposed not to think. Given this predisposition, they believed they had done nothing independently, had merely obeyed orders. These orders allowed them to commit horrendous, satanic evil on a vast scale and with the technological skill of an advanced industrial society by refusing to be thinking people.

Arendt concluded that this new, monstrous evil was previously absent from all law books because it had been nonexistent. One author, Samantha Power, termed it a "problem from hell." A legal expert, Raphael Lemkin, coined the term "genocide."[36] It was not, Arendt thought, philosophically radical in the sense of corruption, that is, sin, which takes people over. Instead, this new kind of evil acted against the universal moral law of humanity's very existence by subordinating it to the state: The Nazi state, ruled by Hitler, commanded death to the Jews.

She noted such evil's politically extreme nature: It takes crimes to their highest level, whether in grand or small deeds. That evil, therefore, may not be both ordinary and extreme. It is always extreme.

Actress Barbara Sukowa, in her role as Arendt, comments in the film *Hannah Arendt* that the court trying Eichmann confronted a new evil, a crime without precedent in human history—the industrial elimination of an entire people. It was not found in any of the historic legal systems, and the new criminal was unknown in any court of law before the Nuremberg Trials.

The court in Jerusalem had to try Eichmann, the new criminal of the new evil, for his new evil deeds. He protested the prosecution's assertions. He had never done these crimes out of his own initiative. Eichmann had no intentions, either good or bad, but only obeyed orders. Every Nazi pleaded that.

The "greatest evil in the world," Arendt wrote, "was the evil committed by nobodies." That phenomenon she called the "banality of evil." Eichmann had surrendered his defining human quality of thinking. He was no longer capable of making moral judgments. That allowed him and other similarly ordinary people to commit small and gigantic evil deeds, like the mass executions of individuals because of their race, using industrial methods. Instead of making commercial products, the Nazi assembly lines gassed millions to death and cremated their bodies.

She concluded that the world had never seen these Eichmanns and their thoughtless crimes before. Only thinking people could give humanity the moral courage in the future to prevent such a catastrophe from happening again in a rare historical moment "when the chips are down," as the film puts it.[37]

In an Age of Infamy, punishments were not always concerned with or connected to crimes like slave labor because exploitation would profit no one but the tyrant, producing only results for the Nazi tyrant's war machine. A camp like Auschwitz became a place where every activity and human impulse was otherwise senseless, and senselessness was produced daily.

For Arendt, the final stage of Nazi totalitarianism confirmed that an absolute, satanic evil had emerged entirely, as it was no longer related to human motives. She believed we would never have known the genuinely extreme nature of this evil without totalitarianism. "Jewry was not the only operative factor in the Holocaust. Totalitarianism in Germany was, in the end, about total terror and its consistency, not just eradicating Jews only."[38] It was the ultimate infamy.

Infamy lies in Arendt's unique understanding of the new evil. It is never as radical as human corruption, but "it is only extreme, [and] it can overgrow and lay waste to the entire world [because] it spreads like a fungus on the surface."[39] An Age of Infamy, if I may borrow Arendt's interpretation, achieved such a rare dimension only due to the immensity of its cruelty committed by thoughtless nobodies.[40]

Between February 16 and March 16, 1963, Hannah Arendt published five articles in *The New Yorker* under "A Reporter at Large: Eichmann in Jerusalem." Later that year she revised and published them with Viking Press as *Eichmann in Jerusalem: A Report on the Banality of Evil*. Both versions sustained hostile waves of criticism. Even as recently as 2011, historian Deborah Lipstadt devoted a chapter to citing Arendt's sins of omission and commission in her book *The Eichmann Trial*. The debate has since subsided.

Three topics troubled Arendt's readers: her criticisms of the prosecution's conduct of the trial, especially Israeli Prime Minister David Ben-Gurion and Chief Prosecutor Gideon Hausner; the role of the European Jewish Councils (Judenrat), especially Berlin's Chief Rabbi, Leo Baeck, whom she initially called the "Jewish Fuehrer;" and, finally, her view of Eichmann as a banal nobody.[41] This last point remains her most controversial discovery, particularly her use of the word "banality." It usually refers to something familiar, trite, or unoriginal.

The Israeli intelligence service kidnapped Adolf Eichmann, an ex-SS lieutenant colonel living in Argentina for seventeen years after fleeing Europe. Israel put him on trial in Jerusalem in 1963. The prosecution insisted he was an anti-Semitic killer and a major war criminal.

Arendt saw him as a mindless, immoral, Kafkaesque bureaucrat whose blind obedience led him to commit horrific acts. Contrary to the prosecution's charge, he probably killed no one with his own hands. The court's psychiatrists found him to be of an average mindset and not a beast acting out of criminal motives. He joined the Nazi Party on a whim and became a Jewish expert who attempted to relocate European Jews to new homelands, such as Madagascar. Countries increasingly refused German Jewish emigration.

By 1942 the Nazis had decided on the "Final Solution," masterminded by Reinhard Heydrich, head of the Reich's main security office, at the Wannsee Conference. As secretary of the conference, Eichmann participated in the specific planning of genocide. He worked with the Jewish Councils on the details of the deportation of Jews to the extermination camps primarily located in Eastern Europe, such as Auschwitz.[42]

Arendt follows Eichmann's transportation system through Europe, showing the differences in regions from the most fervently anti-Semitic, like Romania, to the least, such as Denmark. Often countries like Hungary would deport nonnational Jews while refusing to expel their Jewish citizens, and countries like Italy and Belgium resisted by ignoring orders. Witnesses for the prosecution focused on Eastern Europe, not in areas where Eichmann had little or no jurisdiction.

There were notable personal exceptions to the collapse of traditional morality that the Nazis fostered throughout Europe. For instance, Anton Schmid helped Jews escape Poland, but he was caught and executed. Arendt does not refer to Oskar Schindler. But the actions of both Schmid and Schindler show that totalitarianism was never absolute.

The court found Eichmann guilty, as if he had killed with his own hands. His appeal failed. In Arendt's "Epilogue," she claimed that both at Nuremberg and Jerusalem, the court did not understand the nature of genocide, the new evil, as a crime against humanity: a violation of a community's moral order by attempting to exterminate a race of humans. She believed Eichmann was a thoughtless bureaucrat who committed monstrous crimes against that moral order despite his intentions to obey orders.[43]

Her analysis of Eichmann's banality constituted an innovative, intellectual journey. That trip began accidentally as a first reaction to Eichmann, the man Israel placed in a protective glass booth during the trial. Eichmann did not appear sinister or inhuman. On the contrary, his initial impression startled her. This monster seemed pathetically comic. Was he, she thought, just stupid, or somehow not?[44] She finally concluded that he could not think: "This inability to think creates the possibility for many ordinary men to commit evil deeds on a gigantic scale as one had never seen before, [and] thinking gives people the strength to prevent catastrophes in these rare moments when the chips are down."[45]

What, she had wondered, made this man such a cardboard figure? Her husband, Heinrich Bluecher, suggested that such evil was not an original sin but a historical phenomenon, which prompted Arendt's book's subtitle. This idea had come to him from playwright Bertolt Brecht, who believed that if crooks became powerful politicians, they did not deserve historical fame. "Hitler," Brecht wrote, "was an idiot, and the extent of his enterprises does not make him a great man. If the ruling classes permit a small crook to become a great crook, he is not entitled to a privileged position in our view of history."[46]

Arendt reported on Eichmann's unique "officialese." It betrayed his incapability of telling right from wrong. He could not judge the state's laws as wrong or that the law of humanity's right to exist was higher than the Nazi law denying that right. She agreed Israel was entitled to judge Eichmann. But true justice could only be rendered with new legal and moral categories for Eichmann, who was involved in state-instigated crimes or administrative massacres by industrial means. The Nazis had corrupted all of Europe, including both allies and their victims.

The Israeli court judged Eichmann a liar, an ordinary person aware of his criminality. Arendt's analysis also demonstrated that his conscience had ceased to function. Eichmann was a "bureaucratic murderer who might not be monstrously dedicated to evil, but unable to tell right from wrong."[47]

Norman Podhoretz, editor in chief of *Commentary*, gave a negative summary of Arendt's "perversity of brilliance." He wrote, "In the place of the monstrous Nazi, she gives us the 'banal' Nazi; in the place of the Jew as a virtuous martyr, she gives us the Jew as an accomplice in evil; and in the place of the confrontation of guilt and innocence, she gives us the 'collaboration' of criminal and victim."[48] Arendt had never used the words "collaboration," "monster," and "martyr categories," or wrote about collective guilt or innocence. As her biographer put it, she had not indulged in paradoxes.

War was declared between her and her accusers. After one bitter exchange with Robert Weltsch, journalist and editor, she referred to the "specter of our century" and suggested that joy might eventually come from this pain. He wrote that enough had been said. Most of Arendt's opponents believed she had "wronged the victims, added insult to their injury, and given food for glee and future mischief to the enemies of the Jews."[49]

To repeat, her emphasis was that banality sharply differed from the widely accepted notion that all evil deeds lie in humanity's sinful nature. People do evil things because they are evil, hence, original sin. The court in Jerusalem was "confronted with a crime it could not find in the law books, and a criminal whose like was unknown in any court before the Nuremberg Trial." Even more problematic, Eichmann declared "he had never done anything out of his initiative, that he had no intentions, whatsoever, good or bad, that he had only obeyed orders." She concluded, "The greatest evil in the world is the evil committed by nobodies, the evil committed by men without motive, without convictions, without wicked hearts or demonic wills, by human beings who refuse to be persons. And it is this phenomenon that I have called the 'banality of evil.'"

Arendt pointed out that this evil is not "radical" in the philosophical sense. Rather, the tendency is for evil to become total because it is "unpunishable in that no punishment can be adequate or commensurate; it is rooted in motives so base as to be beyond human comprehension."[50]

C. P. Taylor's play, *Good*, portrays a cultured Eichmann-type, Professor Halder, who is sucked into the Nazi whirlpool. He descends from accepting euthanasia to participating in genocide. The play ends with SS Halder at Auschwitz, complaining that anti-Semitism is the Jews' fault and only a temporary expediency.[51]

Arendt had tried to reconcile Eichmann's "shocking mediocrity [with] his staggering deeds." In Nazi Germany, just about everything had been permitted and possible, and the motives of totalitarian murders became redundant and stale. Simultaneously, totalitarians could also act from calculated wickedness rather than banal or motiveless evil. When that was the case, a person worked from deliberate sin—rather than banality or motiveless evil—and could still distinguish between good and evil. Such evil was only radical— the worst crime found in the law books—but never extreme to the point of being extraordinary. Radical evil was only a privation of the good.[52]

Arendt's friend, the philosopher Karl Jaspers, referred to her book's title when he wrote, "I think: the notion is illuminating, and as a book title, it is striking. It means *this* man's evil is banal; not evil is banal . . ."[53] She never thought of Eichmann as unpunishable or unforgivable. It was more than his misfortune. Eichmann had carried out and supported mass murder, and obedience and support were the same. Because of this, "no member of the human race can be expected to want to share the earth with you. This is the reason, and the only reason, you must hang."[54] As her biographer explained, "His decision to obey and carry out a policy of mass murder was unforgivable: with this decision, he refused to 'share the earth' with the Jews and others." Therefore, no one could be expected to share the earth with him.[55] Some Nazis like Speer had a conscience. They committed radical evil deliberately and knowingly. Eichmann's banality was extraordinary.

4. EXTREME EVIL

Genocide finally became a subject of public discussion in post-war Germany. By the 1960s the debate of formerly taboo subjects was possible in German public discourse, including exile, resistance, torture, and genocide. The contrast was stunning compared to the extraordinary indifference of the 1950s.

In broaching the monstrous subject of Auschwitz, denunciations of the collective amnesia were often as repellent as the previous refusal to discuss it. These discussions constituted a first step in revealing the truth. Victims of Nazi brutality spoke out about the terror visited upon them. No compensation was adequate. They broke through the silence imposed on them by public amnesia.[56] Novelist W. G. Sebald summarized victim Jean Améry's position: "The persecution and extermination of a largely assimilated minority, as planned and put into practice in the German Reich, is 'singular and irreducible' in the very fact of its 'total inner logic and appalling rationality' and that in the last resort the question is not so much one of constructing a plausible etiology of terror as of achieving some ultimate understanding of what it means to be marked out as a victim, excluded, persecuted, and murdered."[57]

The survivors continued to be victims of a "pathological hypermnesia in the past otherwise emptied of content." Whatever content remained of those fixed points were traumatic scenes that recurred with a painful clarity of memory and vision. What was remembered from the brink of death reminded one of a "monumental madness of the procedure inflicted [on them] rather than the emotional aspect of [one's] suffering." It was Dr. Caligari's madhouse of a world turned upside down.

Once people have endured extremes of torture and pain, they are carried forever in their psyche. Sebald explained that this experience was much more than the standard explanation. It was a national perversion. Six million had been helpless before the objective lunacy of history. This power was the SS state towering monstrously above its victims.[58]

Jean Améry's essays, collected in *At the Mind's Limits: Contemplations by a Survivor on Auschwitz and Its Realities*, bring a parting of the ways with Hannah Arendt's banality of evil. Améry concluded that genocide results from the unchecked and limitless lust for power with its intended use of evil means. Arendt's Eichmann simply carries out the tyrant's orders with or without malice toward the victims. He employs technology, such as how the rails were used for the Nazi victims' transportation to the camps or how the camp executioners completed the monstrous crimes of gassing (using Zyklon B) and cremating millions.

Art Spiegelman put it this way: "Here it was the *live* showers, not the dead gas showers what we heard sometimes as rumors." As to caps, Spiegelman said the guards "grabbed" them away and then shot the prisoners for running to pick them up.[59]

Eichmann's moral compass, according to Arendt, had been reduced to zero by a totalitarian regime in which right and wrong had been subverted and turned topsy-turvy, replaced with Nazi ideology. When the chips were down, as Arendt put it, Eichmann could not do what the few, such as Oskar Schindler, did by taking on the moral responsibility to save lives at significant risk to himself.

Améry had been subjected to repeated torture, often bringing him to death's doorstep. He did not observe a mindless bureaucrat using neutral technology to carry out millions of exterminations on behalf of an ideology that substituted itself for God. He saw up close the individual torturer's intensity and pure joy in using power. A historian, Lord John Dalberg-Acton, once observed this sinful human capacity: "Power tends to corrupt, and absolute power corrupts absolutely."[60] Arendt called that evil "radical," not "extreme." She labeled the latter as state-ordered and bureaucratically carried out by banal people like Eichmann.

Some of Améry's most direct accusations about German guilt, meaning a national responsibility shared by all, broke the post-war silence. Améry tolerated no excuses for deferring what happened among the Germans: a people of high intelligence, industrial capability, and unequaled cultural wealth—a people of "poets and thinkers." That was the brutal fact, no matter how much one indulged in clarifications. Forget he demanded such clarifications as German national character or fascism or late capitalism. Don't bother blaming the aftermath of the 1929 economic crash because other European countries avoided their "Day of Potsdam" when Hitler's Reichstag first took power on March 21, 1933. Améry also condemned all academic excuses, theories, or justifications for Hitler's triumph.[61]

He put his position bluntly: "There is nothing that provides enlightenment of the eruption of radical Evil in Germany . . . this Evil is singular and irreducible in its total inner logic and its accursed rationality." Hitler and the Nazis remained a dark riddle. All he could say about evil's origin under the Nazis was that they were a "spontaneous generation, from a womb that bore it as a perversion." That perversion remained silent in the post-war until the 1960s when there appeared to be no anti-Semitism in Germany. Or, if it did exist, it either shut up or became philo-Semitism. That also was disgusting. By then, both the victims and the hangmen were dying out.

The new generation renewed both camps, and a chasm opened between them. Only time would close it. In the meantime, the old anti-Semitism hid in anti-Zionism. It was anchored in a collective psychological infrastructure traced back to repressed religious sentiments and resentments.[62] Améry decided to speak out.

There was his wartime life in Auschwitz. Without practical skills, he was assigned to the worst labor detail, nearest the gas chambers and crematories. He had to learn camp slang. As an intellectual, he was almost alone. The SS state and structure stole his mind and seized the German world from its cultural icons—from Johann Sebastian Bach to Richard Strauss. Améry could no longer claim German culture.

Camp life was deintellectualized and dehumanized into a dystopian world of SS logic, where Big Brother denied natural rights and moral categories. Some Nazi generals in far-off Russia commanded the camp while piling up bodies along the Volga River. Inmates were crushed under the SS wheel while doffing their caps to their murderers. "The power structure of the SS state towered up before the prisoner monstrously and indomitably, a reality that could not be escaped and therefore finally seemed reasonable." Contrary to Marxist theories, that life had nothing to do with capitalism or any other economic system. "It was the monstrous product of sick minds and perverted souls."[63]

Torture, Améry asserts, "is the most horrible event a human being can retain within himself. [It] was not an accidental quality of the Third Reich, but its essence [and] the enormous perception at a later stage, one that destroys all abstractive imagination, makes clear to us how evil overlays and exceeds banality. For there is no 'banality of evil,' and Hannah Arendt, who wrote about it in her Eichmann book, knew the enemy of humanity only from hearsay, saw him only through the glass cage." Améry continues, "When an event places the most extreme demands on us, one ought not to speak of banality. At this point, there is no longer any abstraction and never an imaginative power that could even approach its reality [because] one is carried off, shackled, to the torture cell. Its first blow indicates your helplessness and loss of dignity. Your trust in the world disappears. It's like rape, a crime without consent." Torture was Nazism's essence. In that, the Third Reich materialized.

Améry elaborates that Hitler's vassals only achieved their complete identification if they were "quick as a weasel, tough as leather, hard as Krupp steel. No golden party badge made him a valid representative of the Fuehrer and his ideology, nor did any Blood Order or Iron Cross. He had to torture and destroy to be excellent in bearing the suffering of others. He could handle torture's instruments, so Himmler could assure him his Certificate of Maturity in History; later generations would admire him for having obliterated his feelings of mercy."[64]

Some indignantly objected to Améry's torture theory. They say it wasn't Hitler who embodied torture but something called totalitarianism. They defined communism and National Socialism as two very different manifestations of the same thing. "Hitler and Stalin, Auschwitz, Siberia, the Warsaw Ghetto Wall, and the Berlin-Ulbricht Wall were named together, like Goethe and Schiller, Klopstock and Wieland."[65]

Communism, at least, retains an ideal of humanity. Fascism had none but depravity. It couldn't claim a single idea. It was merely confusing and crackbrained. It hated the word "humanity." It was the only political system of this century that, up to this point, had not only practiced the rule of the anti-man, as Red or Red and White Terror regimes also did, but it had established it as a principle. The terrorists exterminated and enslaved. The Nazis tortured not only for information but also for the good conscience of depravity itself. They tortured because they were torturers, and torture is their most terrible aspect. It stays with one forever.

Political torture has no metaphysical or theological excuses. These torturers are not just bureaucrats and banal, ordinary types or merely sadists in the narrow pathological or sexual sense. Instead, "National Socialism in its totality was stamped less with the seal of a hardly definable 'totalitarianism' than with that of sadism." The Nazis lived in a world where torture, death, and destruction triumph and can't exist except because "the sadist does not care about the continued existence of the world."[66] These fascists wanted to nullify the world by negating humanity and creating hell out of their absolute sovereignty. Torture was brought to the edge of nothingness.

Torture represents the total inversion of the social world. In such a world, man exists only by ruining the other person standing before him. That evil isn't banal. Even if one insists on it, such torture was done by the bureaucrats of torture. "I saw in their serious, tense faces," Améry wrote, "which were not swelling, let us say, with sexual-sadistic delight, but concentrated in murderous self-realization. With heart and soul, they went about their business, and the name of it was power, dominion over spirit and flesh, an orgy of unchecked self-expansion." These self-made gods reduced their victims to "whimpering preys of death."[67] It was midnight in the garden of infamy.

Améry considered collective guilt as a sound hypothesis. It referred to the sum of individually culpable conduct. He meant that it grew out of an individual German's responsibility for everything: from the guilt of deed, omission, utterance, and the guilt of silence to a people's real shame. It was a vague statistic because no one could determine how many Germans recognized, approved, or themselves committed the crimes of National Socialism or, in helpless revulsion, allowed them to pass in their name. All knew, and evidence was all around. "Whether I wanted to or not, I had to accept the notion of collective statistical guilt, and I am burdened with this knowledge in a world and a time that has proclaimed the collective innocence of Germans."[68]

Though the world forgives and forgets, Améry could not forget, least of all forgive, those who murdered or allowed the murder to occur. The "murderer generation just grew old, and the younger generations are tired of it. They equate it with the Allied bombings as equal to Auschwitz." He believed that to be faulty moral mathematics, though an understandable equation. Genocide was still an undeniable part of Germany's history, like other events or parts of the national tradition. Hitler and his deeds will remain a part of German history and tradition. Healing over time was something Améry considered anti-moral. Améry meant the German people should remain sensitive because they could not allow a piece of their national history to be neutralized by time. Otherwise, Hitler would never be disowned, nor would the disgrace be eradicated.

Améry did not mind being called an anti-historical reactionary. Every evil should not be lumped together in a "Century of Barbarism." Germany, he insisted, was unique in this respect: "But such murder of millions as this, carried out by a highly civilized people, with organizational dependability and almost scientific precision," was unique and should not be submerged with the century's other atrocities.[69] Germans still, as historian Samuel Moyn put it, "will cordon off the interlude, as if it were 'an accident in the factory,' as Germans after World War II described their twelve-year mistake."[70]

5. GENOCIDE

In Christopher R. Browning's *Ordinary Men: Reserve Police Battalion 101 and the Final Solution in Poland,* the author considers why most German men who killed routinely were 90 percent of Battalion 101, while only 10 percent did not. He explains many reasons behind wartime barbarity, from war's brutalization to racism. War crimes, especially when aggravated by negative racial stereotypes, added to a massive scale of killings. The crimes of battlefield frenzy do not represent official government policy. Whether tolerated, condoned, or tacitly encouraged by the command structure, these atrocities, in Browning's opinion, did not represent official governmental policy. They were not standard operating procedures.[71]

But there are "other kinds of atrocity, lacking the immediacy of battlefield frenzy and fully expressing official governmental policy, [and they] were standard operating procedure." Browning names some: firebombings, slave labor, reprisal shootings—these were not spontaneous or cruel actions of brutalized men but the methodically executed policies of governments. As such, atrocity by policy requires a different state of mind, one of calculation.

For Browning, the example is the Reserve Police Battalion 101. It systematically carried out the Nazi policy of exterminating European Jewry and was a standard operating procedure because it represented official governmental policy. Once carried out, it brutalized the perpetrators, and by becoming more manageable, they got into a routine.[72] They are not Améry's sadists.

Modern bureaucratic life fosters the administrative aspects of such a destructive process. Many holocaust perpetrators were desk murderers, or what Arendt called banal evildoers, and the bureaucratic nature of their participation facilitated their role in mass executions. Browning uses such words as "segmented," "routinized," and "depersonalized" to characterize a governmental policy of mass murder. The Reserve Battalion 101was not selected but was instead the dregs of the German workforce still available at that stage of the war. They could not even be classified as having authoritarian personalities. Instead, evil arose from ordinary thinking and was committed as a norm, not an exception.[73] Most killers from this unit were drawn randomly from German society. They were not coerced, nor were they morally different. They represented a cross section of Germany. In my opinion, Browning might also say that the allied bombing crews fit into this category, as they were not coerced and followed standard procedure. Those few Germans who refused to execute the executions suffered no dire consequences.[74]

Another influential holocaust scholar, Daniel Goldhagen, in his book *Hitler's Willing Executioners: Ordinary Germans and the Holocaust*, differs from Browning and Arendt in two crucial aspects: first, in his assessing of the role of anti-Semitism in German history, including the Nazi era; and, second, in his consideration of the role of ordinary Germans who were holocaust killers. Goldhagen maintains "that anti-Semitism 'more or less governed the ideational life of civil society' in pre-Nazi Germany, and when the Germans 'elected' Hitler to power, the 'centrality of anti-Semitism in the Party's worldview, program, and rhetoric [also] mirrored the sentiments of German culture.'"[75] They were on the same page. Hence, the Nazis unshackled Germany's preexisting anti-Semitism and unleashed the Holocaust.[76]

Since anti-Semitism already existed, Goldhagen continues, it did not appear, disappear, and reappear.[77] It increased or decreased according to conditions. Given educational, legal, and institutional efforts, Germany could and was transformed after 1945. If this is the case, it wasn't for three or four pre-Nazi decades when anti-Semitism was prevalent.

According to Browning, there are anti-Semites in the plural. For Goldhagen, German negativism should eventually disappear or be eliminated by conversion, assimilation, emigration, or extermination.

As Goldhagen proposed, if this was the case under Hitler, the variations of this organic malignancy all fused into extermination. "Germany," as Browning quotes Goldhagen, "was 'of one mind' with Hitler on the justice and necessity of the Final Solution."[78]

Browning parts company with Goldhagen, as Arendt probably would, on this issue. "Neither the election returns nor any plausible spin put on them suggests that in 1932 the vast majority of Germans were 'of one mind' with Hitler about the Jews or that the 'centrality of anti-Semitism in the Party's worldview, program, and rhetoric . . . mirrored the sentiments of German culture.'"[79] Instead, with the reign of Hitler, all factors increased anti-Semitism.

The success of the Nazis in their campaign to intensify anti-Semitism varied greatly. Nevertheless, researchers like Sir Ian Kershaw, Otto Dov Kulka, and David Bankier agree: "For the 1933–39 period, these three historians distinguish between a minority of party activists, for whom anti-Semitism was an urgent priority, and the bulk of the German population, for whom it was not."[80]

Browning writes that most Germans responded negatively to the 1933 boycott, the vandalism of 1935, and the Kristallnacht of November 9–10, 1938. That majority remained increasingly apathetic, passive, and indifferent to Germany's Jewish minority, less than 1 percent of the population.[81] Furthermore, most Germans wanted to limit or end the Jewish role in German society. That was a major Nazi accomplishment. It did not mean that ordinary Germans would approve or participate in the "mass murder of European Jewry, that the 'onlookers' of 1938 would become the genocidal killers of 1941–42."

Their attitude continued in the war years. The historians Browning cites "knew how to distinguish between an acceptable discrimination . . . and the unacceptable horror of genocide." News of it filtered in. There remained "a strikingly abysmal indifference to the fate of the Jews as human beings." That indifference gave the regime the freedom to push for a Final Solution. Browning quotes Ian

Kershaw's memorable phrase: "The road to Auschwitz was built by hatred but paved with indifference."[82]

Daniel Goldhagen declared indifference did not mean having any views and being utterly and morally neutral to mass slaughter. Germans were "not apathetic" and "indifferent" but "pitiless," "unsympathetic," and "callous," and their silence, according to Goldhagen, amounted to approval.[83] During the war years, "Germans may well have disliked Jews more while caring about them less."

There was a valuable and essential distinction between the Nazi core and the general population. At the war's front, especially in the East, ordinary Germans were more willing executioners than at home, where they were indifferent and apathetic. In the East, they were killers. Eastern Jews were not the assimilated, middle-class German Jews.[84] Browning concludes his remarks on Goldhagen with this comment: "Central to Goldhagen's interpretation is that these men were not only 'willing executioners' but, in fact, '*wanted* to be genocidal executioners' of Jews."[85]

Goldhagen states that "concerning the motivational cause of the Holocaust, for the vast majority of the perpetrators, a monocausal explanation does suffice, [namely the] demonological anti-Semitism [that] was the common structure of the perpetrators' cognition and German society in general."[86]

He has received widespread acclaim, even in Germany, though some condemned his methodology, use of sources, and overgeneralizations. When confronted with criticisms, Goldhagen replied that there were no other national genocides in Denmark or Italy, and only Germany operated as an eliminationist. Max Frankel of *The New York Times* concludes in his review of Goldhagen's book that "yet here we are closing out probably the most brutal century ever . . ."[87]

Goldhagen gives a vigorous defense of his book in "A Reply to My Critics."[88] He states, "The purpose of the central investigation of my book is to uncover and explain the perpetrators' pattern of actions, which includes the pattern of their choices." He shows that ordinary

Germans from all walks of life, at least one hundred thousand or more, were willing, even eager, executioners with a pervasive view of eliminationist anti-Semitism. To them, Jews differed racially from Germans as immutably evil and powerful. They had done great harm to Germany and would continue to do so. They had to be eliminated. The perpetrators' believed extermination was necessary and just.

Although reactions to his book varied, Goldhagen objected to the angry and disparaging ones. They were, he felt, either loosely connected to the book's contents or simply false, such as those that claimed his explanation was monocausal and deterministic or even ahistorical and racist about Germans. "None of these allegations," he claimed, "is true." Critics not only avoided the main issues but made untenable and implausible claims. Above all, a central question remained unanswered: Why did thousands upon thousands of typical Germans kill, torture, and degrade Jews "gleefully" while only a few withdrew when it was easy to do so?

By answering this fundamental question, Goldhagen's book confronted most other holocaust literature by refocusing attention from institutions and abstractions to the perpetrators themselves. They were not automatons and puppets but individuals who made choices and took responsibility. Their beliefs and values led to their actions against the Jews. So, he asks, what did ordinary Germans believe about Jews, and did that justify their actions?

Previously, these questions were avoided or indirectly answered with a laundry list of excuses: obedience to authority, peer pressure, routinization, rationalization, a siege mentality, brutalization, intoxication, totalitarianism, the banality of evil, industrialization, and technology. Goldhagen proposed to uncover and explain the perpetrators' pattern of actions, which included the pattern of their choices. These Germans were responsible agents who inflicted maximum cruelty upon their Jewish victims. Their brutality to beat and degrade was ubiquitous and committed by most Germans. It was singular to the Jews and not, generally, to other victims: euthanasia to other races or nationalities.

Ordinary Germans were "motivated by a virulent form of anti-Semitism that led them to believe that the extermination of Jews was necessary and just. They bragged and boasted about their torturing, took photos, and celebrated over it." Goldhagen put it simply: "They had a ball!" In other words, "anti-Semitic hatreds led them to want to revenge themselves for the harms that they fantasized that Jews had done to their country." By 1941–42, a "consensus existed that the Jews must be gone."

Goldhagen argues that a culturally shared model of Jews held them unalterably different from Germans and dangerous. They had to be eliminated somehow if Germany was to be secure and prosperous. That is the crucial model for understanding German readiness for genocide that culminated in the 1930s and 1940s.

He does not claim Germans are inherently evil, a monster nation, or that post-war Germany could not become democratic and free of anti-Semitism. The Holocaust did arise from Nazi Germany. It was mainly its phenomenon. No Hitler, no Holocaust! Hitler's moral authority was crucial for leaping to the genocidal variant of eliminationist ideology, which most Germans would never have contemplated. That point is central to Goldhagen's argument.[89]

For Hitler and those who implemented his genocidal plans, they shared a single source: virulent anti-Semitism. The most virulent Germans, the Nazis, took state power and turned that into the basis of their state policy as shared by the majority. Only Nazi Germany was in a geo-military position to carry out genocide. Even though gas accounted for 60 percent and shooting for 40 percent, the result would have been the same if gas chambers had not been employed.[90]

FOUR
STALIN'S INFAMY

> A single death is a tragedy. A million deaths is a statistic.

JOSEPH STALIN

I t was a warm, sunny Moscow day on August 2, 2001, when we—Dr. Eugene P. Trani and I—casually strolled into Mikhail Gorbachev's office at the Gorbachev Foundation on 39 Leningradsky Prospekt. It is a dull-gray, poured-cement affair of a building. Even before shaking Gorbachev's hand, the first thing we noticed was the large portrait of his late wife Raisa hanging behind his desk. She had been a patient at Virginia Commonwealth University's (VCU) hospital, where Dr. Trani was president.

1. MEETING EX-PRESIDENT GORBACHEV

Gorbachev came forward to greet us, warmly shook our hands, and said, "Hello, please sit down." We sat in two large, red leather sofas opposite each other—one for Dr. Trani and me and the other for

President Gorbachev and his translator, a thin, middle-aged lady. We were also seated with our Russian companion, Sergei Porshakov.

Gorbachev was a warm, friendly person, the guy you think you have known for a long time, though Soviet diplomat Andrei Gromyko once said he had "teeth of steel." British Prime Minister Margaret Thatcher believed you could do business with him.

Our Moscow friend, Sergei Porshakov, had arranged this interview through a one-time schoolmate and friend of his, Professor Viktor B. Kuvaldin, Gorbachev's right-hand man and senior political advisor. Dr. Trani had conferred an honorary doctorate on Gorbachev in the spring of 1993 for his contributions to world peace at VCU's commencement. Dr. Trani and I tried to avoid controversy and keep to questions that allowed Gorbachev to speculate about Russia's future and relations with the US, which proved impossible. Initially, we expressed our condolences to Gorbachev on his wife Raisa's death, who had passed away in 1999. Dr. Trani, as president of VCU, reminded Gorbachev of their meetings there. Gorbachev's archenemy, Boris Yeltsin, had replaced him in 1991. That had followed a failed Committee for State Security (KGB) August coup against Gorbachev, though he was blamed. The Soviet Union collapsed in December 1991. Then, in 2000, Yeltsin was substituted by his handpicked successor, Vladimir Putin. So our questions were often "softballs" and pitched "gently."

Nevertheless, Gorbachev was expansive, engaging, and took hardballs generously. It quickly became a warm, friendly, and intimate affair, but also a good give-and-take session. Generally, we started with domestic policies and ended with international relations. Among those who still favored a milder version of the Soviet Union rather than its destruction by Yeltsin, Mikhail Gorbachev had a Swedish model of socialism for continuing the USSR, we quickly discovered. As he told us in this 2001 interview and repeatedly to everyone else, "Some say over and over that the Soviet Union's collapse was inevitable, but I keep saying that the Soviet Union could have been preserved." Then, he added, "You criticize me: weak as JELL-O, more or less, in those terms. But what if that JELL-O wasn't in that position at that time? Who the hell knows what might have happened to us."

Gorbachev complained that he had thought more decisive steps would come from the American side to support his initiatives in glasnost (openness) and perestroika (restructuring) after he became general secretary of the communist party in 1984. He was after Western financial support. Given the volume of corruption then and now, Russia was a monumental risk.

Dr. Victor B. Kuvaldin, the director of the Gorbachev Foundation for political studies, had invited us as researchers to converse with Gorbachev for about an hour. Gorbachev was witty and robust. However, he was nearly seventy years old. He supported private ownership, a market economy, democracy, and nonviolence. Gorbachev expressed his optimism due to democracy's rise in contemporary Russia, its foreign relations' stability, international investments, and Russia's debt adjustments. He spoke of corruption during the Yeltsin administration, with politicians, security forces, and oligarchs dividing the USSR's properties among themselves in a scramble for privatization. He also felt Yeltsin's government tried to democratize without adequate preparation.

Although Russia recovered from its 1998 financial meltdown, Gorbachev still believed it needed foreign credits to speed stability, democratization, and a functioning market economy with the government at the "commanding heights," like Lenin's New Economic Policy (NEP) of the 1920s.

On foreign relations, Gorbachev thought the internal war in Chechnya was unnecessary and counterproductive. He emphasized Russia serving as a bridge between East and West and reminded us of his efforts at creating world peace with President Ronald Reagan.

We warmly shook hands upon leaving and had a group picture taken.[1] Dr. Trani and I hoped that Russia would again turn to Gorbachev's style of reforms and the Petrine example of Westernization that Gorbachev favored. Instead, Vladimir Putin has steadily moved to the authoritarianism reminiscent of the nineteenth century Slavophiles and courted the People's Republic of China (PRC), as well as snatching a piece of Georgia, taking Crimea, and invading Ukraine.

Gorbachev instituted changes: glasnost (openness) and perestroika (restructuring). He was cut short by his own security service's (KGB) rebellion against Westernization that these changes implied. The country rose against the KGB, thought Gorbachev was responsible, and replaced him with Boris Yeltsin, who failed after nine years and appointed Vladimir Putin, who, in return, promised the "family"—Yeltsin and friends—legal immunity.

Yeltsin had faced down the "Gang of Eight" conspirators from the top of a tank on August 19, 1991. Afterward, the USSR collapsed on December 25, 1991. Down came the hammer and sickle and up went Peter the Great's naval tricolor. As president of the Russian Federation, Yeltsin immediately moved into the now-defunct Kremlin office of ex-president of the USSR, Mikhail Gorbachev.

Then fools rushed in to cure Russia of its Soviet hangover. Treatments varied from Harvard's Jeffrey Sachs's economic "shock therapy" to Yeltsin's siege of the Russian White House on September 21, 1993. By August 17, 1998, all these efforts, foreign and domestic, failed to save the patient. The ruble crisis all but terminated experiments in Western-style democracy and capitalism in the Federation. Instead, a Russian-style "managed economy" (state capitalism) and a "sovereign democracy" (state authoritarianism) emerged.

Yeltsin appointed Yevgeny Primakov as prime minister and Vladimir Putin as the Federal Security Service (FSB) director. In August 1999, Yeltsin made Putin prime minister. Russia's president resigned on December 31, 1999. On New Year's Day 2000, Putin succeeded him, first as Russia's acting president and then as its elected president on May 7, 2000. He was reelected president from 2004 to 2008 and again from 2012 to 2018. Putin and Prime Minister Dmitry Medvedev were "tandemocracy" presidents or prime ministers until 2020.[2]

Yeltsin promoted renewed collaboration with Europe and signed arms control agreements with the US. Amid growing internal pressure, he resigned by the end of 1999 and was succeeded by his chosen successor, Prime Minister Vladimir Putin. On August 8, 2008, Russian forces began the invasion of Georgia. Six years after the Russo-Georgian War, Russia seized Crimea in 2014 and prepared for a comprehensive military campaign against Ukraine. Moscow continued the occupation of Crimea and, on February 24, 2022, began an invasion of Ukraine, capturing large swathes of Eastern Ukraine's Donbas region. Putin placed the North Atlantic Treaty Organization (NATO) in a dangerous diplomatic situation. Surprisingly, the war went badly for Russia, with Ukraine threatening to retake occupied areas with armament's help from the West.[3]

I am reminded of Sarajevo in June 1914 and the "Guns of August" that same year. Putin challenged what he interpreted as NATO's expansionism by demanding Ukraine remain Russia's client state. He invaded Ukraine by annexing Crimea in 2014 and then launched a wide-ranging attack on Ukraine on February 24, 2022. In response, NATO deployed additional forces to Eastern Europe, and tens of thousands of people fled the country, while others remained to fight. Instead of surrendering, Ukraine offered stiff resistance. NATO sustains a sanction regime, arms donations, and financial aid for Ukraine against Russia. The thirty-one NATO countries prepared to further defy Russia's threat of a potential European-wide war by rapidly rearming. America may militarily return to Europe in force, prepared to fight a land war with traditional military means, even tactical nuclear forces, if provoked by Russia. President Donald Trump seemed to reverse these indicatives of President Joseph Biden's administration. Since 2022, Finland and Sweden have joined NATO.

In 2020 the "tandemocracy" ended suddenly, and Mikhail Mishustin, then head of the Federal Taxation Service, took Medvedev's job. Medvedev was blamed for the stagnating economy. Constitutional changes of the two-term rule in July 2020 allow Putin to run for president twice more until 2036.[4]

Russia came a long way from Stalin's days to what Gorbachev tried. His successors opened things up "Russian-style" at the cost of corruption and heavy-handed bureaucracy. A modern-style Peter the Great might come along and drag Russia into the West again—a place where it seems to belong. Instead, Putin has returned Russia to its Pan-Slavic roots of nineteenth century obscurantism by pivoting east to China (PRC). The Russo-Ukrainian War returns Russia to increasing isolation, as well as threatening world peace. Neo-Stalinism has become popular again. Russians should think twice about that, as the following examples reveal.

2. THE KREMLIN MOUNTAINEER

Nadezhda Mandelstam mercilessly exposed Stalin's communism in her 1970 memoir *Hope Against Hope*. In her explosive opening, she recounts how her famous poet-husband Osip publicly slapped one of Stalin's literary favorites, the "Red Count" Aleksey Tolstoy. "I have punished the hangman," Osip explained, "who ordered the beating of my wife!" Tolstoy went whimpering to playwright Maxim Gorky, who reportedly said, "We'll teach him to strike Russian writers."

In 1932 Tolstoy excused novelist Amir Sargidzhan (who published under the pen name of Sergei Borodin) at the comrades' court for hurting, and some say, raping Nadezhda. Tolstoy, in his acquittal judgment, called out, "I couldn't do anything! We had our orders." Nadezhda recalled that her husband believed "the man ought not to have obeyed the orders."[5] His slapping of Tolstoy was Osip's outward sign of his inner grace, according to Nadezhda.

That grace returned to Osip during his vacation to Armenia in 1930, when he denounced the socialist formula for literature, "national in form, socialist in content," as stupid and illiterate. It was his sense of being right, of recreating his inner freedom. That gave him the power not to obey orders and write his 1934 poem against Stalin, "The Kremlin Mountaineer" (or "The Stalin Epigram").

That poem caused his arrest a few days later and, eventually, his death. After his arrest, Nadezhda devoted her life to the cause of her husband's censored poetry. It seemed as if his published poetic career of three books and an essay had reached its peak by 1928: *Poems*, an essay *On Poetry*, *The Noise of Time*, and *The Egyptian Stamp*. During their exile to Voronezh, Osip completed three notebooks. Nadezhda's memoir underlines the battle between Osip's humanist values and the Stalinist totalitarian system that ordered collectivization in 1928 and ran by decrees enforced through terror.

When and where in the world could a man, by decree, be sentenced to die for reciting a short poem to a few friends? In 1934, in Moscow! Osip Mandelstam wrote, "Poetry is respected only in this country—people are killed for it. There's no place where more people are killed for it."[6] Nadezhda Mandelstam noted this Russian leader's one remarkable feature was his boundless, almost superstitious respect for poetry. The first to hear her husband's poem, "The Stalin Epigram," were horrified. They begged Osip to forget it and called it a suicide note. They knew its self-evident truth against Stalin. His apologizers forgave the tyrant of his massacre of the peasantry in his five-year plans and of dissidents in the "Great Terror" of the 1930s, as well as his megalomania. They bestowed on him the myth of his building communism and stubbornly clung to it, shedding no tears for Mandelstam or the collectivized peasantry.[7]

The first listeners had different views of Mandelstam's dangerous, electrifying poem. A young friend, Boris Kuzin, believed it did not square with Mandelstam's earlier ideas of Bolshevism, the Russian version of Marxism. "Scrap that poem," he told Mandelstam. "Put up with Stalin." Writer and journalist Ilya Ehrenburg also thought the poem was atypical of Mandelstam's earlier, sophisticated verses due to its brutal simplicity. Some complaints annoyed Nadezhda. Kuzin, she thought, had never understood her husband's poetry.

Ehrenburg, who considered the poem a freak, did not see it as a logical progression of Mandelstam's thinking. Even Boris Pasternak, poet and novelist, did not like it because a Jew like himself wrote it, which would encourage anti-Semitism and be especially bad for children. Nadezhda rejected these notions as misunderstandings.

Yet the poem's accusations directly confronted Stalin. Mandelstam was arrested in 1934 and sent to Cherdyn in Siberia, then Voronezh, about 320 miles south of Moscow. He was rearrested in 1937 and condemned to Kolyma's labor camp in the Far East. He died in transit from there to Vladivostok in December 1938. One of Russia's greatest poets lies in an unmarked mass grave. His inflammatory poem reads as follows:[8]

The Kremlin Mountaineer

We live, deaf to the land beneath us,
Ten steps away, no one hears our speeches,

But where there's so much as half a conversation
The Kremlin's mountaineer will get his mention.

His fingers are fat as grubs.
And the words, final as lead weights, fall from his lips,

His cockroach whiskers leer
And his boot tops gleam.

Around him a rabble of thin-necked leaders—
Fawning half-men for him to play with.

They whinny, purr or whine.
As he prates and points a finger,

One by one forging his laws, to be flung
Like horseshoes at the head, the eye or the groin.

And every killing is a treat
For the broad-chested Ossete.

This translation retains the original text as eight alternating rhymed couplets of two lines each, totaling sixteen. As one critic suggested, Mandelstam's Russian is purposefully overt, colloquial, and conversational and contains the poet's neologisms.[9] The poem's meter is alternating anapest: a metrical foot consisting of two short syllables followed by one long syllable or two unstressed syllables followed by one stressed syllable. The first-person plural "we" is intended to remind us of folk couplets.

The first couplet gives a sense of running and looking back from fear while being deaf and dumb to the land itself. Stalin is revealed as the mountain boy who not only gets everyone's attention in the second couplet, but also in the third and fourth. His appearance and manner of speech are cynically illustrated: grubby fingers and screeching voice. That illusion is carried over to his cockroach-like mustache and his military-style boots of a commander-in-chief.

The next two couplets characterize Stalin's lieutenants as worse than half-men, but as fairy-tale-like demons who praise and catcall at his command. They make his terrible laws to maim and kill the opposition and amuse this non-Russian Ossete. In the next to last line, Mandelstam uses the Russian word for raspberry (*malina*), which was a slang word for a criminal whose ill-gotten gains provided a good life.[10]

In his biography, *Stalin: The Court of the Red Tsar*, Simon Montefiore gives both a penetrating analysis of the dictator's grasp of literature and an interpretation of Mandelstam's fate at Stalin's hands. He notes that Stalin not only admired but appreciated great literature. He had a way of separating commonplace from literary genius. The dictator was a voracious reader, with a thirst for mastering literature almost as great as his devouring of Marxism. Like Hitler with architecture, so Stalin with literature: It was his obsessive hobby. Montefiore even claims it would be no exaggeration to say that Stalin was the best-read ruler of Russia from Catherine the Great to Vladimir Putin, including Lenin.[11] Though he banned Dostoevsky as bad for children, Stalin enjoyed Mikhail Zoshchenko's satires. He recognized Boris Pasternak and Mikhail Bulgakov as geniuses, but Stalin suppressed their works even though he never arrested them. Mandelstam was just too much.

Genrikh Yagoda, head of the secret police (OGPU), recited Mandelstam's poem to the dictator. This poem damned and mocked him as the bewhiskered Kremlin's cliff dweller, a peasant slayer, and maggoty fat-fingered Ossete. His coterie was only a rabble of thin-necked bosses. Stalin ordered Yagoda to "preserve but isolate" Mandelstam.[12]

On May 16–17, 1934, Mandelstam was arrested and sentenced to three years of internal exile beyond the one-hundred-kilometer "safety" ring around Moscow and Leningrad. When interrogated, he admitted to authoring the poem.[13] His friends, writer Boris Pasternak and poet Anna Akhmatova, appealed to Nikolai Bukharin, editor of *Pravda*, and Avel Yenukidze, member of the Central Committee. Bukharin wrote Stalin that Mandelstam was a first-class poet, though abnormal. Pasternak, he further noted, was flabbergasted. Bukharin continued, "Poets are always right, history is on their side." Stalin muttered, "Who authorized Mandelstam's arrest? Disgraceful."[14]

Stalin's attitude appeared to have softened before Mandelstam's appearance at the Writers' Congress. The dictator made a personal call to Pasternak to calm the waters and told Pasternak to quote him. "Mandelstam's case is being reviewed," he told Pasternak. "Everything will be all right. If I were a poet and my poet friend found himself in trouble, I would do anything to help him." Pasternak interrupted Stalin to clarify "friendship."

"But," Stalin continued, "he's a genius, isn't he?"

Pasternak replied, "But that's the point."

Stalin replied, "What is the point, then?"

Pasternak wanted to come to the Kremlin and explain. Stalin asked, "About what?" And Pasternak said, "About life and death."

Baffled, Stalin abruptly hung up.

Mandelstam spent a short time in Cherdyn and three years in Voronezh. Rearrested in 1938, Mandelstam went to Kolyma prison camp near Vladivostok.

Nadezhda chronicled her husband's life and death in Soviet Russia. It is a moving, penetrating portrait of her husband and their lives in a totalitarian state, and it opens with the famous slap.[15]

By May 13, 1934, the Mandelstams had nothing to cheer about in life. "They've come for Osip," Nadezhda reported. Chekists, the secret police of the Joint State Political Directorate, were considered the avant-garde and supermen of the new Soviet people, "Homo Sovieticus," like Hitler's SS. They arrived at 1:00 a.m. with topcoats covering their uniforms. Two witnesses accompanied them. They began by checking Mandelstam's papers, making an apartment search, serving arrest warrants, interrogating the couple, and passing sentences on the accused.

Nadezhda thought these raiding bandits were the sort who put a "tiny hole" in the skull of one of Soviet Russia's greatest short story writers, Isaac Babel.[16]

David Brodsky, a translator, was visiting the Mandelstams and probably had been ordered there as a stooge to prevent the destruction of evidence. Nadezhda helped sort papers, and Osip recited his poetry to pass the time.

Unlike his arrest in 1934, Mandelstam's second arrest in 1938 was abrupt. One might say they threw him and his writings into a sack and dragged them off. Arrests had become so frequent that suspects ceased asking what they were being arrested for; they treated that question as forbidden.

The Mandelstams never doubted what their arrest was for, as it was because of that poem, "The Stalin Epigram." Osip Mandelstam would pay for it with his life.

Nadezhda recognized no other standard of law that applied to Soviet rule. People were picked up wholesale by categories and age groups to be destroyed. The remainder would create the unanimity needed for the communist millennium. The exterminating profession had a saying: "Give us a man, and we'll make a case." Nadezhda learned on one May night that though she could not save her husband, she could keep his work, but only by memorizing it all.[17]

Her friends, primarily the poet Anna Akhmatova, rescued whatever manuscripts remained and carried them off in their pockets or shopping bags. They stopped using taboo words such as "arrested," "picked up," or "taken away." Any scraps were left where they had fallen as the Chekists (secret police) returned for a second round, looking for something specific. Then there were the "tails"—special agents following her as common informers.

Nadezhda and Anna distributed copies of small batches of his works to friends for safekeeping. Most, Nadezhda wrote, were lost, but their fate was inconsequential compared to their efforts at saving poems.[18] There was no third search or arrest. Soon both the Mandelstams were arrested.

Nadezhda again appealed to Nikolai Bukharin, editor of *Pravda*. He asked her pointedly if Osip had written anything rash. She lied purposely and excused herself because that poem was no worse than whatever else her husband had written, and her lying got a lesser punishment: exile to Voronezh. Though she remained ashamed of it, she believed it was necessary, typical of the infamous times, and had a satisfactory result under such conditions.

Bukharin was not yet frightened off. Besides, Bukharin confessed that slapping Tolstoy could not have gotten Osip arrested. Nadezhda continued going to Bukharin, but these were the last meetings. She discovered that Bukharin had told Ilya Ehrenburg the Yagoda story of reciting the poem to Stalin. Yagoda had signed the warrant for Osip's arrest.

Sensing his doom, Bukharin finally refused to see her anymore. By then, he had done everything he could to save her husband. He wrote Stalin asking for clemency. The best advice from then on was to keep mum and show no signs of life. Nadezhda noted that Mandelstam had offended Stalin, the most awesome person in the land.[19] No wonder everyone avoided Osip.

Within a couple weeks of Osip's arrest, Nadezhda visited him in the Lubyanka, the headquarters of the secret police. They told him of her arrest as a lie to soften him up. When they brought him to the interview room, he appeared wild-eyed, distraught, and malnourished. The interrogator was familiar with the first draft of the poem, but he misquoted the fourth line: "All we hear is the Kremlin mountaineer, the murderer, and peasant slayer."

The authorities called the poem a "'counter-revolutionary document without precedent' and referred to me [Nadezhda] as an accessory to the fact. Although he was charged with a crime and punishment mentioned, [Nadezhda] heard the phrase 'isolate and preserve.'" That indicated a supreme act of compassion coming from the top. There would be no forced labor on the White Sea, and Mandelstam's sentence was commuted to Cherdyn. She could accompany him.[20]

They began a life of inescapable doom in a land of nonbeing. Ghosts of the liquidated would never rise and call their persecutors to account. Besides, the liquidators were—like Eichmann—supposedly just carrying out orders.

The Mandelstams expected to be shot whenever convenient. People took no notice, fearing being infected by a criminal virus. They were forgotten outcasts, struck from the living rolls, stripped of their names, and marked as numbered and registered. Their first place of exile in the minus twelve (Russia's twelve central cities) and out of the hundred-kilometer zone from Moscow was Cherdyn, near the Kama River's upper reaches.

Nadezhda recounted "that we were saved by a miracle that gave us the three-year lease on life in Voronezh." Cherdyn had been full of resettled peasants and deported kulaks (middle-class peasants) as a result of the five-year plans' collectivization.

In desperation, while suffering hallucinations and delirium, Osip Mandelstam tried to kill himself by jumping out of a hospital window. He survived with a broken arm. His peasant guards believed him to be a conspirator who brought death to those who heard him recite his poems. Other exiles believed that Cherdyn was a bottomless pit where officials, like Hitler's SS, destroyed people without leaving a trace.

The Mandelstams' brief stay there ended when they selected Voronezh. A friend had once suggested Voronezh, and to those in Cherdyn, it sounded like paradise. The miracle was exceptional because officials broke promises. People lost trust, "the first sign of the atomization of society in dictatorships of our type, and this was just what our leaders wanted." Voronezh was a grim place, often lacking much food.[21]

Like Cherdyn, Voronezh depicted a scene of mass deportations. In Soviet Russia, they resulted from Stalin's collectivization. This enormous uprooting, Nadezhda claimed, "destroyed our culture in the process and reverted to savagery." On the trip there, her husband regained his sanity while she contracted spotted typhus.

Three years in Voronezh required securing and maintaining official papers like residence permits, identity cards, and temporary housing permits. Each had separate renewal dates. They needed food and work. Dispossessed farmers begged in the streets. Though not a criminal, Nadezhda could only remain in Moscow for short periods, and she did not regain her right to live there until 1964. Denunciations were rampant with people, like their landlords, writing whatever came into their heads. These accusations subsided after the fall of Nikolai Yezhov, Yagoda's replacement and head of the People's Commissariat for Internal Affairs (NKVD) in 1939, the new name for the OGPU.

At five different times, they selected smaller rooms with twelve square meters in Voronezh and lived, like everyone else, on potatoes, cabbage soup, and eggs. They could not depend on kindness since it had disappeared like everything else. The State Publishing House still gave them occasional translation work.

Stalin's 1930 article in the party magazine *Bolshevik* demanded ideological purity and completely prohibited unsuitable books. All they could do was, as Russians say, "scream under the Kremlin walls." Only the grandees of literature found work, and Mandelstam was expected to write hymns of praise to Stalin. For local performances, Mandelstam composed program notes for pay. However, "life in Voronezh was happier than any we had ever known. M. was very fond of the town itself."[22]

In Voronezh, Mandelstam wrote most of his last poems, the *Voronezh Notebooks*. Often, he was nearly insane and required his wife's presence. They managed their financial affairs, helped by friends and a few weeks of rest at Zadonsk. Though almost unemployable, Mandelstam wrote local radio scripts.

The assassination of Politburo (executive committee of the communist party) member Sergei Kirov on December 1, 1934, marked the beginning of the Great Purge. The resulting increased vigilance meant virtually no work for Mandelstam. He tried to write an "Ode to Stalin" as a desperate measure, but it failed.[23] "To write an ode to Stalin, it was necessary to get in tune like a musical instrument by deliberately giving way to the liturgy, which in those days blotted out all human voices."[24]

When the exile sentence ended, they returned to Moscow but could not get their old apartment back. The tenant, wanting the rooms for himself, denounced them. Their Moscow registration ended, and they lived in towns nearby.

On April 30, 1938, Mandelstam was rearrested while staying at a sanatorium, sent to Butyrka prison, and shipped to the camps. He died at a transit camp near Vladivostok on December 27, 1938.[25]

Mandelstam's death is, in concentrated form, a Stalinist example of the twentieth century's infamy. It spared no one, not even one of Russia's most significant modern poets. Stalinism lingered on even after Stalin died in 1953, with cruel consequences.

Timothy Snyder's book *Bloodlands: Europe Between Hitler and Stalin* shows the "historical overlap *between* German and Soviet aspirations and power." Hannah Arendt had focused on mass industrial society's "dehumanization" rather than how these two states similarly and systematically exterminated undesirables, most famously, people like Mandelstam. The fate of captured soldiers for Snyder was not "progressive alienation" but a means of "extracting labor." Further, the Nazis separated death by exhaustion after transport and forced labor from death by extermination at camps like Belzec. Stalin put them in the state administered camps (gulags) or executed them in Moscow's Lubyanka prison. For Snyder, the first meant hunger, endless work, and the rare event of survival. The second meant immediate and certain death by gassing or a shot to the head. He concludes that "the vast majority of Jews killed in the Holocaust never saw a concentration camp." But Auschwitz combined both concentration and extermination. Each totalitarian state signified dysfunctionality and destructiveness, so the infamy of each—Nazi or Soviet—overlapped. Still, Snyder maintains, the crucial question remains: "How could (how can) so many lives be brought to a violent end?"[26] The twentieth century answered: New technological possibilities added a quantitative measure to the new quality of destructiveness.

3. THE PASTERNAK AFFAIR

On October 23, 1958, Anders Oesterling, permanent secretary of the Swedish Academy, announced the Nobel Prize for Literature to Boris Pasternak "for his notable achievement in both contemporary poetry and the field of the great Russian narrative tradition."[27] The Academy had short-listed three candidates: Alberto Moravia, Isak Dinesen, and Boris Pasternak. Oesterling told the Academy it could "make its decision with a clear conscience—regardless of the temporary difficulty that Pasternak's novel, so far, cannot appear in the Soviet Union." In additional remarks, he singled out the novel as a "great achievement to have been able to complete under difficult circumstances a work of such dignity, high above all political party frontiers and rather apolitical in its entirely human outlook."[28]

Max Frankel of *The New York Times* explained how Pasternak reacted to his "new role, a new heavy responsibility. I am thrilled, but you must understand this new lonely role as though it had always been so." He told Frankel that only the Poles gave him translating work in

the year following the Italian publication and that the prize would add
to his difficulties. "I am," he said, "not a victim of any injustice. I have
not been singled out for special treatment. Under the circumstances,
nothing else could be done." On the day of the announcement, he told
another correspondent, "This is a great joy for me. I don't feel any
tremendous emotion. I'm just delighted." And to another, "To receive
this prize fills me with joy and also gives me great moral support. But
my joy today is lonely."

Nevertheless, he still seemed to believe a trip to Stockholm was
possible. "If I do travel to Stockholm, at least I will have a month and
a half to relax and rest." Pasternak's formal reply to the Swedish
Academy expressed his gratitude: "immensely thankful, touched,
proud, astonished, abashed."[29] If he went, he would be stepping out of
the Soviet writers' village of Peredelkino, a "cocoon of comfort," but
surrounded by a network of spies. Even Pasternak had asked in a
poem, "What century is it outside?" After all, other writers had been
called out of a Peredelkino-like existence and murdered: Boris Pilnyak
in October 1937, Mandelstam in 1938, and Isaac Babel in May 1939.
Why not Pasternak? Stalin had said, "Leave him alone, he's a cloud
dweller."

His friend, the philosopher Isaiah Berlin, wrote about the novel
that it was a "magnificent" masterpiece in the central tradition of
Russian literature, "a personal avowal of overwhelming directness,
nobility, and depth." It was, as author Frances Stonor Saunders put it,
"a miraculous retrieval of the past in an age that had outlawed
history."[30] But the prompt Soviet reaction to Pasternak's Nobel Prize
appeared hasty, harsh, and heartless. He had earlier submitted his
manuscript of *Doctor Zhivago* to the literary journal *Novy Mir* (New
World) for serialization in its pages. The editorial board refused to
publish it. In a September 1956 letter, the members explained why.
They maintained that it was the spirit of Pasternak's novel that they
objected to, not its literary or aesthetic value. That would only be a
matter of personal tastes or one of likes and dislikes. They found that
Pasternak's novel did not accept the socialist revolution. "The general

tenor of your novel is that the October Revolution, the civil war, and the social transformations involved did not give the people anything but suffering and destroyed the Russian intelligentsia, either physically or morally." The novel, in their opinion, concluded that "the October Revolution was a mistake, that the participation in it of sympathizers from among the intelligentsia was an irreparable disaster, and that everything which happened afterward was evil." Dr. Zhivago's life and death, they further insisted, is a "story of the life and death of the Russian intelligentsia, a story of its road to the revolution and through the revolution, and of its death as a result of the revolution."[31]

The revolutionary year 1917 acted as both the watershed of the novel and of Russia itself. The novel's first third was acceptable because it did not contain a clear nonacceptance of Great October, the Bolshevik seizure of power, but the remaining two-thirds did. Only in a vague and general way, they argued, did Pasternak disown bourgeois, pre-revolutionary Russia as unjust.

The author, so they claimed, had the intelligentsia only living in an atmosphere of revolution. Real suffering, however, seemed unknown to them as the revolution itself exploded in their faces. They regretted it because they had to face personal discomforts. Zhivago, his friends, and Lara, his love, also sought only their own well-being. That made Zhivago an intellectual philistine. He was bloated with self-importance but removed from the people to the point of betraying them. Such people did not deserve Pasternak's "unqualified apologia and surrogates to echo a diatribe against Russia."[32]

The editors believed section 4 of chapter 11, "The Forest Brotherhood," was the novel's key. It was where Pasternak and his hero Zhivago were the same person. It showed Pasternak's complete sympathy for the doctor and his unqualified justification of his hero's thoughts and actions. That chapter was where Zhivago entered a tortuous, treacherous path of compassion with the counterrevolutionary Whites, especially a young White Guard soldier he failed to kill and then let go.[33]

The editors also considered the "Epilogue," which consisted of Zhivago's poems. In these, Zhivago emerged as an essentially immoral man and a superman who betrayed his duty to the people. In their opinion, Pasternak's Dr. Zhivago was the acme of the Russian intelligentsia's spirit: He was a "slough." Pasternak's intelligentsia "went astray from their true goal by serving the people, spiritually destroyed themselves, and created nothing worthwhile."

The editors concluded that the book was "profoundly unjust and historically prejudiced." They claimed Pasternak's view of the October Revolution was that it "brought nothing but evil and hardships."[34] Therefore, at the time of the award, the newspaper *Literaturnaya Gazeta* shot a vicious volley at *Doctor Zhivago* in an article titled "A Provocative Sally of International Reaction" (October 25, 1958). The anonymous writer believed the novel was filled with lies and hypocrisy. As to the Nobel Prize, "the presentation of the award for an artistically poverty-stricken and malicious work, which is full of hatred of socialism, is an adverse political act directed against the Soviet Union."[35]

The writer reminded his readers that the editorial board of *Novy Mir* turned the novel down as counterrevolutionary and slanderous. Pasternak had to send it to a bourgeois publication house abroad. Dr. Zhivago was a renegade and traitor who scorned the October Revolution and the Russian people. Pasternak was a megalomaniac, and Zhivago was a petty, mean, and useless person. Pasternak had put a weapon in the enemy's hands. David Zaslavsky, who wrote an article in *Pravda* titled "Reactionary Propaganda Uproar over a Literary Weed," (October 26, 1958), called Pasternak a "superfluous man" and an "anti-realistic" writer. He continued that the novel was full of empty rhetoric of a "self-enamored Narcissus." *Doctor Zhivago,* Zaslavsky maintained, was "full of comic and grotesque exaggeration of a Russian bourgeois intellectual with petty feelings and rotten thoughts—a moral freak."[36]

The Union of Soviet Writers expelled Pasternak on October 27, 1958. It characterized the novel as a "cry of a frightened philistine, offended and terrified by the fact that history did not follow the crooked paths that he would have liked to allot to it." V. E. Semichastny, writing for the Central Committee of the Komsomol (Communist League of Youth), said that *Zhivago* was the "slanderous work" of a "mangy sheep" and compared Pasternak to a pig who has "fouled the spot where he ate and cast filth on those by whose labor he lives and breathes."[37]

Because of these angry barrages, Pasternak wrote Premier Nikita Khrushchev, the general secretary of the communist party, on November 1, 1958, renouncing the Nobel Prize. "I am linked with Russia by my birth, life, and work. I cannot imagine my fate separate from and outside Russia. Whatever my mistakes and errors, I could not imagine that I would be in the center of such a political campaign as started to be fanned around my name in the West." He "voluntarily" renounced the prize.

In another letter, this one to *Pravda* on November 5, 1958, he repeated the other apologies and acknowledged that *Novy Mir* had warned him, and he regretted not listening. He could not accept the assertions that he had renounced the October Revolution, or that it brought misfortunes, or destroyed Russia's intelligentsia.[38]

One of *Doctor Zhivago*'s best reviews in the West was written by Edmund Wilson, the noted novelist and literary critic. Wilson emphasized Pasternak's central theme: death and resurrection. That, Wilson considered, put Pasternak in the same worldly tradition as Pushkin and Tolstoy. Pasternak avoided dead political abstractions asserted by authoritarian governments and was generally outside Marxism and Soviet writings. Wilson contended that the Soviet experience was only incidental and local to human life itself for Pasternak. Life consists of a free personality, continually renewing itself. The integral unit was the individual, not classes or theories.[39]

On one level, *Doctor Zhivago* relates a story of a man torn between two women's love. It also reveals the author's sensitivity and understanding of Russia's fate under a communist dictatorship on a much deeper level. That destiny meant Zhivago's destruction and that of those he represented: the upper classes and intelligentsia. In a very nostalgic moment at the end of the novel, two of Zhivago's best friends look out over Moscow at the close of World War II and hope for better days after the suffering from 1917–1945.

Wilson concluded his review by calling this novel one of the great works of our time. It is, for him, a religious parable and narrative poem. All are given their due to being caricatured or glorified. When Zhivago loses Lara, that episode becomes the emotional high point of the novel. Wilson finishes, *"Doctor Zhivago* will, I believe, come to stand as one of the great events in man's literary and moral history."[40]

Although Pasternak's Russian critics were brutal in their estimation of the novel and its author, they correctly understood its attack on the history and values of the Soviet state. It may not be as good a novel as Wilson thought, but it and Pasternak's fate grimly remind us of life in a totalitarian state. Another Russian author, one among the many, suffered but chose exile.

4. SOLZHENITSYN AT HARVARD YARD

Aleksandr Solzhenitsyn's life in the West remained controversial. There was his criticism of novelist Mikhail Sholokhov, the Russian version of Leni Riefenstahl. Sholokhov succeeded with Stalin's patronage, like Leni Riefenstahl under Hitler, while Osip Mandelstam and Stefan Zweig perished.

Fyodor Kryukov (1870–1920) was a Cossack White Army soldier in the Russian Civil War. He might be the real author of the acclaimed novel *And Quiet Flows the Don* instead of Mikhail Sholokhov. Literary critics like Aleksandr Solzhenitsyn and Roy Medvedev suggested that Sholokhov may have plagiarized this work. A statistical analysis in 2005 by V. P. and T. G. Fomenko came to the same conclusion.[41] In 1984 Geir Kjetsaa believed Sholokhov was the author of *And Quiet Flows the Don*.

Sholokhov asked *Pravda* in 1929 to prove his authorship by submitting the manuscript. A commission accepted Sholokhov's claim: There was no evidence of plagiarism, and the manuscript's style was Sholokhov's.[42] Nobel laureate and novelist Aleksandr Solzhenitsyn disagreed. That critique caught *New York Times* journalist Harrison Salisbury's eye. As Salisbury recalled, Solzhenitsyn's piece on Sholokhov in London's *The Times Literary Supplement* had claimed that Sholokhov stole the work. There were rumors about it already at the time of its publication. Solzhenitsyn asked, How could a twenty-three-year-old beginner lacking experience, education, or sufficient exposure in the Don River region during the revolution and civil war write such a book? Besides, it was written with extraordinary speed between 1926 and 1928. Sholokhov never again wrote anything of that quality, and various revisions of his are weak. A close examination showed fallacies of slovenliness, forgetfulness, and breaks, and Sholokhov's insertions lack connection with the story. Sholokhov's later work, *Virgin Soil Upturned,* was, as Solzhenitsyn noted, "not the same thing, not the same level, not the same canvas, not the same perception of the world." Solzhenitsyn asked, "Could any artist do that to a work which he has created with so much effort?" Solzhenitsyn gave credence to a Cossack White Guard soldier as the author, who died in 1920 of typhus. He thinks Sholokhov plagiarized Fyodor Kryukov's writings, especially his diaries. Presumably, these materials were found in a box of manuscripts and then lost during the German invasion. Solzhenitsyn also cites an anonymous literary critic, "D," who, before his death, came to the same conclusion but remained quiet, fearing official Soviet retaliation.[43]

Salisbury reviewed Solzhenitsyn's criticism by emphasizing "D's" unpublished scholarship. As Salisbury put it, "The critique by 'D' seeks to establish that the Kryukov work was then used by a coauthor, Mr. Sholokhov, who inserted several new characters, principally Bolsheviks, some ideological passages and a 'bridge' from the original material to the new."[44]

Salisbury also praised Solzhenitsyn as a harsh voice who dared to challenge American values head-on. In Solzhenitsyn's Harvard Yard speech of 1978, he denounced American youth for objecting to the

Vietnam War, criticized rock 'n' roll, indicted the US intelligentsia for cowardice, trashed the Declaration of Independence for evoking the pursuit of happiness, reviled the welfare state, and saw America as indifferent to good and evil. Here was the courage and frankness of one who even defended the right of people not to know.

Solzhenitsyn had, in Salisbury's estimation, poured all of his life into that speech. "I thought," Salisbury remarked, that "he had made a grave but understandable mistake in this conclusion." The conclusion was that "American civilization was not a serious one." Salisbury believed the "New York literary community dropped his name down the memory hole."[45]

Salisbury had previously corresponded with Solzhenitsyn about publishing matters. They first met in person when the Russian gave his "A World Split Apart" address at Harvard Class Day Afternoon Exercises on Thursday, June 8, 1978.

Salisbury came to Cambridge that rainy morning to prepare for WGBH-TV of Boston to analyze the Nobel laureate's remarks. In addition, Tom Whitney, the American who translated the first two volumes of *The Gulag Archipelago* into English, had invited the Solzhenitsyns to his Connecticut home for the following weekend. The Whitneys' guests for Saturday's dinner party included the Salisburys, playwright Arthur Miller and his wife, and novelist William Styron and his wife. Salisbury notes these two occasions capture Solzhenitsyn's critique of the West as not a paragon of virtue but an accomplice in infamy.

Salisbury arrived at Harvard Yard just after Solzhenitsyn had received an honorary degree. He had reviewed an advanced text of the speech, labeling it "a powerful approach, the strongest he has made, and the first in which he has placed his essential criticism of the West in a logical and coherent form." It was, Salisbury thought, also an assault on the evils of communism. The United States was weak, according to Solzhenitsyn, misunderstanding Soviet Russia's threat, unable to summon courage because of America's materialist glut. Salisbury speculated that the Massachusetts Bay Colony's Increase

Mather would have been more receptive to Solzhenitsyn's words than contemporary Harvard dons, especially regarding the speech's good and evil themes.

Solzhenitsyn harshly criticized American liberalism, attacked the press, defended the right not to know, and criticized American ultra-legalism contrary to a higher law. He blamed Renaissance humanism for that. The West offered no model for Russia, and Russians would find their own way out of the suffering caused by communism. Morality had a role in diplomacy.

There were unusual delays as the Harvard crowd reassembled after their post-commencement spreads for Solzhenitsyn's 2:00 p.m. address. Salisbury introduced himself to Mrs. Natalia Solzhenitsyn and said hello to Mrs. Irina Alberti, the factotum of Solzhenitsyn's ensemble. Her chore was to read the speaker's English translation simultaneously over the loudspeakers. She greeted Salisbury warmly and told him to defend Solzhenitsyn in the WGBH-TV show.

The speaker and his Harvard entourage passed down the yard and onto the platform. Solzhenitsyn spoke in Russian at a moderate pace and with gestures. Alberti's flat, technical English reading drowned out the speaker. Salisbury claimed Solzhenitsyn was a speaker of enormous force and range, so Alberti's blotting out was unfortunate. Almost everyone remained seated instead of bolting out over the great author's harsh remarks.

Salisbury recalled that there were twenty-five rounds of applause throughout and a tumultuous ovation at the end. Solzhenitsyn was pleased with how enthusiastically young people responded. Harrison was impressed that Harvard's elders initiated most of the applause, especially over Solzhenitsyn's anti-materialism remarks. He also noted there was no applause when the speaker called for the United States to stand up to Soviet provocations.

Afterward, Salisbury rushed to the platform, tapping Solzhenitsyn on the shoulder. He turned and spoke. "Yes, Gospodin (Mr.) Salisbury."

Salisbury continued, "He brightened, a big smile came over his face, and he continued [in Russian], 'Garrison! At last, we meet.' I told him the speech had been terrific and that I was doing a commentary on it and would see him tomorrow."

Salisbury sauntered over to economist John Kenneth Galbraith's home, where he was meeting with friends. At the doorway, John K. Fairbank and Adam Ulam—Harvard's China and Russia experts—chatted. Ulam maintained Solzhenitsyn said nothing new, and no one was interested in him. For Salisbury, this was "a classic attitude of the Harvard Russian department if ever I heard one."

Salisbury believed the speech was a more precise statement of Solzhenitsyn's views. He now carried his argument back to the Middle Ages. "Oh, says Adam, but there is nothing new in that." Salisbury later wrote that "Solzh's philosophy did not bowl over the Harvard intellectuals; thought it out of tune with the times, etc., etc.—all the usual expectable reaction."[46]

The following day, *The New York Times* ran a brief article on Solzhenitsyn's speech, calling it a "bitter view of a West grown slack, pusillanimous and evil through devotion to man's appetite instead of God's design." The address was exemplary against the Chinese as future Stalinists and "a very Russian speech. A biblical speech. I could see him as a prophet of the Third Rome, pronouncing anathema on the Roman church's infamy and its break with Byzantium." It was delivered, the reporter wrote, "in tones of an evangelist excoriating sinners [and] delivered in Russian and amplified over his voice by an interpreter speaking English [as well as] a philippic against the press."[47]

Harrison criticized *The New York Times* article as too brief and lacking excerpts. "I can't for the life of me understand why *Times* did not run text or at least a half-page of excerpts. I suspect it is due to the genuine Jewish antipathy for Solzhenitsyn, which is based on their feeling, which I think is probably soundly based though not articulated by Solzhenitsyn, uncomfortableness with his blatant and strong Orthodoxy, and a general feeling that he is too radical and absolute for their taste."[48]

Over a lavish Saturday night banquet at the Whitneys, Solzhenitsyn contributed further understanding to his speech. He took, according to Salisbury, "enormous pleasure at the reception in Cambridge. He had regarded his move as very daring, going right into the camp of the enemy." Several times during the evening he referred to the speech's warm applause by young Americans. He thought they were open-minded and could change things. He reiterated that religion was "the very central question of his speech because religion and belief were at the center of the moral dilemma of the day." Salisbury concluded that Solzhenitsyn was "Jovian, apocalyptic, Russian in every drop of his blood. There is nothing like Russia. Nothing like Russia's suffering. Nothing like his experience. Tochka. Period."[49]

Like their German-Austrian counterparts, these Russian examples also did not exempt the West from its participation in mass destruction, even if the motives were far different from Hitler's and Stalin's. The firebombings of German and Japanese cities and the use of nuclear weapons on Hiroshima and Nagasaki call into question America and Britain's morality regarding crimes against humanity. These examples bring to mind a prescient movie.

Stanley Kubrick, in his satirical movie masterpiece *Dr. Strangelove or: How I Learned to Stop Worrying and Love the Bomb,* has fictional US President Merkin Muffley tell his head of the Joint Chiefs of Staff, General Buck Turgidson, "You are talking about mass murder, General, not war. I will not go down in history as the greatest mass murderer since Adolf Hitler." Turgidson had suggested the advantage of a first strike of only twenty million dead, rather than a retaliatory strike killing one hundred million.[50] World War II's allies had been complicit in such questionable military activities as firebombings and nuclear strikes. What were the consequences?

FIVE
ALLIED INFAMIES

> I address this reading to the conscience of the man in
> this beautiful house.

JOHN HERSEY, *HIROSHIMA*

The democracies fell victim to using technological means for the mass extermination of targeted groups. It was wartime. For Nazi Germany, it was not a case of being at war with the Jews, who were not foreign aggressors. In the allies' efforts to win World War II, they engaged in the enemy's total destruction. Selective bombings of specific targets of military value gave way to the indiscriminate use of massive air power to deliver incendiary firebombings and, finally, nuclear weapons against enemy civilian populations. As author Margaret MacMillan wrote, "It was no oversight that mass bombings were not included in the Allied indictment of Nazi leaders at the Nuremberg trials." Nor were they at the Tokyo Tribunal.

1. FIREBOMBINGS

Novelist W. G. Sebald pointed out an eerie quiet among post–World War II Germans regarding their recent past and the firebombings of their cities. As another novelist, Heinrich Boell, put it, there was a collective amnesia. The shortage of contemporary accounts persisted as an aberration, and Germans seemed prohibited from looking at their past.

The allied bombings before Hiroshima and Nagasaki were without parallel in Germany: One hundred and thirty-one towns and cities were bombed, some repeatedly, about six hundred thousand civilians as direct victims; 3.5 million homes were destroyed; 7.5 million were homeless; 31.1 cubic meters of rubble per person in Cologne and 42.8 cubic meters in Dresden. Sebald continued, "It seems to have left scarcely a trace of pain behind in the collective consciousness; it has been largely obliterated from the retrospective understanding of those affected, and it never played any appreciable part in the discussion of the internal constitution of our country."[1]

Essen, Germany, was the opening salvo in the Battle of the Ruhr. Over the next five months, Sir Arthur Travers "Bomber" Harris, marshal of the Royal Air Force, launched more than forty raids. Bomber Command poured thousands of tons of bombs on Germany, more than the Germans had dropped during their "Blitz" of Britain and more than Bomber Command had dropped during the whole of 1942. One by one, the allies turned the cities of the Ruhr into ash and rubble. However, the effects on German war production were minimal.

Two hundred thousand tons of bombs fell on Germany in 1943, five times that of 1942. Even then, German wartime production increased. During the bombing of the Ruhr, there was a slight worker shortage because of imported slave labor, but also consumer production remained high. British historians calculated that during these bombings, about fifty-eight thousand tons were dropped. It only meant a few months of output loss. The price for Harris was 872 aircraft or 4.7 percent of 18,506 sorties. Harris believed the raids succeeded, and he told Prime Minister Winston Churchill about the one hundred cities were knocked out. He even bragged that "staggering destruction [has] been inflicted throughout the Ruhr to the extent that no nation can stick it for long. If we can keep this up, it cannot fail to be lethal within a period of time, which, in my view, will be surprisingly short."[2]

The other side of German apathy was to declare a new beginning by quickly clearing the rubble and claiming that a rebuilt Germany would be greater and stronger than before. Reconstruction was another liquidation of Germany's past. With German focus on the future, it took foreign observations or exiles returning to face the past.

The reality hardly seemed noticed, even though the horror surrounded survivors. There was, Sebald continued, "a tacit agreement, equally binding on everyone, that the true state of material and moral ruin in which the country found itself was not to be described." He emphasized that its "darkest aspects [were] taboo, like a shameful family secret." It was simply too horrific. Germany emerged from a war of annihilation in an extraordinary state of self-anesthesia. The Nazi period was relegated out of existence, as were its corpses, which were built right into the foundations of its economic miracle.[3]

Germans could not question the morality of the all-out allied bombing campaign decided upon in February 1942. As Sebald put it, "the question of whether and how it could be strategically or morally justified was never the subject of open debate in Germany after 1945, no doubt mainly because a nation which had murdered and worked to death millions of people in its camps could hardly call on the victorious powers to explain the military and political logic that dictated the destruction of the German cities."[4] Many considered the bombs' firestorms as a just punishment and act of retribution; protests remained few. It was the curious logic of infamy.

The unrestricted bombing program was pointedly debated publicly in Britain's parliament. Even the military was split over this morally indefensible conduct of annihilation against the dictates of good sense. Sebald quoted Churchill's justification in 1941 to force Hitler back as an "absolutely devastating exterminating attack by very heavy bombers from this country upon the Nazi homeland."[5] The British adopted this area bombing strategy, with its limited accuracy, in early 1942. Selected targets could have been hit, and that may have been more effective.

Nevertheless, the area bombing continued. Neither German morale nor productivity was impaired significantly. The war's end remained the same, not one day closer.[6]

Sebald suggested the continuation of the bombing program after its effectiveness had finished was probably due to the inability to cancel its one-third capacity for wartime production quickly, because it achieved a maximum destructive ability, because of its propaganda value for bolstering morale, and because of the hold of "Bomber" Harris over the prime minister. Whatever scruples they had over the bombardment of defenseless cities, they seemed to have consoled themselves with the notion that "those who have loosed these horrors upon mankind will now in their homes and persons feel the shattering strokes of just retribution."[7]

Hamburg provides an example of the destructiveness of airpower. In 1943 the Royal Air Force (RAF) and US Eighth Air Force hammered the city during Operation Gomorrah, with the aim of reducing it to cinders.

On July 27 at 1:00 a.m., ten thousand tons of high-explosive and incendiary bombs were dropped on Hamburg's densely populated residential areas. A combination of four thousand pounds of high-explosive incendiary bombs and fifteen-kilogram firebombs within minutes caused massive fires over twenty square kilometers, creating a firestorm that rose two thousand meters into the sky on air currents of hurricane force. It burned at full intensity for three hours. The flames rolled like a tidal wave at speeds of more than 150 kilometers per hour. Canal water went ablaze, glass melted, and asphalt gushed from the heat that reached a thousand degrees Celsius or more. Smoke from smoldering fires rose to eight thousand meters.

The central death zone covered disfigured corpses, only cleared by late August when the rubble had sufficiently cooled. Some 1.25 million refugees fled. News of this horror spread despite an information blackout. The returning planes left behind a lunar landscape similar to Cologne's bombing.[8]

These large-scale bombings had a terrible effect on fleeing refugees. They were besieged by swarms of pests—rats and flies fed on them and the piles of corpses. The bombed-out necropolises were filled with the "aimless wanderings of millions of homeless people amidst this monstrous destruction [that made clear] how close to extinction many of them really were in the ruined cities at the end of the war."[9]

Air warfare's systematic destruction on this vast scale demanded social organization and technological development to make such an air warfare strategy possible. Intelligence, capital, and labor went into the planning of the destruction. This machinery of destruction had been imagined in early German Expressionist films such as Fritz Lang's *Kriemhild's Revenge* (1924), which pictures an entire army deliberately wiped out. It also anticipates the fascist rhetoric of a "final battle." The Wehrmacht had planned such battles as part of strategic extremism by creating a new league of men who would prepare and carry out such a strategy against external and internal enemies.

Nazi Reich Minister Alfred Rosenberg wrote about making such a group in his 1933 book *The Myth of the Twentieth Century*. In it, SA (Sturmabteilung) and SS (Schutzstaffel) men are "intended not only to serve the direct exercise of power but also to attract a new elite bound by unconditional loyalty . . ." Already in Russia, a fabricated pseudo-documentary book called *The Protocols of the Elders of Zion* claimed that international Jewry sought to dominate the world by ruining nations from within. Throughout Germany and under Hitler, variants of the manuscript led to the removal of Jewish legal rights, confiscation of property, exile, and systematic destruction.[10]

In another Fritz Lang film, *Dr. Mabuse the Gambler* (1922), this cruel antihero plays various roles as a criminal, gambler, gang boss, rabble-rouser, revolutionary, and hypnotist. The plate on his door reads, "Dr. Mabuse-Psychoanalyst." Mabuse is not motivated by hatred so much as by power and the desire for it. Due to his expert understanding of the human psyche, he gets into his victims' heads and then ruins them. His power is only broken with the army's help.

Lang's film is a paradigm of the xenophobia that spread among Germans from the end of the nineteenth century onward.[11] Sebald claims Germans "actually provoked the annihilation of the cities in which we once lived." Air Marshal Hermann Goering would have wiped out London if he'd had the technology to do so.[12]

Albert Speer relates a conversation with Hitler in 1940 in which the dictator imagined London's destruction. Germans pioneered air warfare in Guernica, Warsaw, Belgrade, and Rotterdam. The battle of Stalingrad previewed Hamburg and Dresden's firebombings when twelve hundred German bombers killed forty thousand in a single raid.[13]

Post–World War II German writers shared in the general amnesia about Nazi rule, even to the point of insisting that internal emigration and fleeing abroad never occurred to them. Many writers disappeared into the bushes when they had a chance. Some even quietly agreed with Hitler's 1944 New Year's message of fighting fanatically to the bitter end. It became commonplace to defend German heroes at Stalingrad, El Alamein, and Cassino or to contend that the Nuremberg Trials absolved Germans of the blame for the regime's war crimes at the camps.

A myth arose during the post-war of the collective innocence of the Wehrmacht. Even in German studies, Sebald contends, there had been "neutralizing operations regularly performed . . ." A famous phrase became part of the German language: *bis zur Vergasung* (until I'm gassed).[14] Recently, journalist Alan Cowell, when referring to novelist

Walter Abish, wrote, "Modern Germany, however sanitized it may seem, cannot shake off its long and often dark heritage" or, as novelist John Updike put it, there is "something inexpugnably suspect about it."[15]

Only by the 1960s were Germans able to break the taboo and speak about their Nazi past. Even then, Heinrich Boell's novel *The Silent Angel* could not be published for fear it would not sell, and it was only printed after he died in 1985.

Moral integrity, critics noticed, contrasted Heinrich Boell's conscience against post-war Germany's materialism. Hans Schnitzler, an AWOL German soldier and hero of *The Silent Angel*, returns to Cologne's bombed-out ruins, his native city, in May 1945. He first discovers altruism and greed. Later he also finds caring and love among the ruins. It is the charred, starved, and broken city that always remains standing starkly before him.

A German non-commissioned officer (NCO), Willy Gompertz, exchanges his uniform with Hans, who can then escape execution as a deserter. Instead, Gompertz, demoralized, chooses death by a firing squad, pretending he is Hans. He has hidden his will in that uniform so Hans can bring it to Willy's widow, Elisabeth. On his way to Cologne, Hans picks up other names. He is starving, and a hospital's elderly nun, serving as a nurse, gives him bread and soup. He borrows a dead man's papers at the ruined hospital, where only a few rooms and a statue of a battered, "silent" angel remain. There, he also puts on a raincoat left behind by someone named Regina Unger. Her address appears on a piece of paper in the raincoat's pocket. After returning Gompertz's uniform to Elisabeth, he sees her cut the will out of its lining. Finally, Hans finds Regina, who also suffers from hunger. Regina has just lost her baby to random gunfire. She takes Hans in after he collapses. As Regina and Hans struggle for food in the leaking and windblown apartment, Elisabeth tries to keep her husband's inheritance to feed the hungry. Gompertz's father and his sister's husband, Professor Fischer, deny Elizabeth the will so they can seize the inheritance.

Hans, who witnessed Gompertz's death, holds the truth, but he is too busy finding refuge with Regina. The two survive, but Elisabeth dies. Hans rediscovers his faith among his boyhood church's ruins when a priest helps him marry Regina.

Meanwhile, Fischer's corruption is connected to the church. He collects religious art for sale and edits a Catholic journal. Fischer fights for the will and takes it from Hans. Gompertz's father and Fischer, grinning at their triumph, stand over the recently fallen, silent angel at the hospital nun's funeral, pressing it down into the mud by their weight as the novel ends.

Throughout the novel, Hans reflects on living in a dream but hungering for bread. The story's bleakness made German publishers reject the novel in 1950, only to be published after Boell's death. Bread, Boell suggests, symbolizes the meaning of life in Cologne, the firebombed city of rubble.[16]

Allied firebombings gave way to nuclear attacks.

2. OPPENHEIMER'S "TRINITY"

It is now just over eighty years since the Trinity test, the day the world first witnessed the tremendous power of atomic energy. It was so incredible that even its primary creator, J. Robert Oppenheimer, was moved to make an astonishing remark from the Hindu scripture, *Bhagavad Gita*: "Now I am become Death, the destroyer of worlds." He later recalled, "A few people laughed, a few people cried, most people were silent."[17] Around Trinity today, the sand is "littered with bits of a green, glassy substance called trinitite. This unique, man-made substance, found nowhere else on earth, was produced when sand and debris were thrown into the air and vaporized in the intense heat of that first nuclear blast."[18]

On that Monday, July 16, 1945, "the plutonium test bomb unleashed at Trinity shook the scientists, soldiers, and people of the nearby towns who witnessed it, but left the delighted officials among them as determined as ever to utilize their destructive new power in earnest."[19] Oppenheimer named this the Trinity test, a label inspired by the poems of John Donne. The site chosen for the test was a remote corner on the Alamogordo Bombing Range known as the Jornada del Muerto, or Journey of the Dead, 210 miles south of Los Alamos. "Why I chose the name is not clear, but I know what thoughts were in my mind. There is a poem by John Donne, written just before his death, which I know and love." Oppenheimer then quoted the sonnet "Hymn to God, My God, in My Sickness" about a man unafraid to die because he believed in the resurrection. Oppenheimer continued, "That still does not make a Trinity, but in another, better known devotional poem Donne opens, 'Batter my heart, three person'd god.' Beyond this, I have no clues whatever."[20]

Preparations for Trinity prompted the June 1945 Franck Report, signed by several of Oppenheimer's collaborators cautioning against the bomb's use. It correctly addressed many future issues of the atomic age: the impossibility of keeping atomic secrets, the likelihood of a nuclear arms race, and the necessity of keeping ahead of adversaries by a successful retaliatory ability in an arms race. Most importantly, the report proposed either inviting the world's representatives to a safe site for a demonstration detonation or keeping the whole thing a secret to outdistance rivals. The Interim Committee ignored the Franck Report, and it advised President Harry S. Truman to use the new weapon immediately with all its attendant consequences.

There is an important story behind this momentous decision. In January 1942 President Franklin D. Roosevelt (FDR) formally approved the development of an atomic bomb. Policy decisions made by scientists were then transferred to Secretary of War Henry L. Stimson, Army Chief of Staff General George C. Marshall, and James B. Conant, a chemist, Harvard's president, and chairman of the National Defense Research Committee (NDRC).

According to author David Cassidy, "all decisions and policy matters regarding the development and deployment of the bomb were taken out of the hands of the scientists who built it."[21] The Manhattan

Project had moved from exploratory to an all-out effort directly under Brigadier General Leslie R. Groves, and, as he noted, it "was based upon using it to end the war." All enemies were potential targets, and US hegemony in the post-war world would be ensured.

By March 1942 FDR sent his science advisor, Vannevar Bush, a note: "The whole thing should be pushed not only regarding development but also concerning time. This is very much of the essence."[22] A governmental crash program ensued. Heading that program was the General Policy Group (Top Policy Committee) under Bush and his associates—Vice President Henry Wallace, Stimson, Marshall, and Conant. The A-bomb became an army weapons project under the command of the Military Policy Committee that handled all general policy questions and issued orders to implement them.

In early 1943 the University of California, Berkeley assumed its role as the sponsoring civilian agency, and its Los Alamos National Laboratory operated as the A-bomb's research center. The civilian and military were now fused with the US government to make policy decisions, not the scientists. J. Robert Oppenheimer headed Berkeley's fast neutron theory group, and by May 1942 he coordinated all bomb theory. His task was "to compare theoretical calculations on the operation of a fission bomb with known experimental data on nuclei to estimate the critical mass, the energy yield, and other information needed to construct such a bomb." His1942 summer research committee preceded the Manhattan Project. Transuranium elements— neptunium and plutonium—were discovered at the University of California, the latter proving long-lived and highly fissionable. Also, it was more readily available than the fissionable uranium isotope U-235.

Oppenheimer's team studied the A-bomb development needed for an explosive chain reaction to trigger the bomb. Theoretically possible but an engineering difficulty, fission was easier than fusion for a new H-bomb or "super," so they concentrated on fission. The overall project's name was taken from the control laboratory heading all US Army construction, hence, "Manhattan" under General Leslie R.

Groves, the engineer in charge of building the Pentagon. Chief of Nuclear Weapons Development James B. Conant was assigned by Bush as a liaison between the military and the scientists.[23]

Groves streamlined his various administrations, stretching from Oak Ridge to Chicago to Berkeley. He met Oppenheimer, his chief partner in constructing the bomb. They were each a good match since both saw the project as making their careers. For starters, they agreed on the need for a central laboratory and located it at UC's Los Alamos in New Mexico, as it had both secrecy and isolation. Then they gathered a team in March 1943.[24]

Historian Martin Sherwin maintained that President Harry S. Truman's decision to use the atomic bomb against the Japanese had more to do with keeping Stalin out of Japanese occupation and intimidating him. "The more frightful it seemed as a weapon of war, the more useful it appeared as an instrument of peace." There had to be an actual example of its tremendous power to make Stalin willing to swap territory to neutralize it. Some scientists working on it warned that its use would limit or negate the future of international control, making the Russians "play ball."

Not only were those warnings of a moral liability ignored; they also contributed to the end of the allied wartime alliance and a post-war arms race. Stimson always asserted that victory with the most negligible loss of American lives was his chief purpose. For President Harry S. Truman and Senator James F. Byrnes, soon-to-be Secretary of State, their two chief considerations were how the bomb would motivate Japan's leadership to end the war and its impact on Stalin. Taken together, they ended any efforts to avoid using the bomb.[25]

Some prominent scientists on the Manhattan Project tried to qualify the bomb's use, mainly Leo Szilard, Walter Bartky, and Harold Urey. They privately met with Senator Byrnes to discuss their concerns: the transition from atomic to hydrogen bombs, the vulnerability of urban areas, systems of controlling raw materials, and international restrictions. Their most significant concern was nuclear weapons would start an arms race with Russia instead of an American plan for world peace, and, therefore, the US weapons' lead must be overwhelming. Byrnes wasn't persuaded. Szilard concluded peace and avoiding an arms race were better served by keeping the bomb secret and not using it.

The Interim Committee's policy rejected the Szilard group and recommended the bomb be used without warning against the Japanese. That decision rested on four assumptions:

1. It was a legitimate weapon because the enemy would use it.
2. It would persuade Japan's fanatical leaders to surrender.
3. The American public would want its use.
4. It would have a positive effect on Stalin.

Nothing else, it seemed, would convince Japan except a real target, even though Oppenheimer described for them the bomb's intense luminescence, its cloud rising ten thousand to twenty thousand feet, and lethal neutron radiation of nearly a mile. Despite these warnings, no advance notice would be made, and the targets would be aimed at war plants with many workers and their homes nearby. Two bombs were readied to be used on Hiroshima and Nagasaki in early August, and they were used on August 6 and 9, 1945.[26]

Truman was informed of these recommendations on June 6, 1945.[27] The Franck Report was rejected out of hand, no matter how indiscriminate the destruction, how negative world opinion, or how dangerous an arms race would be.[28]

Oppenheimer retained hope, but he was scared. No neutral site seemed adequate for technical reasons except direct military use. Only Great Britain and Soviet Russia would receive advanced notice. A minority of scientists went on record against this. Even physicist Edward Teller, "Father of the H-bomb," admitted he could find no way to "tie the little toe of the ghost to the bottle from which we have just helped it to escape."[29]

After the bombs fell in August, at 10:30 a.m. on October 25, 1945, Oppenheimer finally met President Truman in the Oval Office.

"Oppie" hoped to explain the enormous consequences this new weapon presented worldwide unless international control could be placed over atomic technology. Oppositely, Truman sought the scientist's help in passing the May-Johnson bill that would turn atomic energy over to the army. Given these opposing positions, their conversation started and ended badly. Truman insisted Russia would never be able to develop an A-bomb. This position, for Oppenheimer, proved Truman's ignorance of the subject's magnitude. His response angered Truman: "Mr. President, I feel I have blood on my hands." An awkward moment followed. Truman said, "Don't worry, we're going to work something out, and you're going to help us." Later, Truman said to Under Secretary of State Dean Acheson, "I don't want to see that son of a bitch in this office ever again." The president even wrote Acheson and described Oppenheimer as a "cry-baby" scientist who had come to "my office some five or six months ago and spent most of his time wringing his hands and telling me they had blood on them because of the discovery of atomic energy."

It was a remarkable encounter, given that Truman decided to drop the two A-bombs on Japan and that the buck would stop at his desk, no matter who recommended it. The authors of the Pulitzer Prize–winning Oppenheimer biography, *American Prometheus*, Kai Bird and Martin J. Sherwin, concluded, "Men as different as [John J.] McCloy, [Isidor] Rabi, and Oppenheimer all thought Truman's instincts, particularly in the field of atomic diplomacy, were neither measured nor sound—and sadly, certainly were not up to the challenge the country and world now faced." They realized the nature of warfare had radically changed and required a new kind of international relations. Oppenheimer's anguish over his creation and its use remained a deeply felt personal responsibility. He came to believe "the United States had 'used atomic weapons against an enemy which was essentially defeated.'"[30]

3. LITTLE BOY

Little Boy was a ten-thousand-pound uranium-type atomic bomb dropped by the United States on the Japanese city of Hiroshima at 8:15 a.m. on August 6, 1945. "No simple device in the history of warfare," wrote President Truman's biographer, Alonzo L. Hamby, "had ever displayed an ability to kill so many people so indiscriminately."[31] It is again worth repeating what J. Robert Oppenheimer, the father of the American atomic bomb, famously said: "I am become Death, the destroyer of worlds." After all, he had just witnessed for the first time the "unspeakable power" of his Frankenstein monster.[32]

At ground zero, everything incinerated immediately. A rapidly spreading fireball scorched Hiroshima while a spiraling tornado shot shards of debris everywhere. Hiroshima's people and property instantly turned into a vast, tangled, smoldering wasteland.

Three days later, a second and more powerful nuclear weapon, a plutonium-type bomb, Fat Boy, destroyed Nagasaki. It is estimated the atomic bombings in Hiroshima and Nagasaki killed between 129,000 and 260,000 people, mostly civilians. Over a few months, additionally, radiation (atomic poisoning) killed between another 90,000 to 146,000 in Hiroshima and 39,000 to 80,000 in Nagasaki, or about 486,000 totally.[33]

President Truman made a stark, straightforward announcement: "Sixteen hours ago, an American airplane dropped one bomb on Hiroshima, an important Japanese army base. That bomb had more power than twenty thousand tons of TNT, [and] it is an atomic bomb." He followed with these threats: "We are now prepared to obliterate . . . every productive enterprise . . . We shall destroy their docks, their factories, and their communications, [and] we shall completely destroy Japan's power to make war . . ." Either Japan surrendered unconditionally, or it would face "prompt and utter destruction."[34]

The Japanese answer reached Truman at 4:05 p.m., August 14,

1945. Finally, at 7:00 p.m., the president told reporters, "I have received this afternoon from the Japanese government, [and] I deem this reply a full acceptance of the Potsdam Declaration, which specifies the unconditional surrender of Japan."[35]

The American plans for the invasion of Japan had proceeded right up to the last moment when, suddenly and almost out of the blue, Truman ordered an atomic bomb on Hiroshima. General George C. Kenney, allied Air Forces Commander in the Southwest Pacific, wrote in his war journal on June 6, 1945, of the intense, hurried efforts preparing for the bombing of Kyushu, Japan's southernmost isle. They had set the "Olympic" operation for the invasion of Japan for November 1, 1945, and it "would be on us before we made the landing."

Commander of US Army Forces in the Far East, General Douglas MacArthur had a plan. It required landing an initial six divisions fully equipped on Kyushu. The navy, worried over kamikaze suicide attacks, wanted sufficient aircraft to destroy Japanese airdromes and rid the air of their fighters before the "Olympic" started. That fear initiated moving the Seventh Air Force to Okinawa as rapidly as fields and hangers were readied.[36]

Allied European Air Power Commander General Jimmy Doolittle, head of the Eighth Air Force, prepared for deployment in the Far East with his B-59s. General Curtis LeMay's Twentieth Air Force would constitute the Strategic Air Command, nominally under General Henry H. Arnold but detailed to General Carl A. Spaatz, commander of Strategic Air Forces in Europe. The initial plan was to move the whole Far East Air Forces into conquered Kyushu. Okinawa and the Philippines would be used as backup bases of airpower to keep Formosa and Japanese forces in China neutralized, and Japanese shipping blockaded.

The Americans prepared a scheme for bombing Japan for six months before landing in Kyushu and hoped "to see if the Japanese for the next six months . . . would not quit without an actual invasion." Kenney believed he would be surprised if Japan sued for peace short of an actual invasion. Their plans to invade Kyushu continued. Failing Japanese surrender, troops, shipping, and supplies would be on hand for the occupation forces. The bombing of Japan required intensification to the maximum immediately, with immense bomb storage capabilities.[37]

On July 10 B-29s were moved to form the Twentieth Air Force, now called the US Strategic Air Command, directed by General Spaatz. Admiral Chester Nimitz turned over his Seventh Air Force to the Far East Air Forces. Simultaneously, the British planned to recapture Singapore.

Throughout July Okinawa was filled with aircraft, and a final sweep of Japanese shipping intensified the blockade. B-29s battered Japan's big cities. General Kenney used fifteen hundred planes daily to strike targets from Borneo to Kyushu. As late as August 2, 1945, Kenney and Spaatz planned attacks on Osaka and Honshu, while Doolittle should hit targets farther west. Suddenly, on August 4, "word came in that the first atomic bomb would be dropped on Hiroshima the morning of the 6th."[38]

Given the importance and intensity of invasion plans, it seems likely other factors played into Truman's sudden decision to drop the first two atomic bombs. There was the Soviet declaration of war against Japan and its invasion of Manchuria on August 8 and 9, 1945 (Stalin's announcement to Truman at the Potsdam Conference, July 17 to August 2, 1945, to fulfill promises he made at Teheran and Yalta); the readiness of two atomic bombs; the fear of seating Stalin as part of the occupation of Japan; the lack of knowledge of radiation effects; and Truman's desire to win the war promptly. The disastrous results of these two nuclear weapons stunned the allies.

As news of the horrendous killing machine let loose by the Americans spread, the government "was not eager to 'get the reputation for outdoing Hitler in atrocities' as the country's secretary of war put it."[39] It became evident these two bombs were not just another artillery weapon. Japan had gotten much more than it deserved.

The US government went into overdrive to contain news of the nuclear holocaust. Japanese Emperor Hirohito in his surrender broadcast of August 15, 1945, said, "By employing a new weapon destined to massacre innocent civilians, the Americans have opened the eyes of the world to their sadistic nature." It was, he continued, a new and most cruel bomb that could destroy civilization. General Douglas MacArthur, heading the occupation of Japan, shut down the news of it. General Leslie Groves, who headed the Manhattan Project to create the bomb, and its leading scientist, J. Robert Oppenheimer, either denied the bad news or admitted that only small numbers were dying of nuclear poisoning.

However, the two bombs deeply affected people, the so-called *hibakusha*, who lost hair and skin, vomited blood, had wounds that would not heal, black blotches on their bodies, diarrhea, and reproductive processes made abnormal, resulting in miscarriages, physical anomalies, and shorter longevity. General Groves and others tried taking back their statements about it being "a pleasant way to die." They claimed what the Germans pleaded about Nazi atrocities: They knew nothing.[40]

Historian Robert H. Ferrell, in his biography *Harry S. Truman: A Life*, summarized the pros and cons of the arguments on Truman's use of the atomic bomb: "The most controversial act of Truman's presidency beyond all doubt," he states, "was the use of nuclear weapons upon Japan during the days following the Potsdam Conference." Even General Dwight Eisenhower wondered whether it was necessary to "hit them with this awful thing."[41]

Already, city after city had been taken out by US airpower, including the firebombing of Tokyo that leveled almost sixteen square miles, created a fire reaching over 1,800 degrees Fahrenheit, and killed more than 150,000 by May 1945. Japan was blockaded, and only a few cities remained relatively undamaged. Ferrell wondered whether waiting a few weeks, or even months, would have led to Japan's surrender. But, he argued, was that realistic given how obstinate Japan was to give up?

Truman based his decision on two reasons: The first was the atrocities Japan had committed. When confronted, he often replied, "You should do your weeping at Pearl Harbor." He might have added: What about the Bataan death march, prisoners' treatment, random shootings, and beheadings? His other reason was a calculation of the cost of invading Japan. As Ferrell notes, "It seemed so high as to justify the use of any new weapons in the American arsenal."

Based on the Iwo Jima and Okinawa battles, the joint war plans committee made wildly varying estimations that invading Kyushu would cost 25,000 killed, 105,000 wounded, and 2,500 missing. Or, if followed by attacking Honshu, the cost would be 40,000 killed, 150,000 wounded, and 3,500 missing. Or, if Kyushu and Honshu were taken, the totals would be 46,000 killed, 170,000 wounded, and 14,000 missing. No one's set of figures matched, so they preferred the second atomic option. These "educated" guesses meant a delay in that Japan would not be conquered until the fall of 1946.

Admiral William D. Leahy spiked these speculative figures. He suggested a force of almost 800,000 to take Kyushu, and casualties ran at 268,000. Anticipating a massive Japanese buildup on Kyushu, American casualties would probably increase.

Ferrell concluded, "Truman may not have been wrong when he said after the war that an invasion would have cost 250,000 American casualties and the same number of Japanese." General George C. Marshall suggested one million.

Truman was vilified. A sense of guilt followed him. "One must say," Ferrell wrote, "that now, in the 1990s, when at least much of the debate is over, when, to use the cliché, almost all has been said and done, Truman's decision does not appear as outrageous or stupidly foolish."[42] Nevertheless, it has remained a sudden and naive decision. "Quite simply," wrote historian Gar Alperovitz, "it is not true that the atomic bomb was used because it was the only way to save the 'hundreds of thousands' or 'millions of lives' as was subsequently claimed."[43]

Ferrell made a more modest argument around three questions:

1. Did Truman try to warn Japan?
2. Did the two atomic bombs or Russia's entry into the war against Japan force Tokyo's surrender?
3. Did dropping the two nuclear bombs mean what America said—to force unconditional surrender—or rather the threat of their possible post-war use?

As to the first, Truman would not explicitly reveal America's possession of nuclear weapons, even though the military was reluctant to use them. Japanese leadership remained unimpressed with "prompt and utter destruction" threats, though they did not know about nukes.

As to Russian entry on August 8, the Nagasaki bombing occurred the next day, and the Japanese cabinet was still deadlocked. At that point, Emperor Hirohito stepped in and forced the decision for peace by August 14, even though he would be subjected to the Supreme Commander's authority, namely MacArthur's. Russia's entry surprised and shocked Japanese leadership, as it counted on using Russia as a mediator. Instead of the three-month promise after the war ended in Europe, the Soviets jumped the gun.

As to the last question, Ferrell calls it an "extraordinary claim." It suggests the US would do anything to confound the Russians, but such a claim lacks evidence, although Ferrell and historian Gar Alperovitz agree with the extraordinary claim. Yet Kai Bird and Martin Sherwin suggest otherwise. That admission leaves one with the sad issue of America's culpability in using the bomb at all. We are brought face-to-face with J. Robert Oppenheimer's remorse and a quote from the *Bhagavad Gita*. The immediate and lasting damages were extraordinary.

4. HERSEY'S *HIROSHIMA*

The controversy over John Hersey's article and book *Hiroshima* in 1946 and its renewal in Lesley Blume's work, *Fallout: The Hiroshima Cover-up and the Reporter Who Revealed It to the World,* demands a fuller account.

Ferrell left the question open with a closing remark that "these issues may never be resolved."[44] Bird and Sherwin considered Truman unaware, even ignorant, of the full consequences of nuclear warfare.[45]

The most nagging problem was the stunning, immediate effect of atomic poisoning and its significant and lingering impact on the victims. The Japanese wartime leadership shared some of the blame for its stubborn intransigence. America's cavalier treatment of the unprecedented destruction and, especially, deadly radiation's effects on innocent civilians lends credence to what Hersey had uncovered and Blume recounted.

Hiroshima tells the story of six ordinary Japanese citizens on August 6, 1945, when the first atomic bomb was dropped.

Mr. Tanimoto was a minister educated in America who volunteered to organize air-raid defenses. He had just moved a friend's daughter's belongings from the city's center. Tanimoto lived two miles from the blast, which leveled his house; he took cover in a garden.

Mrs. Nakamura, another of the characters cited by Hersey, ignored the warning. The blast struck near her home and killed her neighbor.

Dr. Fujii woke up early. The bomb's blast hit his clinic and dumped it into the river.

Father Kleinsorge and his comrades survived because his mission was earthquake-proof.

Dr. Sasaki had not taken his regular train, or he would have died in the blast.

Miss Sasaki was in her office when the bomb hit. The bookcase fell on her, breaking her leg and knocking her out.

Employers refused to hire those with radiation sickness, and they faced poverty. Thirty years after, a law finally granted a monthly allowance to those affected. The victims became known as *hibakusha* (explosion-affected persons).

After the blast, Dr. Sasaki helped the *hibakusha* until 1951, when he set up a private clinic. In 1963, he nearly died after one of his lungs had to be removed, and his wife died from breast cancer.

After years of struggle, Ms. Nakamura joined a carpentry program for housing *hibakusha*. She also used a deserted street shop to make children's toys and gained employment at a chemical company. After retirement, she lived on government aid for the *hibakusha*.

Father Kleinsorge took the name Father Makoto Takakura and became a Japanese citizen. He never recovered from radiation sickness. He worked helping people affected by the blast.

Miss Sasaki underwent operations to repair her leg but was never active again. She worked in an orphanage under Father Kleinsorge and eventually became a nun.

Dr. Fujii rebuilt his clinic in Hiroshima.

Mr. Tanimoto traveled to America to give speeches and raise money for the victims of Hiroshima and built a peace center in Japan. He eventually met author Pearl Buck and worked with her. Employers continually refused to hire those with radiation sickness.

In *Fallout*, Lesley Blume tries to prove that John Hersey's article and book *Hiroshima* were the scoop of the century that exposed a giant US government's cover-up of the magnitude of its wrongful nuclear attack on Hiroshima and, by implication, Nagasaki, in August 1945. Truman had staunchly defended his actions. He did not want to get a reputation for outdoing Hitler's atrocities.

The American government went into overdrive to contain news of the human cost of the bombings. At first, officials denied the radioactivity's aftermath, then maintained it was minor, and finally claimed it had no way of knowing because of the bomb's experimental nature. Besides, the Japanese needed something jarring to surrender and were prepared to defend themselves if the atomic alternative had not been taken.

Hersey's recounting of the story of a city of three hundred thousand immediately vanishing, perhaps one hundred thousand dead, and the remainder suffering a cruel atomic disease stands as a stark reality and a dire warning to the present. Hersey wrote his story by carefully accounting for the lives of those six survivors and their physical and psychological agonies as examples of the rest. Increasingly, the American excuses sounded like the German claims of ignorance. Harvard President James B. Conant's counterattack and the article he inspired from former Secretary of the Army Henry L. Stimson were not enough. How necessary, as they claimed, was the atomic bombing to force capitulation? Even Stimson came to doubt his own story. Incredibly, Blume maintains, peace feelers were not sufficiently pursued. Both Conant and Stimson sidestepped discussion of the intense and deadly radiation aftermath.[46]

Katie Hafner's review in *The Washington Post* called Blume's book meticulously researched and brilliantly written for the seventy-fifth anniversary of the bombing of Hiroshima, especially "the idea that a democracy's highest officials might use verbal sleights of hand to distract citizens from a crisis has been cropping up of late."[47] Blume claimed Hersey's story of the six survivors was the most important journalistic work of the twentieth century.

Hersey's book was made possible by Managing Editor William Shawn and Editor in Chief Harold Ross of *The New Yorker*. The way they got it to the press is also worthy of retelling. Blume's book, the reviewer noted, was the "most gripping when Blume described the article's immediate, dramatic impact on a public that had been kept in the dark about the human devastation in Hiroshima." Newsstands sold out, and Albert Einstein ordered a thousand copies for distribution.

Alfred Knopf soon published it as a book. "Editors and columnists across the country were quick to denounce the silence and secrecy that had shrouded the aftermath of the nuclear attacks on Hiroshima and Nagasaki." The government's spin failed.[48]

Another reviewer was also quick to praise Blume's book. William Langewiesche, writing in *The New York Times,* noted the immense physical devastation and dangerous doses of radiation Blume claimed and Hersey's use of six survivors in telling the story. He points out that Hersey's work "exists as something of an artifact, a stunning work that nonetheless has lost the power to engage largely because the stories it contains have permeated our consciousness of nuclear war." The reviewer praises Blume for her outstanding research and writing to remind us of this horror; it is too important a story to be forgotten. He does expose, in his opinion, two flaws: The first was that far from a cover-up, the military's "ineffective obfuscation occurred during the months following the atomic bombings [that] resulted for the same old stuff—a mixture of authentic ignorance, reflexive secrecy, and incompetent military spin."

The other flaw was her "unnecessary claim that Hersey's work altered the course of history, changed attitudes toward the arms race, and has helped the world avoid nuclear war ever since." He calls that claim "just silly." What changed history was the accumulation of better nuclear weapons despite the suffering described. The curse of nuclear weapons remains. A potential nuclear conflict could end life on the planet, and, quoting the author, "We have learned so little from the greatest tragedies of the 20th century."[49]

Although Hersey maintained his neutrality, letting his characters tell their stories, he privately believed the atomic bomb deserved to be renounced immediately after its unveiling. In a 1965 visit to the White House, he read an excerpt from *Hiroshima* and added, "I address this reading to the conscience of the man in this beautiful house."[50]

A couple of the most infamous dates of the twentieth century stand before us: August 6 and August 9, 1945, the atomic bombings of Hiroshima and Nagasaki, two of the largest cities in wartime Japan. They represent, perhaps, an unforgivable wrong committed over three-quarters of a century ago, and they are the direst warning to the twenty-first century: the atomic bombings of Hiroshima and Nagasaki, two of the largest cities in wartime Japan. These weapons of mass destruction contained uranium-235 and plutonium-239, releasing massive amounts of heat (ten thousand degrees Fahrenheit) and deadly gamma radiation. About a quarter of Hiroshima's population died immediately, and radiation poisoning killed another quarter in those subsequent months. Nagasaki's destruction was similar. The nuclear genie, once out of its bottle, has never been put back into it.[51]

Today we live under the threatening shadow of a doomsday policy of deterrence called Mutually Assured Destruction (MAD). If a nuclear deterrence policy destroys all life on earth, it is difficult to say what it has deterred. It has become evident that these two bombs were not just another artillery weapon.

America continues avoiding a Frankenstein reputation. The threat of a nuclear holocaust remains the curse of the twentieth century into the twenty-first. August 6 and 9 seem to pass over Americans—and the world—almost unnoticed. How sound the good intentions were or how evil the evil ones were could be debated. In each instance, there was a certain amount of naivete mixed with realism. Could a more effective diplomacy, even with dictators, avoid war? The Russo-Ukrainian War of 2022 raises the question of a nuclear option, especially the use of tactical nuclear weapons.[52]

Americans have forgotten, according to Stephen Wertheim, World War II and Cold War lessons while countering Moscow and Beijing's territorial ambitions. Thus, Americans have lost their "healthy fear" of World War III, and though not directly engaging in Ukraine, they may get involved in a war with China over Taiwan. War models suggest lengthy, escalating battles into nuclear warfare if this comes to pass. This time, if I may paraphrase Wertheim, lessons will have to be relearned without the ghostly shadows of World War II and the Cold War.

Have we, the children and grandchildren of the greatest generation, or the Russians and Chinese, really forgotten the lessons of Hiroshima, Nagasaki, and the policy of Mutually Assured Destruction (MAD)? Does anyone not believe that civilization collapses, that the earth becomes uninhabitable while firestorms pulverize cities, and that radiation decimates humanity with a permanent worldwide nuclear winter descending?

If Putin uses tactical nuclear weapons, he risks that they might escalate into a global holocaust. If Xi invades Taiwan, he risks the same thing.[53]

Neville Chamberlain tried to win peace with Hitler by selling out the small Czechoslovak state. Franklin Roosevelt attempted a grand settlement with Stalin only to sacrifice Eastern Europe to the Soviet empire. Henry Kissinger met Zhou Enlai, and Richard Nixon conversed with Mao to contain Russia. These three diplomatic deals had their downsides as a means of excusing infamy: Hitler made World War II; Stalin made the Cold War; Henry Kissinger and Richard Nixon made Taiwan a permanent hostage to the People's Republic of China.

SIX
EXCUSING INFAMY

" I believe it is peace for our time.

NEVILLE CHAMBERLAIN

There were different reasons, some might say excuses, for collaborating with totalitarian regimes. The deals' necessities seemed reasonable, doable, and likely to yield beneficial results. British Prime Minister Neville Chamberlain believed the price for appeasement with Hitler, sacrificing Czechoslovakia's Sudetenland, was worth the fuehrer's guaranteeing peace and ending his desire for further territorial acquisitions in Europe. Later, President Franklin D. Roosevelt (FDR) and Prime Minister Winston Churchill sought peace by getting Stalin to agree to a new world organization that would institute international peace, even though Eastern Europe would remain in the Soviet sphere of power. For a final example, National Security Advisor Henry Kissinger negotiated with China's Premier Zhou Enlai. They, on behalf of their bosses, American President Richard M. Nixon and Chairman of the Communist Party of China Mao Zedong, reduced the USSR's threat to the PRC. China would obtain relaxed border tensions with the USSR, and the US would support China in preventing a Soviet military strike. China became an American ally instead of a Soviet one.

The negotiating appeasers, from Chamberlain to FDR-Churchill to Kissinger-Nixon, gained a momentary advantage in abating Hitler, Stalin, and Mao's ambitions. It took a world war to remove Hitler and later an internal collapse of Soviet Russia to reduce the power of its successor state, the Russian Federation. As for the People's Republic of China, it strengthened itself to become the second most powerful country globally and a significant challenge against its US appeaser. Germany has reformed itself into a collaborative Western democracy. Russia remained authoritarian. None of the appeasements proved lasting, though none collapsed so swiftly as Chamberlain's agreements with Hitler.

1. "PEACE FOR OUR TIME"

It took the extreme brinksmanship of three last-minute meetings between Neville Chamberlain and Adolf Hitler to achieve "peace for our time." That was the phrase the prime minister announced as he waved Hitler's pledge to abide by the Munich Agreement. That scrap of paper bore their signatures.

Chamberlain's plane landed at the Heston Aerodrome on September 30, 1938, and he spoke to the crowds there:

> The settlement of the Czechoslovakian problem, which has now been achieved, is only the prelude to a larger settlement in which all Europe may find peace. This morning I had another talk with the German chancellor, Herr Hitler, and here is the paper which bears his name upon it and mine [shows the paper to the crowd]. Some of you, perhaps, have already heard what it contains, but I would just like to read it to you: '. . . We regard the agreement signed last night and the Anglo-German

Naval Agreement as symbolic of the desire of our two peoples never to go to war with one another again.'

Later that same day, he stood outside his official residence, 10 Downing Street, and again read from that slip of paper. He concluded with the famous phrase:

> My good friends, for the second time in our history, a British Prime Minister has returned from Germany, bringing peace with honor. I believe it is peace for our time. We thank you from the bottom of our hearts. Go home and get a nice quiet sleep.

That quiet sleep soon awoke to war.[1]

Hitler had announced to his generals an intention to attack Czechoslovakia before the end of September 1938 if he did not get the Sudetenland diplomatically. It would be, he boasted, a "magnificent harvest" because France and England "would not intervene."

British Prime Minister Neville Chamberlain dismissed this leaked news, although he was uneasy and nervous because he remained unwilling to commit to Czechoslovakia's defense. France was shaky on this issue. Jan Masaryk, Czech ambassador to Britain, would resist as long as Britain and France did. Even Hitler admitted his threat was a big gamble. The only deterrent would be an Anglo-French mobilization. Would Chamberlain, followed by French President Édouard Daladier, stand up to Hitler? The fuehrer thought not.[2]

Since Hitler was not interested in Sudetenland's autonomy and self-government, that solution was off the table. Three-and-a-quarter-million Germans lived in this, the most defensible borderland of the Czech Republic.

Chamberlain, nicknamed "the Coroner" and the man "always clinging to an umbrella," had a "Plan Z." It was a dramatic and top-secret gesture to resolve the Czech crisis. He would fly to Germany to see Hitler and negotiate directly with him to save Europe's peace.

Only a few of his intimates knew and approved of the initiative. Plan Z would have to happen quickly because of Hitler's mounting threat.

Chamberlain refused to issue an ultimatum, especially since the French were reluctant to commit. Plan Z appeared to be the only alternative. If he succeeded, he thought, it would solve the crisis and change the threatening international situation to a peaceful one. This bold solution seemed especially doable since he believed that Sudetenland's removal from Czechoslovakia was inevitable. Not even a plebiscite would do. Chamberlain sent Hitler a message suggesting Plan Z: "I propose to come across by air and am ready to start tomorrow." Hitler replied on September 14, 1938, that he was at the prime minister's disposal.[3]

Chamberlain left Heston airfield on the morning of September 15 and arrived in Munich to enthusiastic crowds. From there, he took a three-hour train ride to Berchtesgaden. Along the wet, cloudy way, he thought of how unprepared Britain and France were for war. They could do nothing to prevent Germany's seizure of Sudetenland. Peace was essential, but at what price? If it were Hitler's last territorial demand, then that was acceptable, but if not, then what future demands lay ahead?

Hitler met him with a warm handshake. He was, Chamberlain later wrote, "the commonest little dog he had ever seen." After tea, they repaired to Hitler's private study with only a translator. Hitler waved away any further clarifications. Instead, he demanded an immediate solution that avoided so-called Czech atrocities against the Sudetenland German minority by bringing them into the Third Reich.

But Chamberlain wanted to know if there was anything else, for instance, dismembering Czechoslovakia. Hitler denied that, but he ranted on about the German minorities elsewhere. The prime minister responded by saying that had Hitler wanted war all along, then why did he come here in the first place? Otherwise, they could work out the details of self-determination. Hitler backed off, saying they could meet again soon at Bad Godesberg near Bonn to do so. He promised not to give any marching orders.[4]

Chamberlain came away realizing Hitler's brutality but also, curiously, with the impression of a man who kept his word. Hitler said that he had "maneuvered this dried-up civilian into a corner."

Chamberlain had given in by turning Sudetenland over to the Reich. He now had to convince his cabinet, France, and the Czechs. The prime minister had acceded to one power dominating Europe to pay for the price of peace. Didn't Bismarck once say that whoever controlled Bohemia held Europe? Even France thought that deserting Czechoslovakia was the worst part of valor. Chamberlain sent a joint Anglo-French note to Czech diplomat Jan Masaryk: "The entire Sudetenland must be handed over to the Reich." He had abandoned them to their fate.[5]

On September 22, 1938, Hitler and Chamberlain met again at Bad Godesberg to the relief of the British and French, even though the prime minister had thrown a small state to the German wolf. Chamberlain clarified that the same claims could not be used again for Hungary and Poland. Hitler flatly refused because, as he said, the Czech situation could not be delayed. That put Chamberlain in a quandary if Hitler had further demands against those countries.

He requested Hitler write out his demands. They were Czech evacuation and German occupation of Sudetenland within three days. Seeing Chamberlain's consternation, Hitler extended his deadline to ten days.[6]

Returning to London, Chamberlain asked for his government's acceptance. After all, he had Hitler's pledge of "no further ambitions in Europe." Still, one-third of his cabinet favored resistance and openly revolted. The Czechs also rejected Godesberg. Hitler threatened to smash the Czechs. Both sides prepared. Chamberlain urged the Czechs to accept.

Hitler then promised not to move beyond what the Czechs had agreed to and permit a referendum. Chamberlain told Hitler he would get all the "essentials" without war. The prime minister offered to fly to Berlin to discuss arrangements for the transfer alongside French and Italian representatives, a four-power peace conference. Hitler conceded and invited the parties to Munich for the following day.[7]

Chamberlain received a hearty send-off for his third trip with a round of cheers on September 29, 1938. He spoke to the crowd gathered at Heston airfield about trying repeatedly but wags at the foreign office, paraphrasing an old proverb satirizing him by saying if you can't concede, then fly, fly, fly again.

Chamberlain wanted peace with honor. Even so, the Czechs were barred from attending. Jan Masaryk told the prime minister, "If you have sacrificed my nation to preserve the peace of the world, I will be the first to applaud you. But if not, gentlemen, God help your souls."[8]

Munich again cheered as Chamberlain's group landed, and the conference took place in Hitler's party headquarters. Benito Mussolini, the Italian dictator, presented the deal as if it were his own on September 29, 1938, and Hitler gave Chamberlain a double handshake as a friendly gesture. The document related that the final deadline of the October 1 occupation would now begin and be completed by October 10. No reservations or delays were accepted. When Chamberlain asked about compensation, Hitler exploded. The matter was dropped. By the evening of September 29, 1938, an agreement was reached, and the next day the document was signed.[9]

Chamberlain asked for another meeting with Hitler. They met at the dictator's private apartment. Chamberlain had written three short paragraphs for Hitler to sign. The critical statement was that they regarded the Munich Agreement "as symbolic of our two peoples never to go to war with one another again."[10] Hitler signed that infamous piece of paper that the prime minister waved about on his final return to Britain.

The next day Hitler told his foreign minister, Joachim von Ribbentrop, "Oh, don't take it all so seriously . . . That piece of paper is unimportant." Chamberlain appeared with the royal couple on Buckingham Palace's balcony as the crowds sang "Rule, Britannia!" and "For He's a Jolly Good Fellow."[11]

When Hitler attacked Poland in September 1939, this appeasement policy failed. Chamberlain was forced out of office in May 1940, and Winston Churchill headed a coalition cabinet. At first the war went amazingly well for the Germans. Poland was subdued in three weeks and divided between victorious Germany and neutral ally Soviet Russia. In April 1940 Germany quickly took Denmark and Norway. In May Germany invaded the Low Countries and, by the middle of the month, drove deep into France. Fascist Italy entered the war on Germany's side in June, and France fell on June 22, 1940. In August 1940 the Germans opened an air offensive against Britain designed to destroy England's air strength. By late June 1941 the German air attack subsided as Hitler prepared for an invasion of Russia. In April 1941 Germany occupied the Balkan Peninsula, and on June 22, 1941, invaded erstwhile ally Soviet Russia. At first the war went well in Russia, but by December, the German advance was halted outside of Leningrad and Moscow, though the Germans were able to seize Kyiv. In the spring the offensive resumed, with the Germans occupying the Crimean Peninsula and attacking Stalingrad on the Lower Volga in August 1942. The Russians counterattacked in November and, by February 1943, lifted the siege of Stalingrad as well as Leningrad and Moscow. At this time, in October 1942, the Germans were pushed back from El Alamain in North Africa and, by 1943, chased into Italy. Mussolini's government was forced to resign in July 1943. In June 1944 the allied invasion of Normandy began. The Russians, advancing from the east, began the Battle of Berlin in April 1945, and after Hitler's suicide on April 30, 1945, Germany surrendered on May 7, 1945. The allies, meeting at Yalta in the Russian Crimea in February 1945, signed an agreement to divide defeated Germany, try major war criminals, form a United Nations, and bring Russia into the war with Japan after Germany was defeated. The Yalta Agreement established the structure of post–World War II Europe until divided Germany was reunited on October 3, 1990. The Soviet Union dominated the Eastern Bloc of countries until 1989, when they established freely elected governments.

The disaster that followed Chamberlain's attempted appeasement was finally halted. At later dates were FDR, Winston Churchill, Henry Kissinger, and Richard Nixon also "jolly good fellows?"

2. YALTA'S BIG THREE

Whereas the "Riga Axioms" were defined and supported by Russian specialists who were institutionally based within the State Department, the so-called "Yalta Axioms" were more amorphous and lacked an institutional basis. Diplomats at Riga, an American listening post of the USSR in the 1920s, held that the "Soviet Union is a monolithic, world revolutionary state, single-mindedly geared to expansion."

FDR and Churchill went to the Yalta Conference (February 4, 1945 – February 11, 1945) in the Russian Crimea to meet Stalin. They considered the "Soviet Union less a world revolutionary state than a more conventional imperial power . . . it is still," thought historian Daniel Yergin in 1977, "a relatively cautious power, concerned with protecting what it has, and much more to gain from stability."[12] Beyond the president and his closest advisors, they had no enthusiastic cheering section. Relying on public opinion was dicey, and the president's Russian policy had determined critics or, at the very least, mildly querulous foes.

Some were excluded by FDR and thrown into diplomatic exile. The exiled Riga diplomats remained opposed, with the notable exception of Charles "Chip" Bohlen, who translated for FDR at the Tehran Conference (November 28, 1943 – December 1, 1943) and Yalta. The founder of the Russian section of the State Department, Robert F. Kelley, cooled his heels in Ankara. At the same time, his colleagues, Loy W. Henderson and George F. Kennan, remained in Baghdad and Lisbon, respectively. William Bullitt, America's first ambassador to the USSR (1933–1936) and a Riga convert, warned FDR that Stalin would communize Europe after Hitler's defeat.

By 1943, according to Daniel Yergin, FDR had developed his "grand design." Yalta was to be its verification. The "Yalta Axioms" rested on accommodating the Soviet Union but in a realistic way. The basis of "working with" instead of "against" the USSR rested on the "factor of power" within a new world organization. The United Nations (UN) would have an upper chamber, or Security Council, consisting of the Great Powers—the United States, Great Britain, Soviet Russia, and China, which, acting in concert, would have to maintain the peace through force, if necessary. France was later added.

This line of analysis, designating FDR as a realist in contrast to President Woodrow Wilson's idealism in 1919, led to understanding the Yalta Conference primarily as gaining Russia's UN adherence along Roosevelt's lines. All remaining issues were of secondary importance to FDR. Hence the Polish and German questions, which occupied most of the time, were of lesser value to FDR. Both eyewitnesses and others subtracted the Japanese issue because it was not formally discussed at Yalta and had been informally agreed to previously.

But Japan was also part of FDR's accommodation. He had to give in to Russian requests for a pre–Portsmouth Treaty (1905, ending the Russo-Japanese War) for Russia to get Stalin's acquiescence to the UN and his participation in the war against Japan. So, a quid pro quo linked the two issues. Stalin got Sakhalin, plus railway rights and port leasing on the Yellow Sea that Japan had occupied since Portsmouth.

The remaining "Yalta Axioms" boiled down to treating the USSR as a conventional Great Power rather than what was thought to be essentially an ideological phenomenon, with its Marxian world plan for domination through the Comintern (dissolved in May 1943).

The "Riga Axioms" had called for avoiding Soviet diplomatic relations, while the "Yalta Axioms" required accommodation through an intimate partnership of personal diplomacy at the highest summitry levels. FDR recognized that Stalin made all the crucial decisions, and it was essential to talk directly to him. His approval alone was necessary if anything substantive was to be accomplished. Russia would behave like a Great Power within its sphere of influence and not as an ideologically driven empire. FDR believed the so-called "break" of the 1917 Russian Revolution was closing and that the gap between the communist East and capitalist West was narrowing. This was shown as Charles Bohlen, FDR's speech writer Robert Sherwood, and Secretary of State Edward R. Stettinius Jr. gave favorable accounts as to the content of the Yalta Conference itself.

On Saturday, February 3, 1945, FDR and Churchill arrived at Crimea's Saky air base. Stalin got in on Sunday morning. He and his foreign minister, Vyacheslav Molotov, made a personal call to the president at the Livadia Palace at 4:00 p.m. According to Bohlen, FDR's translator, they "greeted each other as old friends, and in a sense, they were . . . Smiling broadly, the President grasped Stalin by the hand and shook it warmly. Stalin, his face cracked in one of his rare, if slight, smiles, expressed pleasure at seeing the President again."[13]

After discussing the military situation, they both spoke negatively of leader Charles de Gaulle and the possibility of a French zone in occupied Germany carved out of the British and US zones. At 5:00 p.m. they met in the grand ballroom for the first plenary session.

Though weary, FDR presided while his closest confidant, Harry Hopkins, remained sick in bed. He was to lose eighteen pounds while at the conference. As reported by the military experts, the entire three hours were devoted to the Eastern and Western fronts. The eight-day conference had no orderly organization or approved stenographic report. Instead, "issues were brought up, discussed, then shunted off to the foreign ministers or military chiefs or just dropped for a few hours." There were plenary sessions each day at 4:00 p.m. and daily morning and afternoon sessions of the diplomatic and military chiefs.[14]

At the first plenary session, Sunday, February 4, Stalin suggested Roosevelt preside, and FDR acted as both judge and conciliator. The Big Three and their staffs reviewed the military situation: General A. I. Antonov for the USSR, General George C. Marshall for the US, and Sir Charles Portal for Britain. Portal explained the air war, and Admiral Sir Andrew B. Cunningham detailed the U-boat threat. Churchill once again, as during World War I, suggested a Balkan expedition for the allies, and his proposal was dropped.[15]

Roosevelt hosted a Russian-style dinner, and, as Bohlen reported, "perfect humor" prevailed. During informal conversations, the rights of small nations in the UN were discussed. "Stalin had already made known his views that the three big powers, which had borne the brunt of the war, should bear the responsibilities of the peace and that he was opposed to giving the smaller powers any rights that could in any way contradict the wishes of any great power." There were such moments of "irritation and bitterness" throughout, but the "overall mood of good feeling continued right to the last dinner, given by Stalin." Bohlen remarked, "Yalta is undoubtedly the most controversial conference in United States history."

Stalin paid an excellent compliment to FDR: "There was a third man, Roosevelt 'whose country had not been seriously threatened with invasions, but through perhaps a broader conception of national interest, and even though his country was not directly imperiled, had been the chief forger of the instrument which had led to the mobilization of the world against Hitler,' a reference to Lend-Lease."[16]

On the second day, Monday, February 5, the foreign secretaries met for lunch at the Koreiz Villa, former Count Yusupov's palace, where Stalin's delegation stayed. Molotov emphasized the Soviet expectations of German reparations, a topic argued back and forth throughout the conference. He also spoke of long-term credits from the US.

The second plenary session met at 4:00 p.m., and Hopkins attended this and the rest of the sessions. It was now that the conferees got severe.

Stalin mentioned that he did not object to a French zone in occupied Germany if it were carved out of the US and British zones, leaving the Russian zone as constituted. He remained opposed to the French participating in the Allied Control Commission for Germany. At first FDR agreed with Stalin against the British. But at the plenary's close, FDR was converted and later concluded that the

French should be given a seat on the Control Commission. "At this point, Stalin raised his arms above his head and said, '*Sdaiyous*,' which means 'I surrender.'" As Bohlen remarked, "One result of Stalin's acceptance was to reinforce Roosevelt's idea that he had a great personal influence on the dictator."

Stalin wanted to know if occupation zones also meant Germany's ultimate dismemberment and, if Germany was divided, what kind of government each part would have. This would all have to be part of the terms of unconditional surrender.

Stalin also raised the question of reparations. All agreed to dismemberment, but the details were to be worked out by the foreign secretaries. The surrender terms would not detail this. As to reparations, Russia's ambassador to Britain, I. M. Maisky, suggested in-kind and yearly payments, of which the Soviet Union would receive $10 billion of the total. Arguments over Germany's ability to repay ensued, and the whole matter was referred to a reparations commission representing only the Big Three.[17]

On Tuesday, February 6, both Churchill and FDR appealed to Stalin's "generosity" regarding Poland at the third plenary session. Stalin remained adamant. Though he feared a breach, Roosevelt persisted, suggesting to Stalin that representative Polish leaders meet to form an interim government and pledge to free elections at the earliest moment. He also reassured Stalin that the US would "never lend its support in any way to any provisional government in Poland that would be inimical to your interests."

The Big Three signed a communiqué that avoided the word "dismemberment" but included it in the surrender document. It was also at this plenary that Secretary of State Stettinius detailed FDR's plans for a world organization, beginning with voting and leaning on what had been accomplished at the Dumbarton Oaks Conference the previous August 21 – September 27, 1944: the structure, procedures, especially voting, and aim of preserving world peace and security. The argument over how many votes the USSR should have in the UN Assembly finally boiled down to three by the end of the conference, including Byelorussia and Ukraine. The veto had yet to be decided.

At the fourth plenary session on Wednesday, February 7, Stalin rejected FDR's letter pleading for Poland, in which the president told Stalin he was determined to avoid a breach. Instead, Stalin presented a Soviet plan in which the seeds of a compromise appeared. According to this, the Lublin Committee would add democratic emigrant circles and hold free elections soon. These leaders would be invited to form an interim government of national unity in Moscow. As to free elections, nothing was mentioned of allied supervision.

But Bohlen concluded, "I do not presume to know what was going on in Roosevelt's mind, but from what he said at Yalta and from his actions there, I feel that he did everything he could to help the Poles." The Russians won out on this issue as the Lublin Committee, with some additions from abroad and Poland, became the "Polish Provisional Government of National Unity."

At the fourth session, it was decided to give Byelorussia and Ukraine an assembly vote in the UN and allow France into the Allied Control Commission. The UN should convene as soon as possible, April 25, 1945, in San Francisco. The voting formula included the veto's question, already drafted at Dumbarton Oaks, to be exercised by the four, or five if France were included, on the UN's council.

As to French participation in the Control Commission, US Ambassador to the USSR Averell Harriman privately conveyed to Stalin that FDR changed his mind on the subject, and the marshal "said that since this was the president's decision, he would go along with it." On February 10 Stalin signed the Declaration on Liberated Europe with no argument. The declaration said there would be consultation among the Big Three regarding democracy in free countries.

The fifth plenary session was held on February 8, 1945. Before the plenary, Stalin came to FDR's study for a military discussion and asked about voting in the UN Assembly. The president had agreed to two additional votes for the Soviet Union.

As to the military, certain airfields near Budapest were agreed to for allied bombers. At the plenary, FDR announced his agreement to the additional votes for the USSR. The Big Three accepted that only associated nations who declared war on the axis should be invited to the UN's opening session. The deadline was set on March 1, 1945. The new Polish borders were also discussed, with much of the Curzon Line, drawn between Poland and Russia after World War I, being accepted in the east, with the western border to be determined by the foreign ministers after further study.

On Friday, February 9, the sixth plenary agreed on the Polish formula of including Poles from outside and inside Poland to reorganize into a Provisional Government of National Unity and hold free and unfettered elections as soon as practicable. It also agreed that German reparations would be about $20 billion, with $10 billion, or 50 percent, going to Russia.

Later, the question of whether trusteeships could be invited to the UN would be considered. This vexed Churchill, and he hotly defended the British Empire. A "Declaration on Liberated Europe" was adopted that strictly referred to the Atlantic Charter as not applying to the British Empire. The question of war criminals and the military situation were touched on.

On Saturday, February 10, the seventh and last plenary session was held. Final drafts on reparations and one on Poland were submitted. No sum was mentioned in the former, and the western border of Poland was to be determined later.

With Churchill absenting himself but signing it, FDR and Stalin agreed the USSR would enter the war against Japan within one to three months after Hitler was defeated. Besides, earlier, on February 8, they had settled what was in it for Russia: the southern half of Sakhalin, the Kuril Islands, joint running of the Manchurian and South Manchurian railroads with China, leasing Port Arthur, and the internationalization of the Port of Darien. In these arrangements, China was not consulted until later.

Bohlen, who was present throughout and did all of FDR's

translating, came to the following conclusion: "Regardless of what was said or not said, written or not written, agreed to or not agreed to at the Yalta Conference, there was nothing that could have prevented the breakup of the victorious coalition and the onset of the Cold War once Stalin set his course." [18]

Unlike Chamberlain with Hitler, or FDR and Churchill's failed efforts at a lasting friendship with Stalin, Kissinger and Nixon's attempts with Zhou Enlai and Mao succeeded.

3. BEIJING'S BIG TWO

On July 1, 1971, Henry Kissinger, the national security advisor to President Richard M. Nixon, departed on his fact-finding tour of Asia. For secrecy and because other jets were in use, Kissinger left in a windowless communications plane from the Tactical Air Command. No reporters came, and the story was stuck deep in the July 10 newspapers. *The New York Times* described him as "feeling slightly indisposed."

Instead of going to Nathia Gali, as announced in *The New York Times*, a decoy motorcade went there. Kissinger secretly boarded a Pakistani Boeing 707 with his three aides—Winston Lord, W. R. Smyser, and John H. Holdridge—and two secret service men, John Ready and Gary McLeod. They landed in Beijing just after noon on Friday, July 9, 1971. Shortly after that, Kissinger shook Zhou Enlai's hand, and for the next two days, they held many hours of discussions with each other, some sessions lasting seven or more hours.

Though they only had to settle on Nixon's arrangements, their talks ranged widely, especially their mutual distrust of the USSR. After Kissinger rested, his first meeting started at 4:35 p.m. Each day's schedule covered eleven items, in sequence, through to the last day, July 11. The first agenda item between Kissinger and Zhou, starting that afternoon, was under the heading of "General Philosophy: The US and Chinese Foreign Policy and Relations." Then they proceeded through each item, breaking at 7:55 p.m. for dinner and starting again at 9:04 p.m. to continue to 11:20 p.m. Kissinger turned up with his fat binders of briefing books, while Zhou Enlai arrived with a single sheet of paper.[19]

The July 9, 1971, discussions were wide-ranging. In these exchanges, the conversation between Kissinger and Zhou fell loosely under four headings: the introductory remarks of greetings and agenda settings, the Taiwan problem, the Vietnamese-Indochina issues, and philosophical-geopolitical questions. Zhou took on a grand inquisitor's role, demanding answers or resolutions to fundamental problems that separated the People's Republic of China (PRC) from America. Kissinger became the dexterous counterpuncher, often offering up ways out of impossible dead ends and, occasionally, displaying toughness when confronted by an impasse where compromise was not in the offing.

Later, when Winston Lord reviewed the Memorandum of a Conversation or "Memcon" of the July 9 conversation between the two principals, in his comments dated July 29, he thought the Chinese premier came across "very impressively" but also that his boss acquitted himself well. "One is struck again just how 'searching, sweeping, and significant' these talks were." More pointedly, "[Zhou] is perhaps a little more rhetorical, without being nasty, than we remember him." Zhou played more on history, but he noted that Nixon was not responsible for the mistakes he inherited. Though tough on Taiwan, he was "relatively restrained" on Indochina and a little too preoccupied with Japan.[20]

Kissinger remembered Zhou as "one of the two or three most impressive men I have ever met." He gave off an air of "controlled tension, steely discipline, and self-control, [and he also displayed] extraordinary graciousness."[21] In their first half hour, Zhou set the tone when Kissinger called China "mysterious," and Zhou contradicted him. Taken aback, Nixon's man confessed that the premier was undoubtedly correct: "We had to build confidence to remove the mystery. This was his fundamental purpose with me, as was mine with him." Converging interests, not goodwill, brought America and China together.

"It was not personal friends with Zhou but a commonly perceived danger that fostered the elaboration of our relationship."[22] Zhou never went pawn grubbing. He was a pure power politician. Kissinger commented that neither side asked the other to do what its values or interests prohibited. There ensued conversations with easy banter and a stylized character as if it were a dialogue between two professors of political philosophy. That nearly obscured the penalty of failure and continued isolation for one side. It would also sharpen international difficulties for one side or the other.[23]

The presidential visit became a subsidiary matter. Zhou agreed with Nixon's Kansas City speech of July 6, which announced the US position on the PRC to the world: The Chinese were creative, productive, and one of the most capable people, and that was why it was "essential that this administration take the first steps toward ending the isolation of Mainland China from the world community." Five economic superpowers —the United States, Western Europe, Japan, the Soviet Union, and the PRC—would determine the structure of peace if they acted in unity.

Zhou rejected the "superpower" designation. China would not play that game. Kissinger reflected, "It was both true and prudent; China needed us precisely because it did not have the strength to balance the Soviet Union by itself."[24]

They settled the one practical item quickly: Nixon's forthcoming trip. For the rest, they could "spend their time enjoying conceptual discussions." Most importantly, "the mutual interests they discussed mainly involved their shared distrust of the Soviets." Kissinger showed the Chinese "super-secret intelligence about Soviet military actions and communication intercepts of Soviet installations on the Chinese border."[25]

The Memcon of their first meeting played out differently. It all started with easy chatter about journalist Edgar Snow and the story of his interview with Mao.[26] Kissinger opened by suggesting the order of business and laying some groundwork on mutual Asian concerns and world peace. He set out a seven-point plan and cautiously added an eighth. "I know you are concerned about collusion, or what you call collusion, of other countries against you." Kissinger assured him that the US "will never collude with other countries against the People's Republic of China, either with our allies or with some of our opponents." What if China colluded, say, with Russia?

Both would strive to avoid this. This question of cooperation, or what came to be termed "condominium," came up again in some detail after the dinner break. It started with Kissinger being pressed about Korea and responding, as he had argued, about Washington's presence in Taiwan. US military presence would be gradually solved as America withdrew from Asia, including Japan. Kissinger naively tried to show how his adopted country had spread over the world.

After World War II, there was a vacuum in Europe. Against its inclinations, Washington was driven by a military doctrine that communists had to be promptly dealt with instead of rotting, as fascism had until it was almost too late. America also had to deal with liberal elements, such as zealots for social welfare or trying to improve the economic progress of nations, even before they had an adequate political organization. Nixon thought the defense of faraway countries was primarily their responsibility. He would only use American power to "intervene primarily when a superpower threaten[ed] to establish hegemony" over weaker countries. Prime Minister (PM) Zhou understood. "There is another superpower," he said. Kissinger replied, "Here? To the north?" A dialogue ensued:

> PM Zhou: Yes. We don't believe that a superpower can control the world, and it will also be defeated as it stretches out its hand. You are feeling difficulties now, and they too will also feel difficulties. They are just now following after you.
>
> Dr. Kissinger: With all due respect, I think they triggered us; they caused our actions. Even today, their

constant probing makes it very hard to settle with them.[27]

The friendly banter turned serious as Zhou picked up on Kissinger's agenda. The premier prefaced his remarks with an emphasis on coexistence, equality, and friendship. On the latter, he recalled that the "Chinese and American peoples are friendly toward each other. This was true in the past and will be true in the future." But within fifty years, things had changed.

After the new China appeared and after the Bandung Conference (April 18, 1955 – April 24, 1955), exchanges ceased, and sixteen years of fruitless meetings followed, all 136 of them in Warsaw; the crux was whether there was an intention to solve problems—not peripherals but fundamental ones. That introduction led Zhou to Taiwan. From the Chinese Revolution and the Civil War onward, it was the touchiest subject. Kissinger revealed how agonizing that topic was: "one of the most painful meetings of my career." It occurred on July 1, 1971—the day of his "Polo I" departure to the PRC. The Government of the Republic of China (GRC-Taiwan) envoy, James Shen, came to his office to preserve Taiwan's seat at the UN meeting. He was opposed to a dual seating plan devised by the State Department. Kissinger later explained, "No government less deserved what was about to happen to it than that of Taiwan."[28] Now the president's national security advisor had to deal with the whole Taiwan issue, brought bluntly before him by the premier.

Zhou maintained that Taiwan was the crucial issue to be resolved, and a change in Washington's position had brought it on shortly after the start of the Korean War. Before then, the US had considered Taiwan an internal Chinese matter. "And, therefore," Zhou said, "the US declared that it wouldn't interfere in China's internal affairs and would leave the Chinese people to settle internal questions." Yet the US still faces the Taiwan issue, as the PRC closely watches Western commitment to help defend Ukraine, beginning in 2022.

After the Korean War broke out, the US "surrounded Taiwan and declared the status of Taiwan was still unsettled. Even up to the present day, the spokesman of your State Department still says that this is your position . . ." That meant, according to Zhou, "if this crucial question is not solved, then the whole question will be difficult to resolve." He considered that all other Sino-American questions seemed to rest on this one, and they would have to wait until this was satisfactorily solved. We are still waiting.

If the PRC was the sole legitimate government of China, then the US could make no exceptions; it must withdraw all its armed forces and dismantle all its military installations in Taiwan. All treaties between the US and the Republic of China (GRC) were illegal.[29]

The NSC chief agreed with the premier's historical review; then he proceeded to Taiwan's linkage to Indochina. If the Korean War had not occurred, Taiwan would probably be a part of the PRC. "For reasons which are now worthless to recapitulate, a previous administration linked the future of Korea to the future of Taiwan, partly because of the US domestic opinion at the time." Developments since then created "some principles of foreign policy for us."

Kissinger divided the question into two parts: the military situation and the political evolution between the GRC and the PRC. Of the first, some symbolic steps were already taken: for example, ending the Taiwan Strait's patrol, removing a squadron of air tankers, and reducing the military advisory group by 20 percent. Kissinger recognized these steps were only symbolic, but they indicated the direction of Washington's intentions. Two-thirds of the American military presence was related to "activities in other parts of Asia," while one-third was connected to Taiwan's defense. The US was prepared to remove the former within a specified brief period after the war in Indochina. As to the latter, "we are prepared to begin reducing our other forces on Taiwan as our relations improve so that the military questions need not be a principal obstacle between us," Kissinger said.

America did not advocate for a two-China, one-China, or one-Taiwan solution. Instead, Nixon insisted that Taiwan's political evolution would likely be in China's direction. The president was firm on these principles. Specific necessities had to be observed.

That rankled Zhou; it still rankles Xi. Zhou asked, "What necessities?" Kissinger maintained Washington should not be forced into formal declarations, which would have no practical effect, but the US would not stand in the way of an essential evolution. But could it evolve into war?

Zhou repeated the PRC's position, but because of Kissinger's admission of no two-China, one-China, or one-Taiwan, Zhou opened the door a crack: "This shows that the prospect for a solution and the establishment of diplomatic relations between our two countries is hopeful."

Kissinger slipped himself and Nixon through that narrow opening. Kissinger underlined that the PRC could count on those principles, so Zhou asked what about the time left for Nixon in his first and, perhaps, second term—Nixon could discuss with Mao the establishment of diplomatic relations assuming equality and reciprocity despite the years of estrangement.

Kissinger insisted recognition had nothing to do with Nixon's reelection. Still, it was based on Nixon's "lifelong conviction that there cannot be peace without the participation of the PRC." When Kissinger asked the premier if Nixon's meeting with Mao depended on recognition or whether the two could be separated, Zhou replied that they could be parted.

Kissinger suggested the military question could be settled if the war in Southeast Asia were ended within Nixon's first term and the evolution of the Taiwan issue left to the second term. When Zhou asked about a Taiwanese independence movement, Kissinger said the US did not support it. Zhou attached great importance to that statement, but he had to be honest about the PRC's recognition and candidly told the premier there was no possibility of it within the next few years. Kissinger insisted on making peace in Indochina, but the settlement had to follow America's honor and self-respect. Actions in Laos and Cambodia were not, he maintained, aimed at China.

Nixon was ready to set a specific date for complete withdrawal, but to reach such a deadline, an overall settlement had to include a ceasefire in all of Indochina, prisoners' release, and respect for the Geneva Conference and Accords of April-July 1954.[30] Demands for reparations contradicted honor, but voluntary aid might be given once peace was made. After America's withdrawal, a final political solution in South Vietnam could be left to the Vietnamese alone, without external interference.

The premier insisted on all foreign troops out of Southeast Asia and Vietnam to be left alone to resolve its fate. Kissinger agreed. After some quibbling about an advisor's role, Kissinger noted the US likely would not return from ten thousand miles away.

When the premier complained that the US had enlarged the war, Nixon's envoy sidestepped the issue: "That is history, and our problem now is how to end it." Zhou urged the best way to end it forthrightly and leave. Kissinger, miffed, replied, "I have stated our views and don't believe I need to repeat them." At that, they broke for dinner. No one wanted the Peking duck to cool.

The Vietnamese problem continued over dinner. Zhou remarked that even if there were a ceasefire and a US withdrawal, those in power would be removed by democratic elections or overthrown. Nixon's NSC advisor approved the former. Zhou, however, did not believe in the forthcoming elections.

Kissinger noted the North Vietnamese wanted the US "both to withdraw and get rid of the government of [South] Vietnam. To do both of these is impossible." Table talk drifted to the coup in Phnom Penh, which, Kissinger insisted "was not of our doing; it was unfortunate. We did not want Sihanouk overthrown. Why should we lie? What difference does it make now? We were negotiating with North Vietnam at that moment. The coup ruined negotiations that we were conducting and that we wanted to succeed."

Formal conversations resumed at 9:40 p.m. The first day's discussions ended with further comments about Vietnam, especially withdrawal conditions and more geopolitical talk.

Zhou referred to Nixon's recent Kansas City speech on July 6. Nixon had said the US should not concentrate all of its energies on Vietnam, which it had for the last ten years, and should look at things from a global perspective. "One can say in all frankness," the premier continued, "that if it were not for the help given the South Vietnamese puppets, the Saigon regime would have collapsed long ago." Why, he wondered, must the US leave a "tail" there? "So, I cannot quite understand what you mean by wanting to leave a tail there, although you reaffirmed moments ago your complete withdrawal."

When Kissinger asked what Zhou meant by a "tail," the premier replied, "The Thieu regime." Kissinger endeavored to state the US position. No negotiations would mean a long and slow withdrawal, and the Saigon government would be strengthened in the interval. But was not that a conditional withdrawal, Zhou asked?

Again, Kissinger elaborated that the US did not want to maintain a specific government and would restrict its support of the government, but "what we cannot do is to participate in the overthrow of people whom we have been allied, whatever the origin of the alliance." If that government were unpopular, it would soon be overthrown after US withdrawal, and if that were the case, America would not intervene. During withdrawal, Washington would abide by internationally set guidelines for stipulated limits on military aid for a specified period of months.[31]

Zhou raised removing US troops from South Korea, which Kissinger said would evolve naturally in Japan and Taiwan. From that point, the conversation dealt with geopolitics—"triangular diplomacy" with the USSR and PRC—and ended at 11:20 p.m.

They met again on July 10 to clarify details of Nixon's visit: dates, who would be invited, settling on an announcement regarding Kissinger's visit, and agreeing on another visit for him in October.

Kissinger wrote a lengthy memorandum for Nixon on his return trip, dated July 14, candidly evaluating the entire experience. His remarks are divided into fourteen sections. They reveal a keen appreciation of the trip: "My two-day visit to Peking resulted in the most searching, sweeping, and significant discussions I have ever had in government." In more than twenty hours of discussions, he had set a summit meeting before the following May and candidly covered essential issues between the US and PRC. He had established a "major new departure in international relations [and had] laid the groundwork for [Nixon] and Mao to turn a page in history."[32]

About Nixon's later "thunder" out of China, his national security advisor's communiqué of July 15 made all the noise. Kissinger neatly put it, "We all agreed with Zhou Enlai that the announcement now firmly scheduled for the following Thursday at 10:30 p.m. Washington time would 'shake the world.'"[33] Once shaken, the world would not need re-shaking by Nixon's encounter with Mao. The significant realignment, diplomatically called "triangular relations," had been accomplished by Kissinger and Zhou, and global relationships were transformed.[34]

Kissinger recounted how relaxed and constructive the atmosphere and conversations were between equals, unlike those held with the Soviet Union. Both he and Zhou were contemptuous of the USSR. The Chinese, urbane and at ease, contrasted with the "self-conscious sense of hierarchy of Soviet officials." Zhou attacked imperialism, including the Soviet brand, as retold by Kissinger: "[There was] the specter of extensive power collusion, specifically of being carved up by the US, the USSR, and Japan; [there was his] contempt of the Indians, [his] hatred for the Russians, and apprehension over the Japanese, the disclaimer that China is, or would want to be, a superpower like the Russians and we who have 'stretched out our hands too far.' There was," Kissinger emphasized, "none of the Russian ploymanship, scoring points, rigidity, or bullying. They did not turn everything into a contest." There was no maneuvering for petty gains.

When Kissinger mentioned how the Russians had put out their English translation, differing from the American's, of the May 20 Strategic Arms Limitation Talks, Zhou "showed obvious contempt" and noted the Chinese would "never resort to such a gambit."

When the discussion turned toward the actual date, Zhou wished for a time after Nixon's Soviet summit. Kissinger explained the problem to Zhou, and he "was willing to be flexible because [as Kissinger explained] this is a significant sign (and perhaps the most significant) of the Chinese worries about their confrontation with the USSR." Kissinger was often explicit about China's resentment of Russia: "He (Zhou) showed deep bitterness against Russia and contempt for their petty tactics."

About the Chinese, Kissinger noted, behind their "elaborate correctness and courtesy [they were] extremely tough on substance and ideological in their approach, but their dealings were meticulous." Zhou was, according to Kissinger, matter-of-fact, clear, eloquent, at home in philosophy or historical analysis, genial, urbane, considerate, and had a "refreshing sense of humor." He concluded, "In short, Zhou Enlai ranks with Charles de Gaulle as the most impressive foreign statesman I have met."

When Zhou made an "extremely tough presentation" before lunch on the second day and Kissinger "responded very toughly" with a "deliberately brusque point-by-point rebuttal," Zhou stopped him to say again that the "duck would get cold" if they did not eat. Then, during lunch, "Zhou's geniality returned."

Kissinger cited a certain tension between Zhou and his compatriots. He thought the Cultural Revolution was an "anguishing period" for them, and he noticed a "moral ambivalence," a "certain brooding quality," and "schizophrenia" in Zhou's presentations, as well as his "jagged rhythm" in drafting the announcement. These were, he reflected, "men in some anguish. Yet their long history of past suffering gave them inner confidence that was reflected in a certain largeness of spirit."

Beijing's position on Hanoi's support was always ambivalent, without wishing to jeopardize a chance of improving Sino-American relations. Kissinger, the exile from Nazi persecution, had skated through all this "turmoil under heaven" and handed Nixon, the grocer's son, a Beijing summit.[35]

Kissinger chuckled over minor incidents that lent charm to the drama. The first was that he left his extra pair of shirts in Pakistan and borrowed John Holdridge's—a six-footer and former West Pointer. Then *New York Times* reporter James Reston's possible interference, whose visit coincided with his in Beijing. Zhou gleefully delayed Reston's train from Shanghai, and he ended up hospitalized in Beijing for an appendectomy. He was so near, yet so far, from the scoop of a lifetime. When Kissinger deplaned in Pakistan, his security was almost blown because his Chinese gifts of Mao's collected works and photos of the historic trip could not be concealed.

Finally, there was that nostalgic remark of the ever-proper PRC's army, Marshal Zhu De, when, on their way to Peking's airport, the marshal recounted how he had run off to join Mao as a nationalist officer and endured the Long March. None of that little band "ever dreamed of seeing victory in their lifetimes, and they thought their struggle was for future generations. As they reached the boarding ramp, the marshal said, "Yet here we are, and here you are."[36]

By now, Kissinger and his small staff agreed with Zhou—the announcement of Kissinger's secret trip and its purpose would "shake the world."

Nixon awaited his NSC advisor's arrival at El Toro Marine Corps Air Station at 7:00 a.m. on July 13. Kissinger had cabled his mission's success while on his way to Teheran, using the code word "Eureka." From 7:20 to 9:30 a.m., Nixon debriefed Kissinger. Kissinger and Lord prepared a four-hundred-word announcement of seven minutes that Nixon made at Burbank's NBC-TV studios. They repaired to Perino's restaurant to celebrate with crab legs and a bottle of Chateau Lafite Rothschild 1961.

The four-hundred-word announcement that shook the world read in part:

> Premier Zhou Enlai and Dr. Henry Kissinger, President Nixon's assistant for national security affairs, held talks in Peking from July 9–11, 1971. Knowing of President Nixon's expressed desire to visit the People's Republic

of China, Premier Zhou Enlai, on behalf of the People's Republic of China, has invited President Nixon to visit China at an appropriate date before May 1972. President Nixon has accepted the invitation with pleasure.

The meeting between China and the United States leaders is to seek the normalization of relations between the two countries and exchange views on questions of concern to the two sides.[37]

With that, America entered an era of triangular diplomacy: "Equilibrium" Kissinger noted, "was the name of the game. We did not seek to join China in a provocative confrontation with the Soviet Union. But we agreed on the necessity to curb Moscow's geopolitical ambitions." Washington had no reason to be involved in the Moscow-Peking ideological dispute, and it had a "moral and political obligation to strive for coexistence . . ."

What the US could not tolerate was Soviet aggression against China. If that succeeded, "the whole weight of the Soviet military effort could be thrown against the West." Kissinger called this newly assumed American position a balancing act on a tightrope. The US-PRC relationship could not overcome Soviet paranoia, and China had to be assured against any Soviet-American collusion. Mao put it succinctly: America must not "stand on China's shoulders" to reach Moscow.[38]

Chamberlain had failed. FDR and Churchill had only partial success. But Kissinger and Nixon succeeded until 2001. An American founding father, Ben Franklin, had once acknowledged a Puritan divine, Cotton Mather's comment, to stoop to get under a low place, even if incurring a little infamy along the way. Triangular diplomacy ended when Xi and Putin signed the Sino-Russian Treaty of Friendship in 2001.[39]

The twentieth-century Age of Infamy gave rise to fictional infamies in the form of dystopian fantasies, which projected even worse worlds.

SEVEN
DYSTOPIAN INFAMIES

> War is peace. Freedom is slavery. Ignorance is strength.
>
> GEORGE ORWELL, *1984*

Philosopher John Stuart Mill may have been the first to use the word "dystopia." If so, what he meant was something "too bad to be practicable." Then, writers created a new literary genre reflecting actual twentieth-century dystopias. Samples of this fiction are Yevgeny Zamyatin's *We* (1921), Karel Čapek's *R.U.R.* (1921), Aldous Huxley's *Brave New World* (1932), George Orwell's *Animal Farm* (1945) and *1984* (1949), Ray Bradbury's *Fahrenheit 451* (1953), and Anthony Burgess's *A Clockwork Orange* (1962).

Like Hitler's Germany, Stalin's Russia, or Mao's China, the twentieth-century totalitarian states usually collapsed either from external assaults or various internal weaknesses—except for Deng Xiaoping's reformist China. Failed twentieth-century totalitarian states had their successful fictional counterparts, enduring far beyond whatever their imaginary challenges were by instituting the most extreme infamies. Dystopian authors created their twentieth-century totalitarian nightmares to warn the world of the future's ultimate infamies. It was like imagining Dr. Caligari having a nightmare.

1. THE ONE STATE

A hundred miles south of Moscow, Yevgeny Zamyatin, the son of an orthodox priest, taught school. He had studied naval engineering in St. Petersburg, became a Bolshevik member of Lenin's Marxist party, was arrested on numerous occasions, and finally finished his engineering degree in Finland.

Zamyatin first wrote fiction as a hobby. In 1916 he came to the United Kingdom to supervise the construction of an icebreaker. He returned to Russia at the time of the October 25, 1917 (November 7, 1917) Revolution. Afterward, he edited journals, wrote, and lectured. Zamyatin opposed party censorship. "True literature," he wrote, "can exist only when it is created, not by diligent and reliable officials, but by madmen, hermits, heretics, dreamers, rebels, and skeptics."

In 1923 he smuggled his novel *We* out of Russia, and E. P. Dutton published an English version. Later, in 1927, the writer gave his Russian text to literary critic Marc Slonim in Prague, who published that version. Copies circulated in Russia, and he was blacklisted. He asked for and received an emigration visa to Paris. Zamyatin wrote, "I do not wish to conceal that the basic reason for my request for permission to go abroad with my wife is my hopeless position here as a writer [and] the death sentence that has been pronounced upon me as a writer here at home."

Zamyatin collaborated with the French film director Jean Renoir on the 1936 adaptation of Maxim Gorky's play *The Lower Depths*, cowritten for the film by Zamyatin. He died of a heart attack in 1937.[1]

Karel Čapek, the Czech playwright, predicted, "Some of the future can always be read in the palms of the present." He referred to his 1921 play, *R.U.R.* (Rossum's Universal Robots), and he coined the word "robot" from the Czech *rozum*, meaning "reason," and *robota*, for "serfdom." In his drama, humanized robots plan to seize power from the people, ending humanity's work-free utopia. They succeed.

Recently, Henry Kissinger, Eric Schmidt, and Daniel Huttenlocher published *The Age of AI: And Our Human Future*. They discuss AI with computers that not only can be programmed to win games and solve problems, but newer ones that learn on their own and then employ their logic independently of humans. Have Čapek's robots come to haunt or help us?[2]

In that same year, 1921, Yevgeny Zamyatin's dystopian novel *We* had savages attempting to overthrow the scientifically ordered One State. They fail. That year marks the serendipitous centenary of *We* and *R.U.R.*, according to writer Dorian Lynskey.[3] A new literary genre, or negative utopia, had been created: dystopia. Was it too bad to be practicable?

Zamyatin sets his futuristic novel one thousand years ahead, where a mathematically perfect society, the One State, exists but is separated from the world outside by a seemingly impenetrable Green Wall. People are known only by numbers, and they live in glass buildings with the shades up. They have almost nothing to hide except sex. Then they pull the shades down. A universal Time Table regulates their lives.

A spaceship, the Integral, is being built by D-503, which will carry his diary and other praises of the mathematically perfect One State throughout the universe. As Zamyatin puts it, D-503 is "one happy cog of a big machine"—that is, until he meets seductress I-330. He is aroused beyond sex to love her. Promiscuous sex for procreation is okay, but love is not. State factories raise children.

Instead of free sex with anyone and then only with the shades down, they secretly meet in a museum of the past, the opaque Ancient House. I-330 smokes, drinks, skips work, and plots a revolution with savages beyond the wall. She manipulates D-503, planning to capture the Integral. D-503 denies these severe crimes because he is insanely in love with her. As an accomplice, he fears being captured by the Guardians (secret police) and executed. As the author puts it, his passion makes him lose everything: his friends, his former sex partner, and his faith in the One State.

On Unanimity Day, while the numbers vote for their Benefactor, the revolutionaries strike, cast their ballots against the leader, and incite a revolt. For D-503, this is the greatest catastrophe in history. They attempt to seize the Integral but fail. The rebels blow up parts of the Green Wall, but the Guards hold them back. They take the rebels to a unique auditorium, like Orwell's Room 101 in his novel *1984* or Stalin's Lubyanka prison, and subject them to the Great Operation, which removes imagination from their brains, turning humans into machines.

D-503 becomes an obeying citizen, betrays the rebels, and turns them in. The Guards torture and execute them, including I-330. He writes that some rebels still fight, but the One State is winning. Zamyatin says, "There is nothing greater or more beautiful than the One State, where reason prevails. 'For reason must triumph.'"[4]

Novelist George Orwell, writer of *1984*, commented on *We*: "The authorities announce that they have discovered the cause of the recent disorders: Some humans suffer from a disease called imagination. The nerve center responsible for creativity has now been located, and the disease can be cured by X-ray treatment. D-503 [betrays] his confederates to the police."[5] However, there are other "cures" for dissidents besides extermination and lobotomy: drugs.

2. THE WORLD STATE

After graduating from Oxford in 1916, Aldous Huxley published short stories and poems and edited *Oxford Poetry*. He also wrote travelogues, satires, and screen scenarios. He lived in Los Angeles from 1937 until he died in 1963. His novel *Brave New World*, published in 1932, made him famous.

It opens in London, the World State city, in the year 632 AF (After Ford or 2540 CE). Citizens are created through artificial wombs, and childhood is indoctrinated by programs to predetermine a person's caste. It is based on society's needs for intelligence and labor.

Lenina Crowne, a birthing worker, is sexually hot and liked. Bernard Marx, a psychologist, is neither. His short stature for his high caste gives him an inferiority complex. He works with sleep-learning that gives him an understanding and disapproval of the World State's methods of keeping citizens peaceful. Society constantly consumes a soothing, happiness-producing drug called "soma."

Bernard is noisy and arrogant in his social criticisms, and his boss wants to exile him to Iceland because of this. He has a friend, Helmholtz Watson, a talented writer who also finds it difficult to use his creativity in a soma, pain-free society.

Bernard goes on holiday with Lenina outside the World State to the Savage Reservation in New Mexico. They observe a primitive world of naturally born people with diseases and the aged. There are other languages and religions. Their folk culture is Native, regional Americans of the descendants of the Anasazi and Pueblo peoples.

Bernard and Lenina witness violent public rituals and meet Linda, a person from the World State who lives with her son, John. She once visited the reservation on holiday, became separated from her group, and was left behind.

She got pregnant by a holidaymaker who is Bernard's boss, the Director of Hatcheries and Conditioning. She did not return because of the shame of her pregnancy. Her son John has never been accepted by the villagers. Their lives are difficult and unhappy. Linda taught John to read from her two books, a science textbook and Shakespeare.

John's feelings are shaped by Shakespeare. Linda wants to return to London, while John hopes to experience London's "brave new world." Bernard gets permission to take them back. On returning to London, John meets his "father," an impossibility in the artificially born society. That causes laughter, and the humiliated director quits before exiling Bernard.

Bernard officiates for John, who is now treated as a celebrity by high society. He enjoys the attention while Bernard's popularity wanes. He envies John and turns to his novelist friend Helmholtz.

Linda spends her time using soma. John stops attending social events organized by Bernard. John understands the emptiness of the World State. Lenina and John become attracted to each other, but John disapproves of Lenina's indiscriminate sex. She tries to seduce him, but he attacks her. John finds his mother on her deathbed.

He rushes to Linda's bedside, but this is not the new society's attitude toward death. Some children who have entered the hospital ward for "death-conditioning" are disrespectful to Linda. John attacks one and then tries to stop the distribution of soma, telling them he is freeing them. Helmholtz and Bernard calm the ensuing riot. The police quell it by spraying soma vapor into the mob.

Bernard, Helmholtz, and John appear before Mustapha Mond, the "Resident World Controller for Western Europe." He tells Bernard and Helmholtz they are exiled to remote islands because of their antisocial activity. Bernard pleads for another chance. Helmholtz chooses the Falklands, believing that "remoteness and stormy weather" will inspire his writing.

Mond tells Bernard that exile is a reward because the islands are full of exciting people who don't fit into the World State's society. Mond summarizes for John the events that led to the present society and argues for a caste system and social control. John rejects this, and Mond says John demands "the right to be unhappy." Mond refuses John's bid to go to the islands, saying he wishes to see John's future.

John moves to a hilltop tower near the village of Puttenham, where he intends to lead a solitary life, purifying himself by flagellation. That draws reporters and sightseers to witness his behavior. Lenina comes. At the sight of her, John attacks Lenina with a whip. This arouses the onlookers, and John is engaged in the crowd's fury.

The next day, he remembers the mob's fury and, filled with remorse, hangs himself. The Zweigs, you recall, had also taken suicide as a way out rather than being temporarily "soma" stoned.

3. OCEANIA

George Orwell, a pen name for Eric Blair, was born in Bengal, India, in 1903. He was educated at Eton (1917–1921) and joined the Indian Imperial Police in Burma in 1922. He left the service in 1927 to return home and become a writer.

After moving to Paris in 1928, Blair described this period in his first autobiographical book, *Down and Out in Paris and London* (1933), published under his pen name, George Orwell. He also used Orwell as the pen name for his first novel, *Burmese Days* (1934).

During the 1930s, Orwell considered himself a socialist and authored a book about the poverty of unemployed miners in northern England, *The Road to Wigan Pier* (1937). He had joined the Loyalists fighting Franco's nationalists and published his Spanish experiences, *Homage to Catalonia* (1938). Orwell worked as the British Broadcasting Corporation's (BBC) literary critic and as the book review editor of *Tribune*. In 1945 he won acclaim with *Animal Farm,* a fable about Stalinism. It became a literary success. Four years later he published *1984*. Orwell died of tuberculosis in 1950.[6]

In *Animal Farm* the creatures revolt to free themselves from farmer Jones's "slavery." Old Major, a domesticated wild pig, writes the seven animal commandments for living free of humans. It starts with, "Whatever goes upon two legs is an enemy." All four-legged creatures and winged ones are comrades. Old Major bans human customs. The freed creatures rename Manor Farm "Animal Farm."

Snowball and Napoleon, two clever pigs who lead the rebellion, soon fall out over bringing electricity to the farm. Napoleon insists it is too expensive and unnecessary. He not only persuades the other animals but also threatens them by unleashing his vicious dogs. Snowball escapes.

Napoleon soon realizes the necessity of electricity. It would bring the millennium by freeing the farmyard workers of drudgery. After setbacks and increasingly enforced labor, the electric plant becomes operational. That takes an extreme effort and requires a dictatorship under Napoleon, using his pigs as bosses and his dogs as police to accomplish it.

The new animal masters, the pigs, even require the help of the once-banned humans. During this effort, the pigs take over human comforts and cooperate with the exiled people from two neighboring farms. The rest of the animals become the pig's slaves, and the farm changes its name back to Manor Farm.

As Orwell puts it, you cannot tell a man from a pig. Along the way to the animal utopia's disintegration, the creatures choose sides, and the once-free animals become downtrodden again. They are treated to various cruel overlords modeled after Stalin's henchmen. Animal Farm became a fabled version of Stalin's totalitarian Russia. Orwell followed this fable with *1984*, where totalitarianism becomes a perpetual dystopia.

We immediately recognize the frightening version of Orwell's totalitarian nightmare by his unique vocabulary and taglines that have become a part of modern languages, such as the superstate of Oceania, one of three such states always at war with each other; its "Inner" and "Outer" party members; and all the rest of the people called "Proles." The population can already see Big Brother (BB) on its telescreens, and they view his face with its bushy mustache posted all over London's shabby walls. His eyes see everyone on those ubiquitous TV monitors.

People must repeat, "War is peace. Freedom is slavery. Ignorance is strength." English socialism's ideology is called "Ingsoc."

Newspeak, the language of Oceania, reduces a person's everyday chatter to simple sentences filled with B-level words invented by the Ministry of Truth (Minitrue). The Thought Police can mind-read people's thoughts, and the super cop, O'Brien, bends them to his wishes. Citizens are forever preparing for BB's frequent "two minutes of hate," watching their telescreens, drinking Victory Gin, and smoking Victory Cigarettes.

Oceania has Four Ministries that are busy vaporizing their opponents—Truth, Love, Plenty, and Peace—while Thought Police

Chief O'Brien accuses his victims of "thought crimes." With this new vocabulary, we can enter Orwell's Oceania.

Winston Smith, O'Brien's next victim, will sooner or later get a bullet to the back of his skull. Even anti-party Emmanuel Goldstein's banned "Brotherhood" can save no one, although he tries with his outlawed book, *The Theory and Practice of Oligarchical Collectivism*. Winston secretly reads a copy given to him by O'Brien and afterward throws it down the memory hole.

Everyone knows that at the Ministry of Love, they'll change traitors into followers. They'll come out with "doublethink" (reality-controlled) brains that can reconcile contradictory thoughts, such as making five fingers equal four, $2 + 2 = 5$, simultaneously accepting both. How long can anyone like Winston hold out against caged rats threatening to bite his trapped, masked face in the infamous Room 101? He might become an unperson and finally betray his loved one, Julia. Winston Smith will give in and declare, "I love BB."

So tortured, Winston surrenders his "independence and integrity" to the state that now owns him. He even feels free, not otherwise aware, like a Čapek robot.

Winston Smith is a low-ranking Outer Member of the ruling party of Oceania (number 6079), who lives in dilapidated Victory Mansions in war-torn London. Oceania is continuously at war in *1984* with Eurasia and allied with Eastasia, but it is about to switch sides. Winston wonders, is it the other way around? They, the world's three superstates, can never destroy each other. War, therefore, is permanent. But the sides could change. Big Brother maintains that "who controls the past controls the future" and "who controls the present controls the past."

Everywhere Winston goes as a "speak writer" at Minitrue, the party watches him through telescreens, even in his apartment. Everywhere he looks, he sees enormous posters of the face of the party's omniscient leader, a figure known only as Big Brother, who is probably just a mythical projection of the party. The party owns and controls everything (an example of oligarchical collectivism) in

Oceania, especially a person's thoughts, history, future, and language.

The party forces an invented language, Newspeak, on everyone. It attempts to prevent political rebellion by eliminating all words related to it and reconciling contrasting thoughts.

The party demands past writings to be rewritten in Newspeak. Thinking rebellious thoughts is illegal, which the Thought Police are on guard against and punish. Such "thought crimes" are the worst of all crimes. Oceania's dictionary is going through various editions to achieve perfection, which is expected in the eleventh edition by 2050. Then, through the destruction of words, thought will be sufficiently narrowed to match Ingsoc's ideology.

Since reality exists only in the human mind and nowhere else, "whatever the Party holds to be the truth *is* truth." The party, maintaining ultimate power, creates its universal reality, and, therefore, it creates the only truth while annihilating all opposing truths through unlimited pain and suffering.

As the novel opens, Winston feels frustrated by the party's oppression and rigid control, which prohibits free thought, sex—except for procreation—and individuality. Winston subconsciously dislikes the party and has illegally purchased a notebook to write a diary of his criminal thoughts. He has also become fixated on an influential party member named O'Brien, whom Winston believes is a secret member of the Brotherhood—the mysterious, legendary group of Emmanuel Goldstein that works to overthrow the party.

Winston works in the Ministry of Truth, altering historical records to fit the party's ever-changing needs. He is troubled by the party's control of history. The party claims Oceania has always been allied with Eastasia in a war against Eurasia. These are the only three remaining countries or "superstates." But Winston seems to recall a time when this was not true. The party also insists that Emmanuel Goldstein, hiding secretly, is the Brotherhood's alleged leader and the most dangerous man alive. This claim does not seem plausible to Winston. He notices a coworker, a beautiful, dark-haired girl, staring at him and worries she is an informant who will turn him in for his thought crimes.

Winston spends his evenings wandering through the poorest neighborhoods in war-torn London, where the proletarians, or "Proles," live squalid lives, relatively free of persistent party monitoring.

One day Winston receives a purloined note from the dark-haired girl that reads, "I love you." Eventually, she tells him her name, Julia, and they begin a covert love affair, always on the lookout for party monitoring. Winston can't divorce his automaton-like wife. Eventually, he and Julia rent a room for "Pornosec" above a secondhand junk store of a party spy, Mr. Charrington, in the Prole's district where Winston bought his diary. Charrington, in faked Oldspeak, likes singing such lyrics as, "Here comes a candle to light you to bed, here comes a chopper to chop off your head."

Winston's relationship with Julia lasts for some time. He is sure they will be caught and punished sooner or later. Winston somehow knows he has been doomed since he wrote his first diary entry. Julia is more pragmatic and optimistic. As Winston's affair with Julia progresses, his hatred for the party grows more intense. Finally, he receives a message he has expected from O'Brien, who wants to see them.

Winston and Julia travel to O'Brien's luxurious apartment. As a member of the powerful Inner Party (Winston and Julia belong to the Outer Party), O'Brien leads a life of luxury that Winston can only imagine. O'Brien makes a fake confirmation to Winston and Julia that, like them, he hates the party and says he works against it as a member of Goldstein's Brotherhood. He indoctrinates Winston and Julia into the Brotherhood and gives Winston a copy of Emmanuel Goldstein's book, the Brotherhood's manifesto, *The Theory and Practice of Oligarchical Collectivism*.

Winston reads the book—an amalgam of several class-based twentieth-century social theories—to Julia in the room above the store. Suddenly, the Thought Police barge in and seize them. Mr.

Charrington, the store's proprietor, is revealed as having been a member of the Thought Police all along.

Torn away from Julia and taken to the Ministry of Love, Oceania's version of Stalin's Lubyanka prison, Winston finds that O'Brien, too, is a party spy. He pretended to be a Brotherhood member to trap Winston into committing an open rebellion against the party.

O'Brien spends months torturing and brainwashing Winston, who struggles to resist. At last, O'Brien sends him to the dreaded Room 101, the final destination for stubborn recalcitrants who still oppose the party after prolonged torture. Here, O'Brien tells Winston he will be forced to confront his worst fear. Throughout the novel, Winston has had recurring nightmares about rats. O'Brien now straps a cage housing two giant rats onto Winston's head and prepares to open the gate and allow the rats to eat his face. Winston snaps, pleading with O'Brien to do it to Julia, not to him.

In giving up Julia, Winston surrenders his ultimate defense of love against the party's hate. O'Brien wanted that from Winston all along. His human spirit is ultimately broken. Winston is released to the outside world. He briefly meets Julia, but he no longer feels anything for her or her for him (she has also had her spirit destroyed). He has accepted the party and has learned to love BB. He knows death awaits him at any moment by a bullet to the back of his skull, and, at the end of a hallway, he finally feels the bullet piercing his brain. Winston has, at last, become an "unperson" and ultimately disappears from history.

Orwell's appendix explains Newspeak. He coined the term "Newspeak" itself in this 1949 dystopian novel. In his fictional totalitarian state, Newspeak was the language favored by the minions of Big Brother and, in Orwell's words, "designed to diminish the range of thought." Newspeak was characterized by eliminating or altering old words, substituting one word for another, exchanging parts of speech, and giving new names for political purposes. The term has caught on and is used to refer to confusing or deceptive bureaucratic jargon.

The aim of Newspeak is simple: to limit and control words

available for ordinary discourse. The party limits thoughts and the ability to communicate. For example, Newspeak expresses "bad" through "ungood." Something terrible is called "doubleplus ungood." Newspeak's B vocabulary contains all words with political or ideological significance, specially tailored to engender blind acceptance of the party's doctrines. Newspeak removes all shades of meaning, leaving simplicities like pleasure and pain, happiness and sadness, good thoughts and thought crimes. They reinforce the totality of Oceania. Newspeak replaces Oldspeak.

A refined film version was made in 1984 and reviewed by film critic Roger Ebert. "Orwell's hero, Winston Smith, lives in a world of grim and crushing inhumanity, of bombed factories, bug-infested bedrooms, and citizens desperate for the simplest pleasures."[7] Yet, is it so unbelievable to think of the ghettos of the world's greatest cities in these terms?

4. BURN, BABY, BURN

Ray Bradbury starts his dystopian novel *Fahrenheit 451* by commenting on the sheer joy firefighter-policemen experience of things smoldering, especially paper burning at 451 degrees. These specialized personnel represent the SS (Nazi Germany) or KGB (Soviet Russia) of Bradbury's futuristic state. Their task is to destroy any remaining books, the evil source of unhappiness within the new state.

Bradbury's state dedicates itself to making its citizens happy through a culture of thoughtless, trivial mass media. This is his version of Huxley's soma, Zamyatin's lobotomy, and Orwell's Room 101. Vanguard firefighters ride around in salamander-shaped cars, armed with kerosene torches, and dressed in black uniforms with Phoenix badges and helmets numbered "451." They systematically torch subversives, their homes, and forbidden books on the banned list of millions.

Fireman Guy Montag and his chief, Captain Beatty, are aided by mechanical hounds that smell the state's enemies to kill them with poisonous injections while helicopters fly overhead for surveillance.

Montag's neighbor, a girl named Clarisse McClellan, challenges Montag's state-inculcated thinking. She exposes him to the world of thought before she and her family are incinerated to prevent them from subverting others. Clarisse senses a fellow believer in the former world of thought, even though most are captivated by simple, pleasure-seeking remedies offered by the state's TV of mass cultural programming.

Even Montag's wife, Millie, feels so trivialized that she attempts suicide. Montag tries to share his illegal, secreted books with her while on sick leave but fails, as she falls back into the daily shows with her relatives and neighbors. He breaks up her TV morning shows with neighbors while reading his poetry to them.

The Montags receive a visit from Beatty, who explains the rationale of the new society. He recites and justifies the firemen's history. It started with the state's digesting of books, then it made digests of digests, and finally, it banned books altogether. Schools dropped book learning and substituted digests. As Beatty says, "Life becomes one big pratfall, Montag; everything bang, boff, and wow."[8] He further discusses the new aims. "Empty the theaters save for the clowns and furnish the rooms with glass walls and pretty colors running up and down the walls like confetti or blood or sherry or sauterne."

The state orders authors to lock up their typewriters, and books are called "dishwater." Readers turn to comics in a thoroughly entertained society. Only then can people stay happy all the time and not be disturbed by evil thoughts. Firefighters enforce peace of mind through book burning, as the Nazis had once done. "That's you and I," Beatty explains. If a fireman gets an itch to read, he can have the story approved for twenty-four hours and then destroy the book. This explanation by his boss still leaves Montag unhappy.[9]

The denouement comes when Montag's wife betrays him and leaves. Montag is sent out on a liquidation mission that turns out to be his own home. The Hound wounds him, but Montag kills Beatty during the episode. Montag discovers other subversives and befriends Faber, and with Faber's help as an ex-professor, he escapes a search and joins a rebel group hiding upriver. The state is at war, and its cities are being bombed. The renegades lay low and hope for a better tomorrow.

5. THE CRIMINAL STATE

As these authors searched to create their fictional versions of a futuristic totalitarian state, we can recognize aspects of fascism and communism they borrowed. Such imaginary states resemble, in even more terrible ways, what Stefan Zweig described in his book *The World of Yesterday*, what Leni Riefenstahl filmed in *Triumph of the Will*, and what Albert Speer collaborated with in his memoir *Inside the Third Reich*. Even more so, one dystopian novel-turned-film caught their essence: Anthony Burgess's novel *A Clockwork Orange* and Stanley Kubrick's adaptation of it in his film.

The dystopias studied here share a common theme: Society is crushing its central hero. In the case of D-503 of Zamyatin's *We*, the One State insists on absolute uniformity of behavior. The Guardians stamp out individualism with lobotomy or, in extreme cases, torture and execution. In Huxley's *Brave New World*, the World State commands uniformity by subversion to ecstasy. Life lives in superabundance, and deviants take the mind-bending drug of happiness, soma, or watch brainless TV in Bradbury's fire-burning world. We would call that soft power in contrast to the brute force of some real and fictional totalitarianisms. Orwell, in both *Animal Farm* and *1984*, makes use of forms of barbarity as practiced by Hitler, Stalin, Mao, and Deng Xiaoping. All of them commanded a uniformity of thought and action. Now comes Anthony Burgess's novel *A Clockwork Orange* and Stanley Kubrick's film of the same name.

The Burgess dystopia reverses the previous scenarios. Instead of a state-enforced uniformity, the role is reversed. The antihero of the novel, Alex, is cured of his violent personality by a rehabilitation program. We find Alex at the film's end, mischievously smiling as he fantasizes about rape. As film critic Roger Ebert says, "Does [Burgess-Kubrick] really want us to identify with the antisocial tilt of Alex's psychopathic little life? In a world where society is criminal, of course, a good man must live outside the law. But that isn't what Kubrick and Burgess are saying. [They] actually [seem] to be implying that in a world where society is criminal, the citizen might as well be criminal, too."

Film director Steven Spielberg put it this way: "It was a very bleak vision of a dangerous future where young people are free to roam the streets without any kind of parental exception [when] you look at the movie right now. Unfortunately, history has caught up to the movie, and the headlines we now live with every day are not dissimilar to the subject matter of the 1970s film *A Clockwork Orange*."[10]

But Ebert missed the point here, and Spielberg was right. The criminals rule and, by ruling, force their state's society to be criminal. It is not necessarily top-down, so I must be a criminal, but bottom-up, so the state is criminalized.

For comparison, we have the Mussolini formula of the criminal state, forcing "everything inside the state, nothing outside the state, nothing against the state." In this situation, if Hitler condones exterminating the Jews as necessary for Germany's well-being, then Germans become the willing executioners of Jews. Alex's fantasizing rape in a dystopian novel becomes Hitler eradicating Jews in the real world. That is what makes *A Clockwork Orange* one of the most devastating of all the fictional dystopias, however bad the others are. Spielberg recognized this horror again, catching up with us in real life. An insidious alternative to Oppenheimer's nuclear catastrophe would be civilization's turning into a dystopia.

Imagine our infamous world as a dystopian nightmare. Its characteristics would mimic some of the features displayed in Zamyatin's, Čapek's, Huxley's, Orwell's, Bradbury's, and Burgess's stories. Advanced medicines, surgeries, and drugs would reduce disease, unhappiness, and pain to the point of making death a pleasant affair. Entertainment would take the place of learning. Big Brother would be an enlightened despot of the Mons variety, and dissidents could be exiled to distant places or, if recalcitrant, shoved down the memory hole or chemically conditioned. Alex and O'Brien could now be chums. The savage could make love to Smith's girlfriend, Julia. We would all communicate in the new universal language, Newspeak, live in glasshouses, and work according to a universal Time Table. Continuous warfare would be eternal bliss as long as no one used nuclear weapons. They would, of course, be rendered harmless by states accepting treaties for their control and elimination or finding a perfect defense to a nuclear calamity.

The list could be endlessly extended as long as the firemen imposed uniformity with their flamethrowers and dogs. Guy Montag could stay in exile with all the other rebels. It would be a world turned upside down while Caligari practiced his psychic cures. Is today's world all that far from Holstenwall? Or will it succumb to nuclear annihilation? Dystopian literature increasingly parallels extreme versions of contemporary society's malaise. Take Kay Dick's 1972 novel *They*. It portrays a barbarian dictatorship shredding its libraries and museums, blinding its artists, making its musicians deaf, cutting out its poets' tongues, and lobotomizing its intellectuals. Margaret Atwood's 1985 novel *The Handmaid's Tale* has a totalitarian, male theocracy subjugating women. Atwood hails Dick's novel as trailblazing.[11] And so, it goes: Dystopia or Armageddon?

EIGHT
NUCLEAR INFAMY

> I urge you to beware of . . . the aggressive impulses of an evil empire. My idea of American policy . . . We win, and they lose.
>
> RONALD REAGAN

To sustain a large and ever-increasing military budget, to maintain and improve a nuclear delivery system, to store a vast and modernized nuclear arsenal—all of these require a believable, powerful rationale. It must seem accurate or appear to be authentic and very persuasive. After all, such monies could be used elsewhere and are denied to many other worthwhile, meaningful, and valuable projects, often screaming for support. But these mighty arsenals, it would seem, can only be used to intimidate or for nuclear blackmail; even small tactical nukes on the Ukrainian battlefield make little or no sense.

Denying the cautionary Franck Report and its implications for openness, transparency, collaboration, and trust, as Oppenheimer subscribed to after August 1945, meant entering the path of an endless nuclear arms race with the deadliest weapons ever invented. The United States had proved its willingness to use them and later, if not in a first strike, then in a projected, massive retaliation of Mutually Assured Destruction (MAD) to deter another's hostile first strike capabilities. This resulted in a nuclear-aggressive peace, blackmail, and intimidation, casting a dark cloud over civilization.

The list of nuclear powers grows. The rationale for having the mightiest nuclear arsenal must be fearsome and sustained. Diplomat Paul Nitze made such a supreme argument in the 1950 US government's National Security Council Paper NSC-68, and it has remained the foundation of all arguments and negotiations ever since. A similar argument is probably the bedrock of all other competing nuclear systems. That makes various nuclear stockpiles and delivery systems a tremendous drag on the world's economy without these horrible weapons ever being used, or will they be?

NSC-68 was opposed by notable moderates such as the father of containment, diplomat George F. Kennan, and his colleagues, Charles E. Bohlen and Louis A. Johnson, President Truman's Secretary of Defense. Nevertheless, they were brushed aside with a rationale driven by urgency, anxiety, fear of an apocalypse, and a nuclear diplomacy of intimidation aimed at driving opponents into submission or destruction. The drama that surrounds denying J. Robert Oppenheimer's security clearance is the cruelest example of this.[1] After sixty-eight years, Oppenheimer's security clearance has been restored by order of then Secretary of Energy Jennifer Granholm.[2] The arguments over atomic weaponry ever since Hiroshima hold to this scenario, which was so well captured in Stanley Kubrick's film *Dr. Strangelove or: How I Learned to Stop Worrying and Love the Bomb*. Also, a biographic film of Oppenheimer was released in July 2023.[3] Over eighty years after Hiroshima and Nagasaki, the dreaded atomic apocalypse still hangs over civilization. The atomic crisis prevented a major hot war, but a Cold War ensued with a policy of containment holding things together. NSC-68 was that policy.

1. NSC-68

As Deputy Assistant Secretary of State for Economic Affairs in 1949, lawyer Paul Nitze was assigned to aid diplomat George F. Kennan in preparing the economic aspects of the ill-fated Palais Rose Conference. The conference was held in Paris in May 1949, in the aftermath of the Berlin Blockade, to discuss German and Austrian problems. Nitze succeeded Kennan as Director of the Policy Planning Staff (S/P) on January 1, 1950, as "head of the division of ideas." It had just been learned in September 1949 that the USSR had detonated its first atomic bomb on August 29, 1949.[4]

The times, Nitze remarked, were ominous. First, there was Stalin's overtly anti-Western speech on February 19, 1946. He had revived the two hostile camps' theory of an inevitable war between socialism versus capitalism. Also, the People's Republic of China (PRC) was established on October 1, 1949. The German Democratic Republic (GDR) was created on October 7, 1949. In the following January, Russia's UN ambassador, Jacob A. Malik, walked out of the United Nations Security Council. On February 14, 1950, the USSR signed a Friendship, Alliance, and Mutual Assistance Treaty with the PRC. British atomic scientist Klaus Fuchs was arrested for espionage that same February. Senator Joseph R. McCarthy (R-WI) made his first charges on February 9, 1950, against 205 supposed communists in the Truman administration's State Department.[5] The times were difficult.

Nitze's policymaking consisted of composing the NSC-68 document, which became the most authoritative statement on how a containment theory could build up US and allied forces to keep the USSR and others restrained and diminished.

NSC-68 expressed quintessential American Cold War and nuclear policy, and its principal architect and author was Paul Nitze. Kennan had called for "containment" or preventing Soviet expansion. Nitze's policy of "rollback" demanded reversing Soviet successes abroad.[6] Indeed, the negativism toward the USSR displayed in NSC-68, which earlier had been renewed by Kennan and the rest of Robert Kelley's boys from the 1920s American listening post at Riga, like Loy Henderson and Charles Bohlen, was expanded by Nitze and Secretary of State Dean Acheson into an all-consuming American phobia. With their growing view of the danger posed by the USSR, Nitze later remarked, "Truman, Acheson, Harriman, Bohlen, Kennan, [Stuart] Symington, [Clark] Clifford, Conant, and I were all in accord—as were the allies."[7] NSC-68 was the bridge between Kennan's "containment" and President Ronald Reagan's "evil empire."[8] An analysis of NSC-68 demonstrates this.[9] It is where the Franck Report feared things would end up, and, somewhat belatedly, Oppenheimer had cautioned against it.

The report starts by stating that by the end of World War II, the earth's political power distribution had become bipolar between the US and the USSR. NSC-68 argued that the Soviet Union was "animated by a new and fanatic faith, antithetical to our own, and seeks to impose its absolute authority over the rest of the world."[10] Conflict, waged by both violent and nonviolent means, had become endemic, reasonable, and terrifying given the onset of weapons of mass destruction, the culmination of the Age of Infamy.

The new polarized balance between the two superpowers was precarious: "Any substantial further extension of the area under the domination of the Kremlin would raise the possibility that no coalition adequate to confront the Kremlin with greater strength could be assembled." Further results of this would mean, according to NSC-68, "destruction not only of this Republic but of civilization itself." The choice was bleak: Accept the possibility of a Soviet-style dystopia dominating the world or gamble on the unlikelihood of a nuclear holocaust.

The report called this Cold War process the "Kremlin design," a phrase used over a dozen times. "The Kremlin will subvert or destroy the government machinery and social structure of the non-Soviet world; it will replace them with subservient ones, first dominating Eurasia's landmass; and then it will confront the US as its principal enemy. [America's] integrity and vitality must be subverted or destroyed by one means or another if the Kremlin is to achieve its fundamental design."[11]

These opening remarks set up a Manichaean dualism between the US and the USSR, an either-or situation with nothing in between an excluded middle. America became the only major threat to the USSR's achievements. In the report's opening comments, it is a fundamental struggle between freedom and slavery, or, as it later intimates, between good and evil—eventually President Ronald Reagan's formula.[12]

The US answer to such a drastic Soviet challenge was to "make ourselves strong" militarily, economically, and politically to "foster a fundamental change like the Soviet system, a change toward which the frustration of the design is the first and perhaps the most important step." Only by developing the West's "moral and material strength" will the Soviets accommodate and coexist. Force was only to be a last resort, although it was noted that military power deters an attack. The report cites "Federalist No. 28" by Alexander Hamilton. If it were to come to war, "the means to be employed must be proportioned to the extent of the mischief." The mischief may be very limited or global. The US and its allies—the free world—must have at their disposal all means to deter the threat on an entire spectrum, from very limited conventional and/or nuclear warfare to total thermonuclear. Otherwise, the US must appease somewhere along the intimidation spectrum rather than meet the intimidator with an appropriate response. NSC-68 looked at the growing Soviet means of intimidation it had at its disposal and proposed graduated reactions.[13]

The Soviet system was described as a militantly worldwide revolutionary movement, a "new universal faith" and a "model 'scientific society:'" the inheritor of tsarist Russia's imperialism in a totalitarian dictatorship. It would resort to war on calculations of practicality and otherwise employ violence, subversion, and deceit without regard to moral considerations. The Russian state was and is seen as amoral and opportunistic.[14] It was antihuman because it ran "counter to the best and potentially the strongest instincts of men . . ." So it might prove "fatally weak." That meant it "cannot relax the condition of crisis and mobilization, for to do so would be to lose its dynamism, whereas the seeds of decay within the Soviet system would begin to flourish and fructify."

Even though the total economic strength of the US to the USSR was 4:1, in specific areas, such as scientific research, an advantage needed to be clarified; the report does point out that the Kremlin focused its economy on a war-making potential. It reduced the gap and ran on a near-maximum production basis, so the US's greater capacity became more inoperative because of the USSR's concentrated efforts in the arms race.

Given this object, the report suggested a potential scenario for 1950 based on the USSR's excessive strength in conventional forces and its new atomic capability. Both serve the USSR as a deterrent and an offensive projection of its power.

The Joint Chiefs of Staff considered the Soviet Union capable of an initial attack that would overrun Western Europe, drive toward the Middle East, and consolidate in the Far East. It would isolate Britain from the air and sea and attack selected targets in North America. Afterward, it could simultaneously conduct further operations in all the above areas to compel surrender or destruction while strengthening its air defenses.

The NSC-68 used this frightening picture to call on a steady and long-term commitment from the West to increase its military strength to deter or delay the USSR. The report also spent time indicating what an atomic attack on the West might accomplish: laying waste to Britain and destruction of Western Europe's and North America's vital centers.[15]

Section VI of NSC-68, "U.S. Intentions and Capabilities—Actual and Potential," considered the possibilities of the West to resist this scenario and painted a grim picture if the whole condition continued as it was and the West did not heed the full implications of containment. Accordingly, containment sought:

[By] all means short of war to (1) block further expansion of Soviet power, (2) expose the falsities of Soviet pretensions, (3) induce a retraction of the Kremlin's control and influence, and (4) in general, so foster the seeds of destruction within the Soviet system that the Kremlin is brought at least to the point of modifying its behavior to conform to generally accepted international standards.[16]

However, NSC-68 argued that the containment policy was that the US must "possess superior overall power" alone or with allies. That superiority once achieved and continually preserved would both guarantee national security and provide the indispensable backdrop to the conduct of the policy of containment. "Without superior aggregate military strength, in being and readily mobilizable, a policy of 'containment'—[which is] in effect a policy of calculated and gradual coercion—is no more than a policy of bluff."[17]

With this statement, NSC-68 intended to flesh out Kennan's fuzzy notion of containment and get down to what it meant in specifics. It must, in Nitze's interpretation, be more than "all means short of war" but be considered in actual dollars and cents, in military hardware, the "superior aggregate military strength" needed for the "calculated and gradual coercion" of the Soviet Union that is credible and not a bluff. When the bluff is called, as any realist knows it will be, the winning hand in military might must be ready at an instant's notice.

That was the heart and soul of NSC-68, which made it qualitatively different from Kennan's containment. Calculated and gradual coercion was aimed at *rolling back* the Soviet Union until it relented or self-destructed. The report suggested a door be left ajar for the USSR's retreat due to the growing pressure of America's superiority.

NSC-68 figured in 1950 that the West could conduct a sufficient military defense of the Western Hemisphere, but it would be inadequate for Britain and the Near and Middle East. If in two to three years, even shorter in an emergency, "the potential military capabilities of the US and its allies would be rapidly and effectively developed, sufficient forces could be produced to deter war, or withstand an initial attack and stabilize supporting attacks, and retaliate with greater impact."[18]

The exciting feature of Section VII, "Present Risks," is it created an either-or scenario because of what it attributed to the so-called "Kremlin design." NSC-68 interpreted that "design" as an implacable system seeking to "impose order among nations by means which would destroy our free and democratic system." What made this design sinister is that "the Kremlin's possession of atomic weapons puts new power behind its design and increases the jeopardy to our system." Since the risks were of a "new order of magnitude," that is, of a "total struggle," it meant "defeat at the hands of the totalitarian is total defeat. These risks crowd in on us, in a shrinking world of polarized power, to give us no choice, ultimately, between meeting them effectively or being overcome by them." The choice of some middle ground or accommodation was excluded. The US and its allies either prevailed or went down; the same held for the other side. Oppenheimer used a metaphor of the two scorpions facing one other, each fearing for its own life. Therefore, the US better have the bigger scorpion.

In the next paragraph, the Kremlin's design was called "evil." NSC-68 anticipated the eventual all-out efforts of the Reagan administration to achieve sufficient superiority to weaken and destroy the "evil empire." It also pointed out that the military readiness of the US and its allies also created choices short of global or total war in the Kremlin's efforts to test the West's resolve at this or that point in the spectrum of capabilities.[19]

In Section VIII, "Atomic Armament," perhaps the most critical part of NSC-68, Nitze considered the uses of nuclear weapons and responded to critics. This oft-quoted section is important because the report talks about 1954—the "year of maximum danger"—as a possible target-date scenario for a nuclear exchange. That was because, at that projected point, America's advantage would disappear, and the USSR could inflict severe damage via a surprise nuclear attack. When 1954 arrived, it was no accident Oppenheimer's hearing for his continued clearance would begin on April 12, 1954, and that it would be denied due to the heightened Red Scare.[20]

Unfortunately, 1954 has often been misinterpreted as a hard prediction. But, as Nitze pointed out, that was incorrect: a "misreading of the paper."[21] He noted that even though 1954 was considered the year of "maximum danger," that was only so because the "Soviets would have atomic weapons and delivery aircraft in sufficient number to threaten extensive (even unacceptable) damage to the United States."[22] There was no international control system, so the Strategic Air Command (SAC) thought it would be enough. There would be no way to verify that because the time-lapse might not allow American retaliation.

The report conceded that only if the Soviet Union moved substantially toward "accommodation and compromise" would such an arrangement be conceivable, but it concluded, "It is impossible to hope that an effective plan for international control can be negotiated unless and until the Kremlin design has been frustrated to a point at which a genuine and drastic change in Soviet policies has taken place."[23] This did not sound likely in the 1950 report. It remains unlikely against the USSR's successor state and its allies.

In Section IX, "Possible Courses of Action," four are listed: continuing current policies, isolation, war, and a rapid buildup. The first three were excused as ineffective or impossible. All four take place within the backdrop of negotiation. Still, negotiation must have behind it a "force sufficient to inhibit a Soviet attack . . ."[24] Even there, negotiations were planned, so proposals must be expected before their acceptance.

The report considers "radical change" in the Soviet design unlikely. Therefore, the Kremlin's three primary objectives would be challenging to meet: its effort to eliminate the US's nuclear capabilities, prevent the mobilization of its superior potential, and get the US to withdraw from its allied commitments.[25] To make negotiations more sensible than using force, a fourth course of action was necessary. Agreements would have to be enforceable, not susceptible to violation without detection, and effective countermeasures readied.[26]

Nitze considered but rejected both the present course and the option of isolation because each would reduce the US to the limited sphere of its hemisphere, shorn of its allies, trade, and communication with the rest of the world. Preponderance would shift to the Kremlin as it dominated Eurasia and threatened to crush the US: "There is no way to make ourselves inoffensive to the Kremlin except by complete submission to its will. Isolation would, in the end, condemn us to capitulate or fight alone and on the defensive, [and] under this course of action, there would be no negotiation, unless on the Kremlin's terms, for we would have given up everything of importance."[27]

As the report suggests, a preventive war would be "unacceptable" and "repugnant" to Americans unless a sufficient counterattack could be delivered.[28] NSC-68 concluded that only a rapid buildup of political, economic, and military strength was possible: "It is clear that a substantial and rapid building up of strength in the free world is necessary to support a firm policy intended to check and to roll back the Kremlin's drive for world domination." By rollback, the report means "a situation to which the Kremlin would find it expedient to accommodate itself, first by relaxing tensions and pressures and then by gradual withdrawal."[29]

Though not noted in the report, it was estimated that a $40-billion-per-year defense would be required for the next four to five years to meet all possibilities, primarily local actions short of total war. Lacking a firm policy, appeasement meant defeat. NSC-68's proposals were costly but affordable. The report itself assumed the trend of increasing Russian power could be reversed, but it would require significant domestic financial and economic adjustments.[30]

The rollback policy was finally announced, which meant the West would actively force the Soviet Union to accommodate, withdraw, and change its system to frustrate its design for world domination.

Criticism arose over the costs. The NSC-68 report itself offered no price tag for its proposed changes. President Truman requested an ad hoc committee to make an estimate. Even Acheson panicked when he saw Nitze's early cost calculations. "Paul," he said, "don't you put that figure in this report. It is right for you to estimate it and tell me about it, and I will tell Mr. Truman, but the decision on the amount of money involved should not be made until it is costed out in detail."[31]

The Bureau of the Budget's representative on the ad hoc committee, William Schaub, led the attack by questioning NSC-68's underlying thinking. According to Schaub, escalating military expenditures diverted resources from domestic needs, making such expenses unproductive. "For Schaub and the people at the Bureau of the Budget, the prospect of tripling military budgets was their worst nightmare come true."[32]

The Council of Economic Advisers "thought that greater defense budgets would be catastrophic."[33] The scholar Samuel F. Wells Jr. cites diplomat Chip Bohlen as giving the "most negative State Department response." That response was [NSC-68] "tends, therefore, to over-simplify the problem and, in my opinion, leads inevitably to the conclusion that war is inevitable." The Soviets wanted to preserve their system and only sought its extension "without serious risk to the internal regime."[34]

At that juncture, the whole issue remained deadlocked. As one thoughtful student of the subject said, "By mid-June, it seemed that the recommendations of NSC-68 were destined to be forgotten and ignored. Tripling defense budgets was too radical an idea."[35]

All this changed at 9:26 p.m. on June 24, 1950, when John J. Muccio, US ambassador to South Korea, telegraphed the State Department from Seoul that North Korean forces had attacked the Republic of Korea (ROK). According to Wells, "the Korean War provided the necessary impetus for adopting the programs implicit in NSC-68. Had the war not intervened, there is strong evidence that no major increase in defense spending would have won administration approval."[36] Currently, many thought Putin's Russo-Ukrainian War could serve as a similar warning. They think Putin has revived Soviet Russia's ambitions. President Donald Trump thinks otherwise.[37]

2. STAR WARS

Ronald Reagan began his presidency as a hard-liner. In March 1983 he gave two memorable speeches: one to the National Association of Evangelicals on March 8, convening in Orlando, Florida, and a nationally televised address to the nation on March 23. In the first, after delivering his standard litany of conservative values, he launched into a morality play on good and evil.

As author Frances Fitzgerald said, this was not the first time Reagan used "evil" when considering the USSR: "In a speech at West Point in May 1981, for example, he had referred to the assembled cadets as a 'chain holding back an evil force.'"[38] Fitzgerald suggested Reagan had trip-wired the whole eschatology of Armageddon for these evangelicals as derived from the biblical books of Ezekiel and Revelation. Since the Bolshevik Revolution, they identified the Soviet Union as an evil empire headed by the Antichrist.[39] The phrase used by Reagan occurs toward the end of his speech:

> So, in discussions of the nuclear freeze proposals, I urge you to beware of the temptation of pride—the temptation of blithely declaring yourselves above it all and label both sides equally at fault, to ignore the facts of history and the aggressive impulses of an evil empire, to simply call the arms race a giant misunderstanding and thereby remove yourself from the struggle between right and wrong and good and evil.[40]

He pointed out that Marxism-Leninism rejected morality based on the supernatural and only recognized it as moral, which furthered its cause. He asked these evangelicals to pray for those who lived in "totalitarian darkness." He finished by calling the real crisis facing Americans a spiritual one, testing the nation's "moral will and faith."[41]

The second memorable speech that month was his televised

"Address to the Nation on Defense and National Security," delivered on March 23, 1983. In it, he first details the enormous Soviet military buildup over the past twenty years. Meanwhile, he notes, America's defenses had atrophied. Besides, a freeze would only make America less, not more, secure by preventing modernization.

Again, at the end of his speech, in which he had enumerated his list of the Soviet's common threats, he shocks his viewers with an announcement known before to only a few of his closest advisors.[42] It was a last-minute insertion in one critical paragraph: "What if free people could live secure in the knowledge that their security did not rest upon the threat of instant US retaliation to deter a Soviet attack, that we could intercept and destroy strategic ballistic missiles before they reached our own soil or that of our allies?"[43]

The specter of retaliation or mutual threat was a "sad commentary on the human condition" and could only be viewed as "fostering an aggressive policy." Therefore, he initiated long-term research on his Strategic Defense Initiative (SDI) so the threat of strategic nuclear missiles could be eliminated.[44] The press immediately labeled it "Star Wars" and called the announcement Reagan's "Darth Vader speech." An antimissile shield, wrote Fitzgerald, was "surely Reagan's most characteristic idea."[45]

Reagan played up the theme of a "security shield" in his second inaugural on January 21, 1985.[46] On March 8, 1985, Reagan went to the hospital to have a polyp removed from his intestine. On March 10 Konstantin Chernenko, general secretary of the communist party of the Soviet Union, died. Vice President George H. W. Bush and Secretary of State George P. Shultz went to Moscow for the funeral and met the new general secretary, Mikhail S. Gorbachev.

In 1984 Reagan's team developed its four-point agenda: End the use of force, eliminate nuclear arms, improve bilateral relations, and promote human rights. Now Reagan and Gorbachev exchanged letters, and soon, the new general secretary invited Reagan to Moscow. After some maneuvering, they met in Geneva, Switzerland, in November 1985. A new era had begun.

In their first private meeting, on November 19, 1985, Reagan clarified to Gorbachev that "countries do not mistrust each other because of arms, but rather countries build their arms because of the mistrust between them." Gorbachev replied that the Soviet Union recognized the role of the US in the world and wished it no harm. Reagan countered that people did not create arms; governments did. Gorbachev maintained the central issue was ending the arms race by finding a formula to do so. Reagan again turned to the question of mistrust and the need to remove its causes.[47]

For Lou Cannon, Reagan's biographer, the immediate breakthrough was that both men found something likable in the other. Though this first encounter was scheduled for only fifteen minutes, it lasted sixty-four minutes. Cannon insisted that for Reagan first impressions were important. "There was a warmth in his face and his style," Reagan later stated, "not the coldness bordering on hatred I'd seen in most senior Soviet officials I'd met until then."[48] Reagan had touched on what had been the heart of the American problem with Russia: a profoundly negative perception of mistrust. Somehow that had to be cleared away, even if it only began at the top between the two leaders themselves.

In their first plenary session later that morning, Reagan returned to the theme of mistrust. Gorbachev called for increased trade by offering the USSR as an excellent market for US goods, rather than a potential outlet for the US military-industrial complex's production and storage of weaponry. Each man gave a litany of the other country's sins. Cannon called it the standard Cold War rhetoric. Each was, at some point, expected to elaborate. There was some substance as each leader drew his line in the sand.

Reagan brought up that the USSR had once been an excellent wartime ally. Due to its mistrust of America, it had thrown away FDR's attempts to bridge the gap between the two alternative systems: capitalism and communism. And when the US was the sole possessor of nuclear bombs, it did not use its threat to gain advantages over the USSR. Reagan concluded, "Most of these times, the United States did not get cooperation from Gorbachev's predecessors." It got the opposite results in terms of mistrust because of the vast Soviet military buildup. "The president said that now the two sides have come to this meeting; he had said frankly why the American people had fears. Maybe not fears of war, but that the Soviet Union could acquire such an imbalance of strength that it could deliver an ultimatum."

That mistrust could be relieved only by deeds: "But deeds can relieve mistrust, if we can go on the basis of trust, then those mountains of weapons will shrink quickly as we will be confident that they are not needed." Given sufficient trust, both sides could research SDI—not even knowing if such a system could ever work—and share their results with everyone so "no one would have a fear of a nuclear strike." A shield would also prevent a madman from starting a nuclear holocaust.[49]

The conversation had gotten hot, and Reagan suggested it was time for the two to take a walk and get a little fresh air. It was a brisk November afternoon, and they soon retreated to the boathouse, where a roaring fire had been prepared. Cannon, leaning on Reagan's estimation, believed the president's invitation to cool off, as well as the ensuing private fireside chat and return walk, were the critical moments at the summit; this was especially apparent when the president got ahead of his delegation and suggested future summits in Washington and Moscow, to which Gorbachev readily agreed.[50]

The boathouse conversation focused on a single subject, the one that usually troubled the Russians: SDI. It remained the core issue. It never went away. It already was the most objectionable feature at the second plenary. Now Gorbachev went one-on-one with Reagan. Reagan handed him an envelope of materials that stressed a 50 percent reduction in strategic offensive arms as a seed for negotiating. Gorbachev agreed it was a good starting point. He pointed out that in January, this would be negotiated with a halting of an arms race in space.

Reagan's standard rejoinder by then was that SDI was strictly a defensive weapon, not a part of the arms race, and its technology would be shared among the other nuclear powers. Regardless, Gorbachev answered, even when talking about the Intermediate-Range Nuclear Forces (INF), what about other land-based systems and the separate French and British systems? Gorbachev wanted to know whether Reagan subscribed to the narrow or broad interpretation of anti-ballistic missiles (ABM). Reagan belonged to the latter because any laboratory system would have to be tested to know in practice whether such a weapon worked. It would, he reiterated, be shared by all. "The worst thing he could imagine was for any one country to acquire a first-strike capability."

Gorbachev queried: It was already declared that nuclear weapons would never be used; was not that enough? The president said he believed him, but what about after they were gone? Gorbachev, "with some emotion," asked the purpose of deploying a weapon as yet unknown and unpredictable. Verification would always be unreliable due to the weapon's maneuverability and mobility, even if called defensive; it would always be regarded as an added threat. "If the goal was to get rid of nuclear weapons," he asked, "why start an arms race in another sphere?" Each side could refrain, open its laboratories, and start the process of a 50 percent reduction of its offensive weaponry.

Likewise, the MAD doctrine would be rendered useless because each side would have an impenetrable shield. Reagan stuck to insistence on the space shield that reminded him of World War I and poisonous gas, which each side rendered useless with its gas masks. Gorbachev, finally, said he believed him personally, but politically "could not possibly agree with the president with regard to this concept, [and he] would urge the president jointly with him to find a way of formulating guidelines for their negotiators with a view to stopping SDI." If both sides deployed layer after layer, Gorbachev warned, "only God himself would know what they were."

As they strolled back from the boathouse, Reagan suggested future summits, and Gorbachev agreed.[51] That was the breakthrough.

Reagan returned home and wrote to Gorbachev. In his letter, he suggested negotiators focus on eliminating first-strike possibilities and offered to cooperate in helping the USSR get out of Afghanistan. Almost simultaneously, Secretary of State George P. Shultz proposed to Ambassador Anatoly Dobrynin that Gorbachev come to Washington the following June.

It was only a month later that Gorbachev responded to these initiatives. He still demanded a ban on SDI, what he considered a space-strike weapon, and he disputed the claim of a Soviet advantage in first-strike weapons.[52] In a January publicized message to Reagan, he proposed a three-stage elimination of nuclear weaponry: 50 percent, followed by further reductions, including other nuclear powers. "Everything was conditioned on an immediate moratorium on nuclear testing and banning 'space-strike weapons' from the start."[53]

Gorbachev's "new thinking" was a little slow in coming. In February he called on Anatoly Chernyaev to become his assistant for foreign affairs. Chernyaev was, perhaps, the most critical of traditional Soviet diplomacy. Like Gorbachev, he believed something new had to be done: Improve agriculture and create work incentives; replace former General Secretary Leonid Brezhnev's people; let Polish leader General Wojciech Jaruzelski solve his problems; renounce the Brezhnev Doctrine (any threat to one socialist state in the Soviet bloc was a threat to all and justified intervention); get out of Afghanistan; remove SS-20s from Europe; shift from a militarized economy to a civilian one; free dissidents; allow refuseniks and Jews to leave.[54]

Yet Gorbachev was cautious and clung to some of the "old thinking." For instance, he still believed in the so-called "narrow interpretation" rather than the "broad interpretation" of the 1972 Anti-Ballistic Missile (ABM) Treaty. The former prohibited testing and developing any ABM components, whereas the latter assumed the right to conduct research, testing, and development but not deployment.

Reagan kept writing to him, even offering to "enter into an agreement to liquidate and ban all offensive ballistic missiles before any strategic defenses would be deployed." These proposals were ignored, and Gorbachev continued railing against the "militarization of space."[55] The stalemate continued into the summer. Finally, Gorbachev suggested a late September or October summit in Reykjavik, Iceland. He needed to get Reagan to ease the burden of Soviet military expenditures to keep pace with the US and, therefore, allow his domestic reforms to continue.

When they met on October 10, 1986, both Reagan and Gorbachev agreed the central issue was a strategic arms proposal. Already, Reagan had picked up the Russian proverb *doveryai no proveryai* (trust but verify). Seeking to "sweep Reagan off his feet," Gorbachev proposed a 50 percent overall reduction of strategic arms; he dropped the counting of French and British INFs, and he offered the Soviet removal of theirs from Europe. He wanted to continue the narrow interpretation of ABM for at least another ten years: only research and testing in laboratories, with a prohibition on all anti-satellite weapons and a ban on nuclear testing.

Reagan countered with a call for eliminating all strategic offensive weapons, ridding Asia of INFs, and replacing the ABM Treaty with one that allowed broad interpretation. He explained why SDI did not fit an "offensive weapons" definition.

After further argument, they reached a reasonable accord on everything except SDI. As Ambassador Jack Matlock admitted, "Progress came to a complete halt when the two went over the tediously familiar ground of SDI and the ABM Treaty. The exchanges seemed almost a replay of Geneva, except that Reagan was now suggesting a complete elimination of all ballistic missiles before strategic defenses could be deployed. Gorbachev would not move off his demand that SDI research be confined to laboratories and that the United States committed itself not to withdraw from the ABM Treaty for ten years."[56]

As they got closer to making "the most sweeping commitments in history to reduce mankind's most destructive weaponry," Gorbachev dug in his heels on the make-or-break issue: "We may as well go home and forget about Reykjavik," he said. Reagan lost patience and blurted out, "Oh, shit!" He was dumbfounded. "Can you really mean that you would turn down a historic opportunity because of a single word?" The word Reagan had in mind was "laboratories." Gorbachev replied, "But for us, it's not the word that counts; it's the principle."[57] And with that, Reykjavik failed.

By 1987 Gorbachev focused on the narrow interpretation rather than getting Reagan to sign off on only laboratories for SDI. He also realized his domestic reforms depended on an arrangement with Reagan, and time was not on his side. He understood that Britain's and France's INFs were unnecessary because there was no war with either of them. Removing the USSR's INFs changed nothing, and Margaret Thatcher drove home the West's legitimate fear of the traditional worldwide communist goal. And finally, "parity" only meant creating a Soviet-style bloated military-industrial complex in which, as Gorbachev noted, "We are stealing everything from the people and turning the country into a military camp."[58]

When Shultz visited Moscow in April 1987, he found Gorbachev would conclude an Intermediate-Range Nuclear Forces (INF) Treaty, leaving the remaining problems for another time. Perhaps more important, he now realized that "maybe for the first time [he] was dealing with a serious man of sound political judgment." The way to a summit in Washington in December 1987 was clear: Reagan's goals now fitted Gorbachev's needs for perestroika.[59]

The twentieth century was coming to an end, not the Age of Infamy. The greatest infamy of all was still left unresolved: nuclear weaponry.

CONCLUSION

INFAMY'S HOUR

> [The twentieth century's] culture was science and technology; its course was unpredictable change; its fate was to suffer two major wars and a confrontation between two visions of mankind that threatened to lead to a third.
>
> EDWARD TELLER, *MEMOIRS: A TWENTIETH-CENTURY JOURNEY IN SCIENCE AND POLITICS*

What if there is no recovery from the two worst infamies of the last century: totalitarianism and total war? The former will reengage in genocide, and the latter will practice nuclear blackmail and warfare.

I still think Hannah Arendt got part of totalitarianism's genocide right: a Kafkaesque kind of human such as Adolf Eichmann—a mindless, desk-style killer, but a killer nevertheless. Jean Améry came even closer by explaining an extreme sadist, a personality enjoying torture, living in a totalitarian society, and Naziism as the ideology of total sadism. Daniel Goldhagen has the whole of it: a long-term German anti-Semitism that only needed a state's official approval to carry it out wholesale. For Goldhagen, those who didn't directly participate silently approved or didn't give a damn.[1]

A newly released exposé, "The Devil's Confession: The Lost Eichmann Tapes," reveals the confidential interviews with Eichmann and shows how he glorified genocide—a character right out of Arendt, Améry, and Goldhagen. Améry, especially, was not in the mood for forgiveness. That part of German history, he believed, could never be erased, excused, or pardoned.[2]

As to total war, Russia's invasion of Ukraine is turning into a protracted affair, threatening the use of tactical nuclear arms, as well as a nuclear holocaust by Vladimir Putin.[3] In 1914 it only took the assassinations of the archduke and his wife to strike the match, setting off World War I. A similar incident, for instance, the assassination of a Russian official while visiting the UN, might well be the celebrated cause. We could think of the war in Ukraine as a prelude similar to the Balkan Wars preceding World War I. Once the nuclear genie gets out of the bottle again, Dr. Strangelove may have his way. And that finds me in Oppenheimer's hot seat: charging President Truman and his numerous allies by equating their point of view with mass murder. I land on the side of Stanley Kubrick's President Merkin Muffley, who told General Buck Turgidson that he would not go down in history as a mass murderer.

Despite Kenneth Clark's fear of this atomic eschaton, he still believed in a modern hero, a version of Charlemagne's rescue of the West. Civilization's survival, he surmised, requires a supreme heroic effort to provide a moral and intellectual center since, as he put it, heroic materialism isn't enough. Humanity, Clark believed, was tied to the incomprehensibility of the universe. A recent writer, Benjamín Labatut, suggests we have reached that point in his book *When We Cease to Understand the World*. For Clark, no one knows our destiny. Labatut thinks it ends in the universe collapsing into black holes. For Clark, it is even "intellectually dishonest" to guess about it. Clark felt baffled by modern civilization: First, we have increased our reliance on machines giving us directions and artificial intelligence (AI) issuing commands; second, with such machines, we have increased our urge to destroy. For Labatut, modern civilization's vast accumulation of junk and poisonous waste dooms us.[4]

J. Robert Oppenheimer may have become a quintessential antihero when the US government took away his security clearance in 1954. When Oppie saw Trinity, the first detonation of an atomic weapon at 5:30 a.m. on July 16, 1945, he quoted from the *Bhagavad Gita* about "Death"—the A-bomb—becoming the destroyer of worlds. He realized that more than winning a World War was at stake. Civilization could die from nuclear suicide. He was frightened and felt responsible.[5]

On February 17, 1953, Oppenheimer made a speech, with President Dwight D. Eisenhower's consent, to a closed meeting of the Council on Foreign Relations. He summarized America's position on using thermonuclear weapons: "We have from the first maintained that we should be free to use these weapons, and it is generally known we plan to use them. It is also generally known that one ingredient of this plan is a rather rigid commitment to their use in a very massive, initial, unremitting strategic assault on the enemy." That meant, according to his biographers Kai Bird and Martin J. Sherwin, the destruction of enemy cities in a "genocidal air strike." Oppenheimer added, "We may anticipate a state of affairs in which the two Great Powers will each be in a position to put an end to civilization and life of the other, though not without risking its own." In closing, he "startled" his audience: "We may be likened to two scorpions in a bottle, each capable of killing the other, but only at the risk of his own life."[6]

Today we should be startled, even terrified, at what Oppenheimer called the "ignorance and folly" of such a doctrine. Civilization's Age of Infamy awaits its "now is the hour" when someone presses the nuclear button, unless Eliot's "hollow men" end it, or we descend into a dystopia. Maybe the Charlemagne miracle occurs.

After all, civilization only requires a modicum of belief in itself, as

Charlemagne discovered, but without it, there is chaos. That belief hid behind the barbarians in the ninth century and in the twentieth century during totalitarianism's reign of war and genocide. Renewal in the twenty-first century, like spring, bursts forth when we allow ourselves to see and smell, to taste and hear its oncoming rush. Only then, the Michelangelos and Leonardos, the Dantes and Shakespeares emerge from infamy's dark shadows. They open our minds and hearts, our treasures and hopes to the rhythms of springtime, reestablishing society's necessary institutions: its foundations and colleges, its schools and communities, which nourish our better instincts with the arts and sciences. Vibrant governments and laws codify civilization's existence. They provide the stability and incentives to resurrect and sustain once again the citadels of a humane society. Then, private and government sponsorships seek and develop talent while preserving the past's traditions in the arts and sciences, in its libraries, museums, and concert halls. Creativity becomes a civilization's livelihood. A commitment to civilization justifies renouncing our past infamies and avoiding future ones.

Instead of the modern miracle of a renaissance saving us, is it preposterous to think of Oppenheimer's prophesy dooming us? Our fears have been "reawakened by Putin's invasion of Ukraine—not to speak of the slide from one 'final solution' to another, from the Holocaust of the Jewish people to nuclear Armageddon." Putin's intimidations and Biden's doomsday reactions suggest how and when our civilization will die. We face infamy's hour, the destroyer of worlds: Death.[7]

A recent estimate of deaths from a full-scale nuclear war amounted to 5.341 billion, and starvation for nearly everyone else after two years. It concluded, "There is nowhere to hide."[8] Putin challenged the West by saying it helped Ukraine strike Russia, and it "must, in the end, understand [that] all this truly threatens a conflict with the use of nuclear weapons, and therefore the destruction of civilization."[9]

In 1939 a popular British songstress, Vera Lynn, sang a hit tune,

"We'll Meet Again."[10] She meant lovers. Stanley Kubrick chose it to end his film Dr. Strangelove. He meant we'll meet that mushroom again on a sunny day.

POSTSCRIPT

THE SUPER

> When the whole world is running headlong towards the precipice, one who walks in the opposite direction is looked at as being crazy.

T. S. ELIOT

As early as 1942 and their first year at Los Alamos, physicists like Edward Teller were already exploring new ideas on the rudiments of a fusion weapon instead of the planned fission one that was finally dropped on Hiroshima in 1945. They nicknamed it "the Super."[1] It got sidelined because an atomic bomb would be faster to make before Hitler did than a hydrogen one. Scientists resurrected the discarded idea after the Soviets exploded Joe-1, their first atomic bomb, on October 5, 1949. America's atomic advantage soon evaporated, and the race was on for the first hydrogen bomb. Lewis Strauss, investment banker, rear admiral, and chairman of the Atomic Energy Commission (AEC), proposed a "quantum jump" to develop a hydrogen bomb. Otherwise, he believed, America would be a victim of the Soviet's hydrogen bomb blackmail. Teller became its scientific champion and the father of the Super.[2]

Two conditions were necessary to produce the Super: enough of physicist Ernest Lawrence's cyclotron's power at Berkeley to produce more tritium and sufficient computing from mathematician John von Neumann's MANIAC I (Mathematical Analyzer Numerical Integrator and Automatic Computer Model I) at Princeton for verifying the calculations of Teller's model. Nevertheless, some were against or were ambivalent about the Super's utility in warfare because they opposed an almost limitless destructive power. Its only purpose, according to the Joint Chiefs of Staff, was for its intimidation value. By getting it first, Teller insisted, the US prevented Soviet intimidation, so his argument went, and kept American superiority in the arms race. That argument persuaded congressional hawks, the military, and President Truman. In their enthusiasm, they considered it intolerable for the US to let the Russians get it first.

Opponents argued it was simply a "Maginot Line" or cheap defense when refurbishing the entire military was called for anyway. Besides, it was as morally wrong as poison gas was in World War I, outlawed by international convention and never again used. Teller countered by insisting—without proof—that the Super was indispensable to America's survival. Oppenheimer initially sat in between those favoring and those against, saying its possibility should be explored, not that it should be done.[3] His opinion would change: Did America, he finally asked, need the Super? It would be seventy times the power of Trinity, the atomic bomb that destroyed Hiroshima.[4]

Teller's mighty Super works as follows:

> In early nuclear bombs, like the ones the U.S. dropped on Japan in World War II, the fission of plutonium or uranium and the fatal energy released were the end of the story. In modern weapons, plutonium fission ignites a second, more powerful stage in which hydrogen atoms undergo nuclear fusion, releasing even more energy. The

U.S. hasn't made these [plutonium] pits in a significant
way since the late 1980s.[5]

Veteran diplomat and Russian expert George F. Kennan believed "it
might be possible to negotiate a halt to the arms race with the Soviet
Union." That was the view of James Conant, who, after the war,
"served on the Joint Research and Development Board (JRDC) that
was established to coordinate burgeoning defense research, and on the
influential General Advisory Committee (GAC) of the Atomic Energy
Commission (AEC); in the latter capacity he advised the president
against starting a development program for the hydrogen bomb."
Conant was the most vital voice in opposition to the Super because of
its "essentially unlimited explosive potential." Its practical effect
would be genocidal.[6] Nevertheless, the generals, congressional hawks,
and Secretary of State Dean Acheson advised Truman to fund the
Super, which he did, as his mind was already made up.[7] It was not
until late 1969 that détente began, and only by the time of Gorbachev
and Reagan that the abolition of nuclear weapons was considered.
"There is every reason to believe," wrote National Security Analyst
Joseph Cirincione, "that in the first half of this century, the peoples
and nations of this world will come to see nuclear weapons as the
'historic accident,' [and] we may finally be able to correct the one
mistake Einstein thought he made." He had persuaded FDR to build
the bomb.[8]

APPENDIX

A BRIEF HISTORY OF THE TWENTIETH CENTURY: AN AGE OF INFAMY

According to one knowledgeable observer, his generalization about the twentieth century is that it was terrible. He uses many other words: brutal, barbarous, violent, desperate, destructive, catastrophic, and cruel. You may also choose a word. This celebrated historian is Eric Hobsbawm, who especially liked "extreme." Further, he calls the twentieth century "the short one" because of its two significant demarcation points, 1914 and 1991. The first marks the start of World War I, and the other the collapse of the Soviet Union. Events within these dates have more similarities to each other than to events before or after. He also considers the two decades of the thirties and forties to be the "hinge" of the last century. The decisive moment when capitalism and communism allied to defeat fascism. Neither could win without the other. However, he considers the Red Army's role as decisive. The allied bombing of Europe, though destructive of cities and their urban populations, was strategically ineffective. Japan and Germany required quick and successful offensives to win. Otherwise, the combined resources of the allies increasingly weighed in their favor. "Hitler's folly" of joining Japan's war against the US, Hobsbawm declares, allowed President Roosevelt (FDR) to enter the war in Europe free from opposition and provide aid for Stalin to overcome Hitler's first assault against Leningrad and Moscow and later to win at Stalingrad.

The twentieth century's greatest infamies occurred during the hinge. Whereas World War I was a mass war because the whole population of countries participated, World War II was both a mass war and a total war. It required efficient and full use of the prominent participants' human, material, and ideological resources. Indeed, World War II was the most significant enterprise the world has ever known. That endeavor needed professional expertise and accelerated technical changes. The resulting destruction was unparalleled. The post-1945 consequences multiplied: a Cold War between capitalism and communism; modernization of the world; creation of a single, unified world economy; a significant leap in transportation and communications; the ending of the Eurocentric world; the making of a global village; and the snapping of generational ties. Hobsbawm summarized the period from 1914 to 1945: Each of these wars had a unique historical profile, as both were episodes of carnage without parallel.

Revolutionary initiatives in European civilization broke radically with the past, anticipating much more significant breaks in Europe's political landscape and socioeconomic fabric. Though the twentieth century officially began on January 1, 1900, Hobsbawm argues it started on June 28, 1914, with Archduke Franz Ferdinand's assassination. On August 3, 1914, the Germans attacked France as planned by General Alfred von Schlieffen. World War I was the culmination of the national animosities and diplomatic intrigues of the nineteenth century. It brought to a close the whole structure of national and international politics created at the Congress of Vienna in 1815.

The Great War exhibited the destructive power of the machine age set loose by the Industrial Revolution on a massive scale. World War I ripped up Western civilization. The whole history of the West unraveled because the war was a technological monster eating itself up. After a twenty-year truce from 1919 to 1939, it continued wrecking everything. Technology affected European life and war-making. Heavy industry organized into corporations by pooling investors' capital, mobilizing labor armies, procuring raw materials, and using new accounting methods. The state regulated more of life's aspects. The theoretical physics of Max Planck and Albert Einstein overturned Newtonianism, but the old political rivalries continued.

France was defeated in a war with Prussia in 1870 but allied with Russia in 1892 and Great Britain in 1904. Russia joined these two powers in 1907 as the Triple Entente and faced Germany, the Austro-Hungarian Empire, and Italy in the Triplice. Europe was now divided into two hostile camps. The action bringing war between them was the assassination of Franz Ferdinand, heir to the Austrian throne, by a Serbian terrorist, Gavrilo Princip, on June 28, 1914.

After some diplomacy, war broke out in early August 1914, and a stalemate resulted, as illustrated at Verdun and the Somme in 1916, costing the lives on each side of about 350,000. Tanks were first used in these offensives, and another four hundred thousand British and two hundred thousand French lost their lives from July to November, and Germans lost four hundred thousand to five hundred thousand men at the Somme. Such losses gained little advantages. The machine gun, tank, gas warfare, submarines, airplanes, and zeppelins were first used. On the eleventh hour of the eleventh day of the eleventh month, 1918, an armistice ensued after the American doughboys turned the tide of war, starting April 6, 1917. Russia quit in the Treaty of Brest-Litovsk with the German side on March 3, 1918. Lenin and his Bolshevik Party made that treaty after seizing power from Alexander Kerensky's provisional government on November 7, 1917 (October 25, 1917, old style). Tsar Nicholas II fell from power in March 1917.

Kaiser Wilhelm II abdicated on November 9, 1918, two days before the armistice. The number of dead was placed at ten million and wounded at twenty million. The direct cost of the war has been estimated at \$180.5 billion and the indirect at \$151.6125 billion. The cost of money, lives, and destruction led to the four great empires of Eastern Europe collapsing: Austria, Germany, Russia, and Turkey. The thirty-two victor states signed five treaties in Paris to punish the five losers: St. Germain with Austria; Trianon with Hungary; Neuilly with Bulgaria; Sèvres (and later Lausanne) with Turkey; and Versailles with Germany. Article number 231 of the Treaty of Versailles made Germany responsible for the war, with total reparations at about one trillion francs. Germany also lost its colonies. They were divided into trusteeships, and the Polish Corridor separated East Prussia from the rest of Germany. President Woodrow Wilson's League of Nations met in Geneva. America never joined.

The war left Italy in economic chaos with significant unemployment and strikes. In March 1919, Benito Mussolini founded the fascist party. It gained three hundred thousand members and thirty-five seats in the Italian Chamber of Deputies. On October 27, 1922, the fascists marched on Rome. King Victor Emmanuel III appointed Mussolini as prime minister. The Chamber of Deputies voted Mussolini, the Duce, full power, and he turned Italy into a dictatorship. His corporate state arose: the organization of the population into syndicates of employers, employees, and professional men under the auspices of labor courts, which dealt with labor disputes. A Grand Council regulated the syndicates.

On November 8 and 9, 1923, Adolf Hitler tried to overthrow the Bavarian provincial government and then march on Berlin. His "Beer Hall Putsch," backed by conservative elements, failed. Hitler was convicted of treason and sentenced to five years, but he spent only eight months in prison. Hitler built a mass party that came to power legally in 1933. General Paul von Hindenburg was elected to the presidency of the Weimar Republic in 1925 after its first president, Friedrich Ebert, died. Gustav Stresemann's death left Weimar fragmenting. Hindenburg asked Heinrich Brüning, a conservative, to form a government. His program in 1929 called for financial restraint to restore Germany's economy during the Great Depression. When his program failed to get a vote of confidence in July 1930, Bruning ruled by decree under article number 48 of the Weimar Constitution. In an election of September 1930, the Nazi Party of eight hundred thousand and twelve seats in the Reichstag, Germany's lower legislative house suddenly became a party of 6.5 million and 107 seats. Brüning governed until 1932.

Through 1931 Hindenburg was forced to sign emergency measures. By March 1932 Hitler challenged the presidency with 11.5 million to 18.5 million votes and 13.5 million to 19 million in a runoff election. On May 30, 1932, Hindenburg dismissed Brüning and appointed Franz von Papen as chancellor. He called for elections to the Reichstag for July. The Nazis received 13.5 million votes and 230 seats out of 32 million and 549 seats. Papen's government committed to bringing Hitler into the government. Through this effort, Hindenburg appointed Hitler chancellor on January 30, 1933. Hitler, ruling by decree, destroyed Weimar after coming to power. In 1933 he dropped Germany out of the League of Nations. Germany began rearmament. Hitler regained the Saar by plebiscite in 1935 and reoccupied the Rhineland in 1936. In 1938 he annexed Austria and provoked the Czech crisis. At the Munich Conference, Hitler got Bohemia and soon seized Slovakia. On August 23, 1939, he signed the Nazi-Soviet Pact, and on September 1, 1939, he attacked Poland. World War II began because Britain and France were allied to Poland.

Poland fell in three weeks and was divided between Germany and Soviet Russia. In April 1940 Germany took Denmark and Norway. In May Germany invaded the Low Countries and drove deep into France. Fascist Italy entered on Germany's side, and France fell on June 22, 1940. In August the Germans opened an air war against Britain. By late June of 1941 the German air attack subsided. Hitler prepared to invade Russia. In April 1941 Germany occupied the Balkan Peninsula, and on June 22, 1941, attacked Soviet Russia. The Wehrmacht advance halted outside Leningrad and Moscow by December, though the Germans seized Kiev (now Kyiv). In the spring the offensive resumed, with the Germans occupying the Crimean Peninsula and attacking

Stalingrad in August 1942. Stalin counterattacked in November. By February 1943 he lifted the siege. In October 1942 the Germans were pushed back from El Alamain in North Africa and, by 1943, chased into Italy. Mussolini's government resigned in July 1943. In June 1944 the allied invasion of Normandy began. The Russians, advancing from the east, began the Battle of Berlin in April 1945. After Hitler's suicide on April 30, 1945, Germany surrendered on May 7, 1945. America dropped the atomic bomb on Hiroshima and Nagasaki on August 6 and 9, 1945. Japan capitulated on August 15, 1945.

The allies, meeting at Yalta in the Russian Crimea in February 1945, signed an agreement to divide defeated Germany, try major war criminals, form a United Nations, and bring Russia into the Japanese war after Germany was defeated. The Treaty of Yalta established post–World War II Europe's structure until divided Germany was reunited on October 3, 1990. The once Soviet-dominated Eastern Bloc of countries finally established freely elected governments by 1989. This action was mainly the work of Mikhail Gorbachev, who came to power in 1985. Gorbachev fell from power in December 1991 when the Soviet Union ended on December 25, 1991, and was replaced by Boris Yeltsin, president of the Russian Federation, until the end of 1999. Vladimir Putin replaced him and remains in power in 2024. He attacked an independent Ukraine in 2022.

From the end of World War II in 1945 to the USSR's collapse in 1991, a Cold War existed between the West, headed by the US, and the East under the USSR. The world lived with another World War III threat, and the policy of Mutually Assured Destruction (MAD) prevented that kind of war. The superpowers, America and Russia, maintained a balance of power. For the USSR, the People's Republic of China (PRC) allied with Stalin in 1949 but reversed that arrangement in 1972 with President Nixon's trip to China.

Détente meant "peaceful coexistence," and Washington and Moscow continued disarmament agreements. Nikita Khrushchev believed communism would bury capitalism. Mikhail Gorbachev, coming to power in 1985, convinced the West to end the Cold War. As

Hobsbawm put it, "That is why the world owes so enormous a debt to Mikhail Gorbachev, who not only took this initiative but succeeded, singlehandedly, in convincing the American government and others he meant what he said." A century of infamy ended at the close of the second millennium. America remained the sole superpower but now contends with a rising China and also Russia at war with Ukraine. NATO's aid to Ukraine has prevented a Russian victory without its direct participation, although Putin threatens the use of tactical nuclear weapons.

NOTES

PREFACE

1. Richard Rhodes, *The Making of the Atomic Bomb* (Simon & Schuster, 1986), 676. For Paris, see Paul Morand, *1900 A.D.* (William Farquhar Payson, 1931).
2. Rhodes, 19, Kindle; W. J. Hennigan, "At the Brink," *The New York Times*, March 4, 2024, https://www.nytimes.com/interactive/2024/03/07/opinion/nuclear-war-prevention.html. This essay inaugurated a special "Opinion" series of articles *The Times* labeled as "Nuclear War Is Called Unimaginable. It's Not Imagined Enough." Hennigan and coauthor Kathleen Kingsbury continued seventy-nine years to the day with what the nuclear arms race looked like to Hiroshima's survivors and their story: "What Today's Nuclear Arms Race Looks Like to Hiroshima Survivors," *The New York Times*, August 6, 2024, https://www.nytimes.com/2024/08/06/opinion/nuclear-threat-hiroshima-survivors.html. See also https://www.nytimes.com/2024/03/04/opinion/nuclear-weapons-bibliography.html and https://www.nytimes.com/2024/03/24/books/review/nuclear-war-annie-jacobsen-countdown-sarah-scoles.html. On the real possibility of incremental nuclear warfare resulting in Armageddon, see https://www.nytimes.com/2024/12/02/magazine/nuclear-strategy-proud-prophet.html.

INTRODUCTION

1. Carl Sagan, *The Demon-Haunted World: Science as a Candle in the Dark* (Ballantine Books, 1997), 25; T. S. Eliot, "The Hollow Men," All Poetry, accessed August 7, 2025, https://allpoetry.com/the-hollow-men.
2. Eliot, "The Hollow Men"; James Temperton, "'Now I Am Become Death, the Destroyer of Worlds.' The Story of Oppenheimer's Infamous Quote," *Wired*, July 21, 2023, https://www.wired.co.uk/article/manhattan-project-robert-oppenheimer; "*Oppenheimer* (film)," Wikipedia, accessed August 7, 2025, https://en.wikipedia.org/wiki/Oppenheimer_(film); Matt Maytum, "Grave New World," *Total Film*, no. 332 (December 15, 2022): 34–39. (Nolan quote on 36.)
3. Kenneth Clark, *Civilisation* (Harper & Row, 1969), 346; Kai Bird and Martin J. Sherwin, *American Prometheus: The Triumph and Tragedy of J. Robert Oppenheimer* (Vintage, 2006), 465; Hoai-Tran Bui, "*Oppenheimer* Is Christopher Nolan's Magnum Opus, and His Apology," *Inverse*, July 30, 2023, https://www.inverse.com/entertainment/oppenheimer-christopher-nolan-dark-knight-apology.
4. "Infamy," *Merriam-Webster*, https://www.merriam-webster.com/dictionary/infamy.
5. Eric Hobsbawm, *The Age of Extremes: The Short Twentieth Century 1914–1991* (Abacus, 1995), 1–17.
6. Aleksandr Solzhenitsyn, "Nobel Prize Lecture," The Nobel Prize, https://www.nobelprize.org/prizes/literature/1970/solzhenitsyn/lecture/.

7. "Hannah Arendt," Wikipedia, accessed August 7, 2025, https://en.wikipedia.org/wiki/Hannah_Arendt; "Daniel Goldhagen," Wikipedia, accessed August 7, 2025, https://en.wikipedia.org/wiki/Daniel_Goldhagen.

8. Michiko Kakutani, *Ex Libris: 100+ Books to Read and Reread* (Clarkson Potter, 2020), 299–301.

9. Bird and Sherwin, *American Prometheus*, 332.

10. Bird and Sherwin, *American Prometheus*, 422.

11. Bird and Sherwin, *American Prometheus*, 307–8.

12. Stephen Wertheim, "World War III Begins with Forgetting," *The New York Times*, December 2, 2022, https://www.nytimes.com/2022/12/02/opinion/america-world-war-iii.html; Bird and Sherwin, *American Prometheus*, 584.

13. Bird and Sherwin, *American Prometheus*, chap. 23 title, 314.

14. Wertheim, "World War III Begins with Forgetting"; Bird and Sherwin, *American Prometheus*, 584.

15. Clark, *Civilisation*, 29, 31.

1. WARNINGS OF INFAMY

1. William L. Langer, *An Encyclopedia of World History* (Houghton Mifflin Company, 1968), 978.

2. Tim Bouverie, *Appeasement: Chamberlain, Hitler, Churchill, and the Road to War* (Tim Duggan Books, 2019), 223.

3. Richard Urbanscheck obituary, *Napa Daily Register*, September 17, 1921; Alfred Cyril Doyle, William Mitchell Haulsee, and Frank George Howe, *Soldiers of the Great War, Volume I* (Soldiers Record Publishing Association, 1920), 145.

4. Siegfried Kracauer, *From Caligari to Hitler: A Psychological History of the German Film* (Princeton University Press, 1947), 66.

5. Kracauer, *From Caligari to Hitler*, 67.

6. Roger Ebert, "A World Slanted at Sharp Angles," RogerEbert.com, June 3, 2009, https://www.rogerebert.com/reviews/great-movie-the-cabinet-of-dr-caligari-1920.

7. Siegried Kracauer, "November Fire Recordings," *The Cabinet of Dr. Caligari* (2011), 66.

8. Ebert, "A World Slanted at Sharp Angles."

9. History.com Editors, "World War I," History.com, October 29, 2009, https://www.history.com/topics/world-war-i/world-war-i-history.

10. Miranda Seymour, *Robert Graves: Life on the Edge* (Henry Holt & Co., 1995), vii.

11. Robert Graves, *Good-Bye to All That* (Knopf, 2018), 5–11.

12. Seymour, *Robert Graves: Life on the Edge*, 179.

13. Seymour, *Robert Graves: Life on the Edge*, 180.

14. Graves, *Good-Bye to All That*, 253.

15. Graves, *Good-Bye to All That*, 360.

16. Graves, *Good-Bye to All That*, 356.

17. H. Stuart Hughes, *Oswald Spengler: A Critical Estimate* (Transaction Publishers, 1992), 133.

18. "The Trial," Wikipedia, accessed August 11, 2025, https://en.wikipedia.org/wiki/The_Trial.

19. James Joyce, *Ulysses* (Shakespeare and Company, 1904), 72–95; Vladimir Nabokov, *Lectures on Literature* (Harcourt Brace Jovanovich, 1980), 315–320; "Episode 6: Hades," UlyssesGuide.com, accessed August 11, 2025, https://www.ulyssesguide.com/hades.

20. Jeffrey Somers, "Top 10 Must-Read Books of the 1920s," ThoughtCo., July 25, 2019, https://www.thoughtco.com/literature-of-twenties-4154491; Emily Temple, "A Century of Reading: The 10 Books That Defined the 1920s," *Literary Hub*, October 17, 2018, https://lithub.com/a-century-of-reading-the-10-books-that-defined-the-1920s/.

21. Anthony Lane, "The Shocks and Aftershocks of 'The Waste Land,'" *The New Yorker*, September 26, 2022.

22. "Eliot's Poetry: *The Waste Land*," SparkNotes, https://www.sparknotes.com/poetry/eliot/section2/.

23. "The Fisher King," Wikipedia, accessed August 11, 2025, "The Fisher King, keeper of the Holy Grail, is an enigmatic figure in literature: a rich king wounded by his own spear. The earliest sources show him suffering a mortal wounding—a result not of an accident but of his own ethical failings. The wound does not heal," https://en.wikipedia.org/wiki/Fisher_King.

24. W. J. Stuckey, "'The Sun Also Rises' on Its Own Ground," *The Journal of Narrative Technique* 6, no. 3 (Fall 1976): 224–32. My brother Robert, literary critic and novelist, was a big help in understanding Hemingway.

25. Ernest Hemingway, *The Sun Also Rises* (The Hemingway Library Edition) (Scribner, 2014), 207. Kindle.

26. Ernest Hemingway, *A Moveable Feast* (Scribner, 1964), 60–62.

27. Hemingway, *A Moveable Feast*, 60–62.

28. Carlos Baker, *Ernest Hemingway: A Life Story* (Charles Scribner's Sons, 1969), 155.

29. Lesley M. M. Blume, "The True Story of the Booze, Bullfights, and Brawls That Inspired Ernest Hemingway's *The Sun Also Rises*," *Vanity Fair*, May 12, 2016, https://www.vanityfair.com/culture/2016/05/the-true-story-of-the-booze-bullfights-and-brawls-that-inspired-ernest-hemingways-the-sun-also-rises.

30. Stefan Zweig, *The World of Yesterday* (Plunkett Lake Press, 2011), loc. 3,180 of 7,067, Kindle Digital.

31. "George Eric Rowe Gedye," Wikipedia, accessed August 14, 2025, https://en.wikipedia.org/wiki/George_Eric_Rowe_Gedye; George Eric Rowe Gedye, *Fallen Bastions: The Central European Tragedy* (Victor Gollancz, 1939), 313.

32. Gedye, *Fallen Bastions*, 305.

33. Gedye, *Fallen Bastions*, 313.

34. Friderike Zweig, *Married to Stefan Zweig* (Plunkett Lake Press, 2012), locs. 3,030, 3,044, 3,069, 3,082, Kindle Digital (hereafter KB Digital); Alexander Nazaroff, "Fouche, Whom Napoleon Called 'The Perfect Traitor'; Stefan Zweig 'Blows the Soul' into His Portrait of the French Revolution's Arch-Villain," *The New York Times*, August 17, 1930, https://www.nytimes.com/1930/08/17/archives/fouche-whom-napoleon-called-the-perfect-traitor-stefan-zweig-blows.html; Donald A. Prater, *European of Yesterday: A Biography of Stefan Zweig* (Oxford University Press, 1972), 174.

35. Zweig, *Married to Stefan Zweig*, locs. 260, 283, 364, 436, 449.

36. Zweig, *Married to Stefan Zweig*, locs. 3,005, 3,046, 3,067, 3,088, 3,084, 3,284, 1,345, 1,517. Barbara Tuchman quotes Zweig as saying that it would only be a matter of

decades before "evil and violence would finally be conquered"; see Barbara Tuchman, *The Proud Tower: A Portrait of the World Before the War: 1890–1914* (Macmillan, 1966), 270.

37. Zweig, *The World of Yesterday*, Locs. 3,430, 3,473, 3,513.

38. Zweig, *The World of Yesterday*, Locs. 3,648, 3,727, 4,590–651, 4,663.

39. Zweig, *The World of Yesterday*, Loc. 5,297.

40. Zweig, *The World of Yesterday*, Locs. 5,350, 5,361, 5,374.

41. Zweig, *The World of Yesterday*, Locs. 5,401, 5,536–549, 5,594.

42. Oliver Matuschek, *Three Lives: A Biography of Stefan Zweig* (Pushkin Press, 2011), locs. 6,160, 6,193, KB Digital; Alberto Dines, Kristina Michahelles, et al., ed. Israel Beloch, *A Network of Friends: Stefan Zweig, His Last Address Book, 1940–1942* (Memoria Brasil, 2014), 9–13; Stefan Zweig as quoted by Klemens Renoldner, "Thoughts About Stefan Zweig's Last Address Book," Beloch, 16.

43. Donald A. Prater, *European of Yesterday: A Biography of Stefan Zweig* (Clarendon Press, 1972), 259.

2. CELEBRATED INFAMIES

1. "FDR's Infamy Speech," USHistory.org, accessed August 12, 2025, https://ushistory.org/documents/infamy.htm.

2. Margaret MacMillan, *War: How Conflict Shaped Us* (Random House, 2020), 146–47.

3. MacMillan, *War*, 147.

4. Daniel Jonah Goldhagen, *Hitler's Willing Executioners: Ordinary Germans and the Holocaust* (Vintage Books, 1997), 14.

5. Iris Chang, *The Rape of Nanking: The Forgotten Holocaust of World War II* (Basic Books, 1997), 215.

6. Chang, *The Rape of Nanking*, "Introduction," 4, 102.

7. "John Rabe's Nanjing Diaries," Hypotheses.org, accessed August 12, 2025, https://rabediaries.hypotheses.org.

8. Chang, *The Rape of Nanking*, 4.

9. "The Rape of Nanking," GradeSaver.com, accessed August 12, 2025, https://www.gradesaver.com/the-rape-of-nanking/study-guide/analysis.

10. Chang, *The Rape of Nanking*, 102.

11. Chang, *The Rape of Nanking*, 225.

12. Thomas Keneally, *Schindler's List* (Touchstone Books, 1982), 114. Rolf Czurda mentioned by Keneally.

13. Art Spiegelman, *Maus: A Survivor's Tale* (Pantheon Books, 2011), 230–32.

14. Spiegelman, *Maus*, 125.

15. Spiegelman, *Maus*, 127–133. By late April or early May 1942, historian Peter Longerich contends, "A decision to murder indiscriminately all European Jews within its reach as quickly as possible" had been made, with the consent of Hitler, by Heinrich Himmler and Reinhard Heydrich. The Wannsee Conference of that January had been the first important step along the way. See Christopher R. Browning, "When Did They Decide?," *The New York Review of Books*, March 24, 2022, https://www.nybooks.com/articles/2022/03/24/wannsee-the-road-to-the-final-solution-peter-longerich/; Peter Longerich with Jeremy Noakes and Lesley Sharpe,

Wannsee: The Road to the Final Solution (Oxford University Press, 2021), 29–31, chap. 3; Siegelman, *Maus*, 187.

16. "Amon Göth," Wikipedia, accessed August 12, 2025, https://en.wikipedia.org/wiki/Amon_Göth.

17. "Amon Göth," Wikipedia.

18. Keneally, *Schindler's List*, 167–68.

19. Keneally, *Schindler's List*, 169–71.

20. "Amon Göth," Wikipedia; on Ford, see Keneally, *Schindler's List*, 173.

21. Keneally, *Schindler's List*, 192–94, picture on 190, 218–19 on gunning people down.

22. Keneally, *Schindler's List*, 219.

23. Keneally, *Schindler's List*, 279.

24. Keneally, *Schinder's List*, 256, 266, 279.

25. "Amon Göth," Wikipedia.

26. Harrison Salisbury, *To Peking-and Beyond: A Report on the New Asia* (Quadrangle, 1973), 31–40.

27. Salisbury, *To Peking-and Beyond*, 43–57.

28. Salisbury, *To Peking-and Beyond*, 61, 70.

29. Harrison Salisbury, *The New Emperors: China in the Era of Mao and Deng* (Little, Brown and Company, 1992), 222–24, 225, 236–37, 243, 247, 254, 270–71, 272, 288–89, 292–302, 305, 306.

30. Harrison Salisbury, *Tiananmen Diary: Thirteen Days in June* (Little, Brown and Company, 1989). (These following paragraphs summarize this remarkably candid eyewitness account.)

3. HITLER'S INFAMY

1. "Totalitarianism," *Merriam-Webster*, https://www.merriam-webster.com/dictionary/totalitarianism; "Totalitarianism," accessed August 14, 2025, Wikipedia, https://en.wikipedia.org/wiki/Totalitarianism; "Nazi Germany Quotations," AlphaHistory.com, accessed August 14, 2025.

2. "Totalitarianism," Brittanica, https://www.britannica.com/topic/totalitarianism; "Is It Fascism? A Leading Historian Changes His Mind." *The New York Times Magazine*, Elisabeth Zerofsky, October 23, 2024, https://www.nytimes.com/2024/10/23/magazine/robert-paxton-facism.html; Robert O. Paxton, *The Anatomy of Fascism* (Vintage Books, 2005).

3. "Albert Speer," Wikipedia, accessed August 14, 2025, https://en.wikipedia.org/wiki/Albert_Speer.

4. Albert Speer, *Inside the Third Reich* (Macmillan, 1970) 519–21.

5. "Nuremberg Executions," Wikipedia, accessed August 14, 2025, https://en.wikipedia.org/wiki/Nuremberg_executions.

6. Spiegelman, *Maus*, 10.

7. Speer, *Inside the Third Reich*, 15–19.

8. Speer, *Inside the Third Reich*, 24.

9. Speer, *Inside the Third Reich*, 24, 26.

10. Speer, *Inside the Third Reich*, 28–31.

11. "Albert Speer," Wikipedia. On Speer's lies about the holocaust and labor atrocities, see Richard J. Evans, *Hitler's People: The Faces of the Third Reich* (Penguin Press, 2024),

232; "Gitta Sereny, PT. 2," CharlieRose.com, October 12, 1995, https://charlierose.com/videos/6845.

12. Speer, *Inside the Third Reich*, 39–44.

13. Speer, *Inside the Third Reich*, 49, 55, 58–59, 67, 69.

14. For a review of buildings and map, see "The Nazi Party Rally Grounds in Nuremberg," Google Arts & Culture, https://artsandculture.google.com/story/the-nazi-party-rally-grounds-in-nuremberg-documentation-center-nazi-party-rally-grounds/9gXBnoIq2KGTIg?hl=en.

15. Speer, *Inside the Third Reich*, 73–75.

16. Martin Kitchen, *Speer: Hitler's Architect* (Yale University Press, 2015), 2.

17. "Albert Speer > Quotes," Goodreads, accessed August 14, 2025, https://www.goodreads.com/author/quotes/13435.Albert_Speer.

18. Bob Carruthers, ed., *Hitler's Wartime Conversations: His Personal Thoughts as Recorded by Martin Bormann* (Pen and Sword Military, 2018).

19. Speer, *Inside the Third Reich*, 231–36, 296.

20. Adolf Hitler, *Mein Kampf/My Struggle: Four and a Half Years of Struggle Against Lies, Stupidity, and Cowardice* (White Wolf, 1925).

21. Adam Gopnik, "Does 'Mein Kampf' Remain a Dangerous Book?" *The New Yorker*, January 12, 2016, https://www.newyorker.com/books/page-turner/does-mein-kampf-remain-a-dangerous-book.

22. Gopnik, "Does 'Mein Kampf' Remain a Dangerous Book?"

23. Neffertia Tyner, "Mein Kampf by Adolf Hitler | Definitions, Excerpts & Quotes," Study.com, updated November 21, 2023, accessed August 14, 2025, https://study.com/academy/lesson/mein-kampf-definition-summary-quotes.html;   "Mein Kampf," Wikipedia, accessed August 14, 2025, https://en.wikipedia.org/wiki/Mein_Kampf.

24. Armond White, "Turner Classic Movies: Enemy of Film-Watchers," *National Review*, March 31, 2021, https://www.nationalreview.com/2021/03/turner-classic-movies-enemy-of-film-watchers/;

Thomas Rogers, "Filmmaker's Private Archive Rekindles Debate Over Her Nazi Ties," *The New York Times*, November 6, 2024, https://www.nytimes.com/2024/11/06/movies/leni-riefenstahl-documentary-nuba-photographs.html.

25. Leni Riefenstahl, "The Last of the Nuba," and Jack Pia, "SS Regalia," University of California, Santa Barbara, History Dept. (1974), https://marcuse.faculty.history.ucsb.edu/classes/33d33dTexts/SontagFascinFascism7.htm

Susan Sontag, "Fascinating Fascism," *The New York Review*, February 6, 1975, https://www.nybooks.com/articles/1975/02/06/fascinating-fascism/.

26. Cooper Graham, *Leni Riefenstahl and Olympia* (Scarecrow Press, 1986), 20, 23–24, 201–2, 177. Riefenstahl https://marcuse.faculty.history.ucsbedu/classes/33dTexts/SontagFascinFascism75.htm contends that Reich's monies were only loans repaid later from box office receipts.

27. David Hinton, *The Films of Leni Riefenstahl* (Rowman & Littlefield, 2000), 47.

28. Graham, *Leni Riefenstahl and Olympia*.

29. Hinton, *The Films of Leni Riefenstahl*, 49–59, 126–29.

30. Graham, *Leni Riefenstahl and Olympia*.

31. Graham, *Leni Riefenstahl and Olympia*.

32. "Campy," *Merriam-Webster*, https://www.merriam-webster.com/dictionary/campy.

33. Sontag, "Fascinating Fascism"; Also see second quote in Susan Sontag, *Notes on "Camp"* (Picador, 2019), first two pages of unnumbered text, Kindle.

34. Richard Meran Barsam, *Filmguide to Triumph of the Will* (Indiana University Press, 1975), 27–28.

35. Barsam, *Filmguide to Triumph of the Will*, 72.

36. "Holocaust," *Merriam-Webster*, https://www.merriam-webster.com/dictionary/holocaust; Samantha Power, *"A Problem from Hell": America and the Age of Genocide* (Basic Books, 2002), 47–78.

37. *Hannah Arendt*, "Eichmann Trial," directed by Margarethe von Trotta (2012), http://www.hannaharendt-derfilm.de.

38. "The Origins of Totalitarianism," Wikipedia, accessed August 14, 2025, https://en.wikipedia.org/wiki/The_Origins_of_Totalitarianism.

39. Elisabeth Young-Bruehl, *Hannah Arendt: For Love of the World* (Yale University Press, 1982), 369.

40. Amos Elon, "Introduction," *Eichmann in Jerusalem: A Report on the Banality of Evil*, au. Hannah Arendt (Penguin Classics, 2006), 13–14, 24. Amos Elon dwells at length on an evaluation of Eichmann as shallow, brainless, or her specific word for his "banality."

41. Arendt and Elon, *Eichmann in Jerusalem*, 337.

42. Longerich, "The Final Solution Becomes a Reality," *Wannsee: The Road to the Final Solution*.

43. Arendt, *Eichmann in Jerusalem*, 9–12. See especially her portrait of Eichmann in chapters 2 and 3, as well as her four chapters on deportations, and, of course, her epilogue "Banality"; "Eichmann in Jerusalem: A Report on the Banality of Evil by Hannah Arendt," GradeSaver, accessed August 14, 2025, https://www.gradesaver.com/eichmann-in-jerusalem-a-report-on-the-banality-of-evil/study-guide/summary.

44. Arendt, *Eichmann in Jerusalem*, 330.

45. *Hannah Arendt*, directed by Margarethe von Trotta.

46. Young-Bruehl, *Hannah Arendt*, 331.

47. Young-Bruehl, *Hannah Arendt*, 342–43.

48. Young-Bruehl, *Hannah Arendt*, 347; Norman Podhoretz, "Hannah Arendt on Eichmann: A Study in the Perversity of Brilliance," *Commentary*, September 1963, https://www.commentary.org/articles/norman-podhoretz/hannah-arendt-on-eichmanna-study-in-the-perversity-of-brilliance/.

49. Young-Bruehl, *Hannah Arendt*, 347, 351–52, 356.

50. Young-Bruehl, *Hannah Arendt*, 369.

51. Cecil P. Taylor, *Good & And a Nightingale Sang . . .* (Bloomsbury, 1982), 1–72.

52. *Hannah Arendt*, directed by Margarethe von Trotta; Young-Bruehl, *Hannah Arendt*, 369. There is the kind of extreme crime that a truly evil mind can only conceive: acts so mighty that they can scar a whole nation for generations. The perpetrators managed to achieve a level of notoriety usually only afforded to Hollywood icons. See Kate Briggs, Tom Briggs, and Phil Clarke, *Extreme Evil: Taking Crime to the Next Level* (Canary Press, 2011), Kindle.

53. Young-Bruehl, *Hannah Arendt*, 370; Karl Jaspers, *The Question of German Guilt* (Fordham University Press, 2001), especially the section "Political Guilt," 55–57 and "Recapitulation," 67–75.

54. Hannah Arendt, *Eichmann in Jerusalem*, 279.

55. Young-Bruehl, *Hannah Arendt*, 372.

56. W. G. Sebald, *On the Natural History of Destruction* (Random House, 2003), 146–47.

57. Sebald, *On the Natural History of Destruction*, 148.

58. Sebald, *On the Natural History of Destruction*, 153–55.

59. Siegelman, *Maus*, 186, 195.

60. Acton, quote, www.acton.ord. For the sheer pleasure, see Siegelman, *Maus*, 195: "Count the blows, if you lose count, I'll start again!"

61. Jean Améry, *At the Mind's Limits: Contemplations by a Survivor on Auschwitz and Its Realities*, trans. Sidney and Stella P. Rosenfeld (Indiana University Press, 1980), 46, 58.

62. Améry, *At the Mind's Limits*, 72, 85, and both prefaces. (In Bernhard Schlink's novel, *The Reader*, he suggests that the second generation of Germans "were silenced by revulsion, shame, and guilt" and then asks, "Was that all there was to it now?", 104).

63. Améry, *At the Mind's Limits*, 11, 14.

64. Améry, *At the Mind's Limits*, 21, 24–25, 27–30.

65. Améry, *At the Mind's Limits*, 30.

66. Améry, *At the Mind's Limits*, 34.

67. Améry, *At the Mind's Limits*, 35.

68. Améry, *At the Mind's Limits*, 72, 75.

69. Améry, *At the Mind's Limits*, 75, 79.

70. Samuel Moyn, "The Trouble with Comparisons," *The New York Review*, May 19, 2020, https://www.nybooks.com/online/2020/05/19/the-trouble-with-comparisons/.

71. Christopher R. Browning, *Ordinary Men: Reserve Police Battalion 101 and the Final Solution in Poland* (Harper Perennial, 1992), 159–61.

72. Browning, *Ordinary Men*, 161.

73. Browning, *Ordinary Men*, 161, 162, 165, 166.

74. Browning, *Ordinary Men*, 192.

75. Browning, *Ordinary Men*, 192, where Browning quotes Goldhagen, *Hitler's Willing Executioners*, 85, 399, 443.

76. Browning, *Ordinary Men*, 192.

77. Browning, *Ordinary Men*, 192.

78. Browning, *Ordinary Men*, 193–94; Goldhagen, *Hitler's Willing Executioners*, 582, 593, 594; Young-Bruehl, *Hannah Arendt: For the Love of the World*, 370.

79. Browning, *Ordinary Men*, 197; Goldhagen, *Hitler's Willing Executioners*, 85, 399.

80. Browning, *Ordinary Men*, 199; Goldhagen, *Hitler's Willing Executioners*, 321–322.

81. "According to the census of June 16, 1933, the Jewish population of Germany, including the Saar region (which at that time was still under the administration of the League of Nations), was approximately 505,000 people out of a total population of 67 million, or somewhat less than 0.75 percent. That number represented a reduction from the estimated 523,000 Jews living in Germany in January 1933; the decrease was due in part to emigration following the Nazi takeover in January. (An estimated 37,000 Jews emigrated from Germany during 1933.)" See "Germany: Jewish Population in 1933," United States Holocaust Memorial Museum, Holocaust Encyclopedia, https://encyclopedia.ushmm.org/content/en/article/germany-jewish-population-in-1933.

82. Browning, *Ordinary Men*, 200; Goldhagen, Hitler' Willing Executioners, 322.

83. Browning, *Ordinary Men*, 200; Goldhagen, *Hitler's Willing Executioners*, 439–40, 592.

84. Browning, *Ordinary Men*, 200–201.

85. Goldhagen, *Hitler's Willing Executioners*, 386, 414.

86. Browning, *Ordinary Men*, 203; Goldhagen, *Hitler's Willing Executioners*, 386, 414.

87. Max Frankel, "Willing Executioners?" *The New York Times*, June 28, 1998, https://www.nytimes.com/1998/06/28/books/willing-executioners.html.

88. Daniel J. Goldhagen, "A Reply to My Critics: Motives, Causes, and Alibis," *The New Republic*, December 13, 1996, Library of Social Science, accessed on August 14, 2025, https://www.libraryofsocialscience.com/assets/pdf/Goldhagen-A_Reply.pdf.

89. Goldhagen, *Hitler's Willing Executioners*, 447.

90. Goldhagen, *Hitler's Willing Executioners*; 447 and fn 214.

4. STALIN'S INFAMY

1. Kevin Jacobs, "ISU Professor meets Mikhail Gorbachev," *The Daily Vidette*, September 5, 2001, 1.

2. "On 16 January 2020, Medvedev was appointed to the post of deputy chairman of the Security Council of Russia. His salary was set at 618,713 rubles (8,723.85 USD). In a July interview with *Komsomolskaya Pravda*, Medvedev said he retains 'good friendly relations' with President Putin, which was in contrast with the opinion of many circles that his departure from the role of Prime Minister was a result of a rift in the domestic policies of the two"; Dmitry Medvedev, Wikipedia, accessed August 15, 2025, https://en.wikipedia.org/wiki/Dmitry_Medvedev.

3. https://www.youtube.com/watch?v=lFWRKxk5Zwk

4. Steven L. Myers, *The New Tsar: The Rise and Reign of Vladimir Putin* (Knopf, 2015); Marvin Kalb, *Imperial Gamble: Putin, Ukraine, and the New Cold War* (Brookings Institution Press, 2015); "Russia-Ukraine War: Key Things to Know About the Conflict," *AP*, March 23, 2022, https://apnews.com/article/russia-ukraine-kyiv-europe-united-nations-nato-40dde8718d5ca5864a1f3bfdba7e9d84.

5. Nadezhda Mandelstam, *Hope Against Hope*, trans. Max Hayward (Penguin Books, 1975) 1, 11–12; Clarence Brown, "Into the Heart of Darkness: Mandelstam's Ode to Stalin," *Slavic Review* 26 (1967): 584–604; Seamus Heaney, "Osip and Nadezhda Mandelstam," *London Review of Books* 3, no. 15 (August 20, 1981), https://www.lrb.co.uk/the-paper/v03/n15/seamus-heaney/osip-and-nadezhda-mandelstam.

6. Mandelstam, *Hope Against Hope*, 190.

7. Robert Conquest, *The Great Terror: A Reassessment* (Oxford University Press, 1990), 304–5.

8. Mandelstam, *Hope Against Hope*, 190–91; translated version on 13.

9. Charles Bernstein, "Ian Probstein: Three Translations of Osip Mandelstam's 'Stalin's Epigram,'" *Jacket* 2, https://jacket2.org/commentary/ian-probstein-mandelstam-stalin-epigram.

10. Bernstein, "Ian Probstein."

11. Simon Sebag Montefiore, *Stalin: The Court of the Red Tsar* (Knopf, 2004), 96, 98.

12. Montefiore, *Stalin*, 96, 98.

13. Mandelstam, *Hope Against Hope*, 88.

14. Montefiore, *Stalin*, 133.

15. Mandelstam, *Hope Against Hope*, 1, 11–12.

16. Mandelstam, *Hope Against Hope*, 4.

17. Mandelstam, *Hope Against Hope*, 13, 15.

18. Mandelstam, *Hope Against Hope*, 18–22.

19. Mandelstam, *Hope Against Hope*, 23–24, 26, 28, 133.

20. Mandelstam, *Hope Against Hope*, 34–36.

21. Mandelstam, *Hope Against Hope*, 54–62, 73–79, 110, 112, 152.

22. Mandelstam, *Hope Against Hope*, 116, 144, 155, 159–69. Writers, as "engineers of the soul," had to show a utopian future, not what life was really like, 96.

23. Brown, Clarence, "Mandelstam:'Into the Heart of Darkness,'" *Slavic Review*, Vol 26, No. 4 (1967) pp. 584-604.

24. Mandelstam, *Hope Against Hope*, 243.

25. Brown, "Mandelstam: 'Into the Heart of Darkness," 584-604..

26. Timothy Snyder, *Bloodlands: Europe Between Hitler and Stalin* (Basic Books, 2010), 381–82, 387.

27. "Nobel Prize in Literature 1958: Announcement," The Nobel Prize, accessed August 15, 2025, https://www.nobelprize.org/prizes/literature/1958/press-release/.

28. Petra Couvée and Peter Finn, *The Zhivago Affair: The Kremlin, the CIA, and the Battle over a Forbidden Book* (Pantheon, 2014), 158–59.

29. Robert Conquest, *Courage of Genius: The Pasternak Affair* (Collins and Harvill Press, 1961), 92, 94.

30. Frances Stonor Saunders, "The Writer and the Valet," *London Review of Books* 36, no. 18 (September 25, 2014).

31. Conquest, *Courage of Genius*, 139–41.

32. Conquest, *Courage of Genius*, 142–47.

33. Conquest, *Courage of Genius*, 155.

34. Conquest, *Courage of Genius*, 159–63.

35. Conquest, *Courage of Genius*, 127.

36. Conquest, *Courage of Genius*, 164–75.

37. Conquest, *Courage of Genius*, 131–35, 161–71, 173, 176.

38. Conquest, *Courage of Genius*, 177, 180.

39. Edmund Wilson, "Doctor Life and His Guardian Angel," *The Bit Between My Teeth: A Literary Chronicle of 1950-1965* (Farrar, Straus and Giroux, 1965), 427.

40. Wilson, "Doctor Life and His Guardian Angel."

41. "Fyodor Kryukov," Wikipedia, accessed August 15, 2025, https://en.wikipedia.org/wiki/Fyodor_Kryukov.

42. "Fyodor Kryukov," Wikipedia; "A 1984 monograph by Kjetsaa and others used statistical analyses that support the view that Mikhail Sholokhov was likely the true author of *And Quiet Flows the Don*, defending the Soviet writer against persistent allegations of plagiarizing. Among his other biographies were works on Yevgeny Baratynsky, Fyodor Dostoevsky, Nikolai Gogol, Maxim Gorky, Leo Tolstoy, and Anton Chekhov"; "Geir Kjetsaa," Wikipedia, accessed August 15, 2025, https://en.wikipedia.org/wiki/Geir_Kjetsaa.

43. Alexander Solzhenitsyn, "Sholokhov and the Riddle of 'The Quiet Don,'" *TLS*, https://www.the-tls.co.uk/articles/sholokhov-and-the-riddle-of-the-quiet-don/.

44. Harrison Salisbury, "Solzhenitsyn Questions Authorship of Classic Novel by Sholokhov, a Fellow Winner of the Nobel Prize," *The New York Times*, September 1, 1974, https://www.nytimes.com/1974/09/01/archives/solzhenitsyn-questions-authorsip-of-classic-novel-by-sholokhov-a.html.

45. Harrison Salisbury, *Heroes of My Time* (Walker & Co., 1993), 35; Donald E. Davis and Eugene P. Trani, *The Reporter Who Knew Too Much: Harrison Salisbury and The New York Times* (Rowman & Littlefield, 2012), 227–29, 238.

46. Davis and Trani, *The Reporter Who Knew Too Much*, 228.

47. Israel Shenker, "Solzhenitsyn, in Harvard Speech, Terms West Weak and Cowardly," *The New York Times*, June 9, 1978, https://www.nytimes.com/1978/06/09/archives/solzhenitsyn-in-harvard-speech-terms-west-weak-and-cowardly.html.

48. Davis and Trani, *The Reporter Who Knew Too Much*, 229.

49. Davis and Trani, *The Reporter Who Knew Too Much*, 239.

50. President Richard Nixon took the opposite view and was scolded by a letter to *The New York Times*: Steven Soter, "Bombing Civilians: The World War II Lesson," *The New York Times*, May 22, 1983, https://www.nytimes.com/1983/05/22/opinion/l-bombing-civilians-the-world-war-ii-lesson-182408.html; W. J. Hennigan, "Sole Authority," *The New York Times*, March 7, 2024,
    https://www.nytimes.com/interactive/2024/03/07/opinion/nuclear-weapons-president.html.

5. ALLIED INFAMIES

1. Sebald, *On the Natural History of Destruction*, 4.

2. Randall Hansen, *Fire and Fury: The Allied Bombing of Germany, 1942-1945* (Doubleday, 2008), chap. 11.

3. Sebald, *On the Natural History of Destruction*, 10.

4. Sebald, *On the Natural History of Destruction*, 13–14.

5. Sebald, *On the Natural History of Destruction*, 13–16.

6. Sebald, *On the Natural History of Destruction*, 17.

7. Sebald, *On the Natural History of Destruction*, 19.

8. Sebald, *On the Natural History of Destruction*, 26–31.

9. Sebald, *On the Natural History of Destruction*, 33–36.

10. Sebald, *On the Natural History of Destruction*, 64–65, 97–101.

11. Siegfried Kracauer, *From Caligari to Hitler*, 81–84.

12. Sebald, *On the Natural History of Destruction*, 100–4; "Dr. Mabuse the Gambler," Wikipedia, accessed August 18, 2025, https://en.wikipedia.org/wiki/Dr._Mabuse_the_Gambler.

13. Sebald, *On the Natural History of Destruction*, 102–4.

14. Sebald, *On the Natural History of Destruction*, 115, 123, 127, and 137; Harald Jähner, "Staying Silent, Talking, Listlessly Closing Ranks," *Aftermath: Life in the Fallout of the Third Reich, 1945-1955* (Borzoi Books, 2022), 302–15.

15. Alan Cowell, "Walter Abish, Daring Writer Who Pondered Germany, Dies at 90," *The New York Times*, May 31, 2022, https://www.nytimes.com/2022/05/31/books/walter-abish-dead.html; John Updike, "Sentimental Re-Education," *The New Yorker*, February 8, 2004, https://www.newyorker.com/magazine/2004/02/16/sentimental-re-education.

16. Heinrich Boell, *The Silent Angel* (Picador, 1995).

17. "Robert Oppenheimer: I've Become death, the Destroyer of Worlds," Curiosity Pulse, YouTube, July 28, 2023, accessed August 18, 2025, https://www.youtube.com/watch?v=k_P7Y0-wgos.

18. Rod Buntzen, "This Is What It's Like to Witness a Nuclear Explosion," *The New York Times*, March 27, 2022, https://www.nytimes.com/2022/03/27/opinion/nuclear-weapons-ukraine.html. The actual quote is from the digital version of this article on March 29, 2022.

19. David C. Cassidy, *J. Robert Oppenheimer and the American Century* (Plunkett Lake Press, 2017), loc. 7,244, Kindle; "The Trinity Test," U.S. Department of Energy, The Manhattan Project: An Interactive History, https://www.osti.gov/opennet/manhattan-project-history/Events/1945/trinity.htm; John Loeffler, "The Manhattan Project and the Experiment That Changed the World," *Interesting Engineering*, November 15, 2021, https://interestingengineering.com/manhattan-project-and-the-experiment-that-changed-the-world.

20. [20] Bird and Sherwin, *American Prometheus*, 99–102 and 111 for Oppenheimer's knowledge of Sanskrit and John Donne's poetry.

21. Cassidy, *J. Robert Oppenheimer and the American Century*, loc. 6,368.

22. Cassidy, *J. Robert Oppenheimer and the American Century*, locs. 6,349, 6,383.

23. Cassidy, *J. Robert Oppenheimer and the American Century*, locs. 6,423, 6,442, 6,478.

24. Cassidy, *J. Robert Oppenheimer and the American Century*, loc. 6,515.

25. Martin J. Sherwin, *A World Destroyed: Hiroshima and Its Legacies* (Stanford University Press, 2003), 193–98.

26. Actually the US had a third bomb ready for shipment and enough nuclear material for a fourth bomb by the end of August and planned to use them immediately; Annie Jacobsen, *Nuclear Warfare: A Scenario* (Dutton, 2024), 13.

27. Sherwin, *A World Destroyed*, 200–8.

28. Sherwin, *A World Destroyed*, 208–211.

29. Sherwin, *A World Destroyed*, 214–18.

30. Bird and Sherwin, *American Prometheus*, 332–33 and 389. In December 2022 Secretary of Energy Jennifer Granholm signed an order vacating a 1954 decision by the Atomic Energy Commission to revoke the security clearance of J. Robert Oppenheimer. For the charges and Oppenheimer's defense, see the following exchange of letters between Oppenheimer and Major General K. D. Nichols, general manager, Atomic Energy Commission (AEC): J. Robert Oppenheimer, "Oppenheimer Replies," *Bulletin of the Atomic Scientists*, July 17, 2023, originally published in May 1954, https://thebulletin.org/premium/2023-07/oppenheimer-replies/; K. D. Nichols, "Nichols Presents Charges," *Bulletin of the Atomic Scientists*, July 17, 2023, originally published in May 1954, https://thebulletin.org/premium/2023-07/nichols-presents-charges/. Even Truman's hometown newspaper recently recognized how unnecessary the Hiroshima atomic bombing was: Michael Childers, "It's Time to End the Myth That the US Needed to Drop Atomic Bombs to End World War II," *The Kansas City Star*, August 19, 2024, https://www.kansascity.com/opinion/article291127690.html.

31. Alonzo L. Hamby, *Man of the People: A Life of Harry S. Truman* (Oxford University Press, 1995), 385.

32. Michiko Kakutani, *Ex-Libris: 100+ Books to Read and Reread* (Clarkson Potter, 2020), 263. Oppenheimer took this well-known line from the *Bhagavad Gita*. Christopher Nolan gave an extended look at his film *Oppenheimer* on April 25, 2023, to CinemaCon. "Nolan said, 'Like it or not, J. Robert Oppenheimer is the most important person who ever lived. He made the world we live in—for better or for worse'": Chris Lee, "We Got Our First Look at *Oppenheimer*, a Movie About 'the

Most Important Person Who Ever Lived,'" *Vulture*, 2023, https://www.vulture.com/2023/04/nolan-previews-oppenheimer-footage-at-cinemacon.html.

33. "Atomic Bombings of Hiroshima and Nagasaki," Wikipedia, accessed August 18, 2025, https://en.wikipedia.org/wiki/Atomic_bombings_of_Hiroshima_and_Nagasaki.

34. David McCullough, *Truman* (Simon & Schuster, 1992), 455.

35. McCullough, *Truman*, 461, 462.

36. George C. Kenney, *Air War in the Pacific: The Journal of General George Kenney, Commander of the Fifth U.S. Air Force* (Lulu.com, 2018), 345–46.

37. Kenney, *Air War in the Pacific*, 360, 363.

38. Kenney, *Air War in the Pacific*, 365, 367.

39. Lesley M. M. Blume, *Fallout: The Hiroshima Cover-Up and the Reporter Who Revealed It to the World* (Simon & Schuster, 2020), 3.

40. Blume, *Fallout*, 23, 31, 44, 79, 89, 97, 104, 128.

41. Robert H. Ferrell, *Harry S. Truman: A Life* (University of Missouri Press, 1994), 210.

42. Ferrell, *Harry S. Truman*, 211–14.

43. Gar Alperovitz, *The Decision to Use the Atomic Bomb: And the Architecture of an American Myth* (Knopf, 1995), 629. This book began the debate over whether the bomb should have been used at all.

44. Alperovitz, *The Decision to Use the Atomic Bomb*, 217.

45. Bird and Sherwin, *American Prometheus*, 332–33.

46. "Stimson on the Bomb," Atomic Heritage Foundation, The National Museum of Nuclear Science & History, accessed August 18, 2025, https://ahf.nuclearmuseum.org/ahf/key-documents/stimson-bomb/.

47. Katie Hafner, "The Reporter Who Revealed the Truth About Hiroshima," *The Washington Post*, August 7, 2020, https://www.washingtonpost.com/outlook/the-reporter-who-revealed-the-truth-about-hiroshima/2020/08/06/bed947e0-c7a4-11ea-a99f-3bbdffb1af38_story.html.

48. Katie Hafner, "The Reporter Who Revealed the Truth About Hiroshima; Deborah Nicholls-Lee, "'It Was the One Great Mistake in My Life:' The Letter from Einstein That Ushered in the Age of the Atomic Bomb," *BBC*, August 6, 2024, https://www.bbc.com/culture/article/20240801-it-was-the-one-great-mistake-in-my-life-the-letter-from-einstein-that-ushered-in-the-age-of-the-atomic-bomb.

49. William Langewiesche, "The Reporter Who Told the World About the Bomb," *The New York Times*, August 4, 2020, https://www.nytimes.com/2020/08/04/books/review/fallout-hiroshima-hersey-lesley-m-m-blume.html.

50. Nicholas Lemann, "John Hersey and the Art of the Fact," *The New Yorker*, April 22, 2019, https://www.newyorker.com/magazine/2019/04/29/john-hersey-and-the-art-of-fact.

51. By 1952, the US had 841 atomic weapons. The USSR had fifty: Annie Jacobsen, *Nuclear Warfare*, 16.

52. Tovah Lazaroff, "Why Has Russia's Ukraine Invasion Triggered the Nuclear War Alarm?" *The Jerusalem Post*, March 17, 2022, https://www.jpost.com/international/article-701620: "Putin has made the threat of a nuclear exchange between NATO and Russia part of his strategy from the start, experts explained."

53. Wertheim, "World War III Begins with Forgetting."

6. EXCUSING INFAMY

1. "Peace for Our Time," Wikipedia, accessed August 19, 2025, https://en.m.
   wikipedia.org/wiki/Peace_for_our_time.
2. Tim Bouverie, *Appeasement: Chamberlin, Hitler, Churchill and the Road to War* (Crown, 2019), 230, 232.
3. Bouverie, *Appeasement*, 235–37, 239, 241, 243–44.
4. Bouverie, *Appeasement*, 248–51.
5. Bouverie, *Appeasement*, 251, 254–55.
6. Bouverie, *Appeasement*, 258–59, 263.
7. Bouverie, *Appeasement*, 263, 267, 274–75.
8. Bouverie, *Appeasement*, 278.
9. Bouverie, *Appeasement*, 284.
10. Bouverie, *Appeasement*, 284.
11. Bouverie, *Appeasement*, 285.
12. Daniel Yergin, "The 'Riga/Yalta' Knot," *The New York Times*, May 23, 1977, https://www.nytimes.com/1977/05/23/archives/the-rigayalta-knot.html.
13. Charles E. Bohlen, *Witness to History, 1929-1969* (W. W. Norton & Co., 1973), 180.
14. Bohlen, *Witness to History*, 179.
15. Edward R. Stettinius Jr., *Roosevelt and the Russians: The Yalta Conference* (Doubleday, 1949), 102–11.
16. Bohlen, *Witness to History*, 181–82.
17. Bohlen, *Witness to History*, 185; Stettinius, *Roosevelt and the Russians*, 121–34.
18. Bohlen, *Witness to History*.
19. Walter Isaacson, *Kissinger: A Biography* (Simon & Schuster, 1992), 343–45.
20. Donald E. Davis and Eugene P. Trani, *Distorted Mirrors: Americans and Their Relations with Russia and China in the Twentieth Century* (Missouri University Press, 2009); "Kissinger and Zhou," Memorandum of Conversation, July 9, 1971, 4:35–11:20 p.m., with a cover memo by Lord, Document 34, National Security Agency (NSA), https://history.state.gov/historicaldocuments/frus1969-76v17/d139.
21. Henry Kissinger, *White House Years* (Little, Brown and Company, 1979), 745.
22. Kissinger, *White House Years*, 746.
23. Kissinger, *White House Years*, 747–48.
24. Kissinger, *White House Years*, 749.
25. Isaacson, *Kissinger*, 345.
26. Edgar Snow, "Interview with Mao," *The New Republic*, February 25, 1965, https://newrepublic.com/article/89494/interview-mao-tse-tung-communist-china.
27. Memorandum of Conversation, "Kissinger and Zhou."
28. Memorandum of Conversation, "Kissinger and Zhou"; Kissinger, *White House Years,* 733.
29. Memorandum of Conversation, "Kissinger and Zhou."
30. History.com Editors, "Geneva Conference to Resolve Problems in Asia Begins," *History*, November 13, 2009, updated May 28, 2025, https://www.history.com/this-day-in-history/geneva-conference-begins.
31. History.com Editors, "Geneva Conference to Resolve Problems in Asia Begins."
32. Kissinger to Nixon, "My Talks with Chou En-lai," Memorandum, July 14, 1971,

Document 40, National Security Agency (NSA), https://2001-2009.state.gov/documents/organization/72581.pdf.

33. Kissinger, *White House Years*, 754, 755.
34. Kissinger to Nixon, "My Talks with Chou En-lai."
35. Kissinger to Nixon, "My Talks with Chou En-lai"; Kissinger, *White House Years*, 750.
36. Kissinger to Nixon, "My Talks with Chou En-lai," 753–55.
37. Kissinger to Nixon, "My Talks with Chou En-lai," 755, 759–60.
38. Kissinger to Nixon, "My Talks with Chou En-lai," 763–66.
39. The Treaty of Good-Neighborliness and Friendly Cooperation Between the People's Republic of China and the Russian Federation (FCT) is a twenty-year-plus strategic treaty that was signed by the leaders of the two international powers, Jiang Zemin and Vladimir Putin, on July 16, 2001.

7. DYSTOPIAN INFAMIES

1. "2001 Sino-Russian Treaty of Friendship," Wikipedia, accessed August 19, 2025, https://en.wikipedia.org/wiki/2001_Sino-Russian_Treaty_of_Friendship.
2. "Yevgeny Zamyatin," Wikipedia, accessed August 19, 2025, https://en.wikipedia.org/wiki/Yevgeny_Zamyatin; Daniel Huttenlocher, Henry A. Kissinger, and Eric Schmidt, *The Age of AI: And our Human Future* (Little, Brown and Company, 2021).
3. Dorian Lynskey, "The 100-Year-Old Fiction That Predicted Today," *BBC*, September 2, 2021, https://www.bbc.com/culture/article/20210902-the-100-year-old-fiction-that-predicted-today.
4. Yevgeny Zamyatin, *We* (Penguin Classics, 1993), summary, loc. 77, Kindle.
5. George Orwell, "Review of *We* by E. I. Zamyatin," Orwell.ru, originally published January 4, 1946, accessed August 19, 2025, https://orwell.ru/library/reviews/zamyatin/english/e_zamy.
6. "George Orwell," Wikipedia, accessed August 19, 2025, https://en.wikipedia.org/wiki/George_Orwell.
7. Roger Ebert, "1984," February 1, 1985, RogerEbert.com, https://www.rogerebert.com/reviews/1984-1984.
8. Ray Bradbury, *Fahrenheit 451* (Simon & Schuster, 2013), 54.
9. Bradbury, *Fahrenheit 451*, 56–57.
10. Roger Ebert, "A Clockwork Orange," RogerEbert.com, February 2, 1972, https://www.rogerebert.com/reviews/a-clockwork-orange-1972; "Steven Spielberg Calls *A Clockwork Orange* the First 'Punk Rock' Movie," American Film Institute, YouTube, https://www.youtube.com/watch?v=aA6kyinCNq0.
11. Blake Morrison, "Prowled and Yowled," *London Review of Books* 44, no. 9 (May 2022), https://www.lrb.co.uk/the-paper/v44/n09/blake-morrison/prowled-and-yowled.

8. NUCLEAR INFAMY

1. Bird and Sherwin, *American Prometheus*, chaps. 34–38. The main culprit in this affair was Lewis Strauss, chairman of the Atomic Energy Commission (AEC) and a major supporter of the "super" (hydrogen bomb).

2. Giulia Heyward, "J. Robert Oppenheimer's Security Clearance Was Wrongly Revoked, Energy Secretary Says," *NPR*, December 17, 2022, https://www.npr.org/2022/12/17/1143896431/j-robert-oppenheimer-security-clearance.

3. "*Oppenheimer* (film)," Wikipedia, accessed August 21, 2025, https://en.wikipedia.org/wiki/Oppenheimer_(film).

4. Paul Nitze, *From Hiroshima to Glasnost: At the Center of Decision—A Memoir* (Grove Atlantic, 1989),
    11, 13, 16, 86; John B. Keogh to Paul Nitze, March 17, 1951, "Paul H. Nitze Papers," Library of Congress, box 29, f. 10, https://findingaids.loc.gov/exist_collections/ead3pdf/mss/2001/ms001027.pdf. Special permission is required to use Nitze's papers, and some boxes remain closed.

5. Paul Nitze, "The Development of NSC 68," *International Security* 4, no. 4 (Spring 1980): 172; Samuel F. Wells Jr., "Sounding the Tocsin: NSC 68 and the Soviet Threat," *International Security* 4, no. 2 (Fall 1979): 117. On February 8, 1950, Nitze presented a paper, "Recent Soviet Moves," published in *Foreign Relations of the United States* I (February 8, 1950): 145. He says the USSR is committed to defeating the US, not immediately, but shows a "greater willingness than in the past to undertake a course of action, including a possible use of force in local areas, which might lead to an accidental outbreak of general military conflict."

6. George F. Kennan's views, see NSC 20/4, in *Foreign Relations of the United States* I, part 2 (1948): 662, ff.

7. John Lewis Gaddis and Paul Nitze, "NSC 68 and the Soviet Threat Reconsidered," *International Security* 4, no. 4 (Spring 1980): 170–76, as found in the section by Nitze, which he calls, "The Development of NSC 68."

8. NSC-68 "portrayed the Soviet Union in a far more dismaying light than Kennan's Long Telegram." Strobe Talbott, *The Master of the Game: Paul Nitze and the Nuclear Peace* (Knopf, 1988), 55. This is explained by Robert W. Tufts: "What the paper called for can be stated in a very simple argument. The Soviet Union, we argued, would devote resources to building up an atomic capability to go with its conventional capability. This would lead to a dangerous military imbalance unless the United States developed conventional capabilities to go with its atomic capabilities. The result, if we were successful, would be a military balance favorable to our interests in successful containment . . . in time bring[ing] about the 'mellowing' NSC-68 saw as the success we looked for." Robert W. Tufts to Steven Reardon, April 14, 1989, "Paul H. Nitze Papers," Library of Congress, box 136, f. 6.

9. David Callahan, *Dangerous Capabilities: Paul Nitze and the Cold War* (HarperCollins, 1990), 510: "In these books [*Foreign Relations of the United States*], dozens of Nitze's memorandums have been reproduced, and from them it was possible to document in detail Nitze's thinking on nearly every major national security issue from 1949 through early 1953." See these documents in Department of State, *Papers Relating to the Foreign Relations of the United States, 1949–1953*.

10. This quote and the remainder are from a complete web posting of the document: https://info.publicintelligence.net/US-NSC-68.pdf. However, most of this document appears in Kenneth W. Thompson and Steven L. Rearden, *Paul H. Nitze on National Security and Arms Control* (University Press of America, 1990), 5–31. Also see *Foreign Relations of the United States* I (1950): 235–92, for the entire NSC-68 document.

11. Thompson and Rearden, *Paul H. Nitze on National Security and Arms Control*, 5–7; Tufts to Reardon, "Paul H. Nitze Papers," box 136, f. 6. Tufts comments on the language used in NSC-68: "The purple prose was intended to make as strong a case as possible for the kind of preparedness we thought was needed." Callahan claims NSC-68 saw the comparison between the US and the USSR as "between good and evil"; Callahan, *Dangerous Capabilities*, 117. Talbott also asserts that "NSC 68 stressed the offensive nature of the threat [and depicted it as] near-term and potentially military"; Talbott, *Master of the Game*, 56–57.

12. Thompson and Rearden, *Paul H. Nitze on National Security and Arms Control*, 15.

13. Thompson and Rearden, *Paul H. Nitze on National Security and Arms Control*, 10–11. Callahan says NSC-68 postulated that "there could never be true coexistence between the United States and the Soviet Union"; Callahan, *Dangerous Capabilities*, 116. In a similar analysis, Talbott says that, according to NSC-68, "peace must now be waged in much the same way that war had been waged in the past—by amassing and deploying military power"; Talbott, *Master of the Game*, 54–55.

14. See Section V. (of NSC-68), "Soviet Intentions and Capabilities," https://info.publicintelligence.net/US-NSC-68.pdf

15. Thompson and Rearden, *Paul H. Nitze on National Security and Arms Control*.

16. Thompson and Rearden, *Paul H. Nitze on National Security and Arms Control*.

17. Thompson and Rearden, *Paul H. Nitze on National Security and Arms Control*.

18. Thompson and Rearden, *Paul H. Nitze on National Security and Arms Control*.

19. Thompson and Rearden, *Paul H. Nitze on National Security and Arms Control*, 14–16; Bird and Sherwin, *American Prometheus*, 465.

20. Bird and Sherwin, *American Prometheus*, chap. 35.

21. Nitze, *From Hiroshima to Glasnost*, 97. However, Talbott does not quibble with this estimate: "Yet, on the advice of the Air Force, the authors of NSC-68 concluded that the Soviet Union already had aircraft of sufficient range to reach the United States and that by mid-1954, it would be able to drop a hundred bombs on the United States, enough to 'strike swiftly and with stealth' and 'seriously damage this country'"; Talbott, *Master of the Game*, 56.

22. Nitze, *From Hiroshima to Glasnost*, 97.

23. https://info.publicintelligence.net/US-NSC-68.pdf

24. Thompson and Rearden, *Paul H. Nitze on National Security and Arms Control*, 18.

25. Thompson and Rearden, *Paul H. Nitze on National Security and Arms Control*, 19.

26. Thompson and Rearden, *Paul H. Nitze on National Security and Arms Control*, 20.

27. Section IX. "Possible Courses of Action," Part C. "The Second Course—Isolation," https://info.publicintelligence.net/US-NSC-68.pdf

28. Section IX. https://info.publicintelligence.net/US-NSC-68.pdf

29. Thompson and Rearden, *Paul H. Nitze on National Security and Arms Control*, 24; Melvyn P. Leffler, *The Specter of Communism: The United States and the Origins of the Cold War, 1917–1953* (Hill and Wang, 1994), 93–94, 96–97, 103, 105; Melvyn P. Leffler, *A Preponderance of Power: National Security, the Truman Administration, and the Cold War* (Stanford University Press, 1992).

30. Thompson and Rearden, *Paul H. Nitze on National Security and Arms Control*, 23, 25, 31.

31. Callahan, *Dangerous Capabilities*, 120.

32. Callahan, *Dangerous Capabilities*, 122.

33. Callahan, *Dangerous Capabilities*; Wells, "Sounding the Tocsin," 135–38: Willard L. Thorp, assistant secretary for economic affairs, is cited as complaining that we are not closing the economic gap, and the US invested twice as much as the USSR in 1949 on defense: $16.2 billion compared to $9 billion. Cost estimates varied from $5.2 billion in fiscal year 1951 to $7 billion in fiscal year 1955. Cost estimates were interrupted because of the Korean War, and on September 29, 1950, the NSC adopted the study's conclusions, approved by Truman the next day. Nitze himself recalled that "Leon Keyserling consistently advocated the view that we could afford programs of the size contemplated on economic grounds and that it was largely a politico-military question as to whether we needed such programs for security"; Paul H. Nitze to Edward S. Flash Jr., May 9, 1960, "Paul H. Nitze Papers," Library of Congress, box 136, f. 6.

34. Wells, "Sounding the Tocsin," 136.

35. Callahan, *Dangerous Capabilities*, 123.

36. Wells, "Sounding the Tocsin," 139.

37. Orlando Figes, "Putin Sees Himself as Part of the History of Russia's Tsars—Including Their Imperialism," *Time*, September 30, 2022, https://time.com/6218211/vladimir-putin-russian-tsars-imperialism/; Archie Bland, "Tuesday Briefing: Trump's Statements About Putin Have Changed. Will His Actions Catch Up?" *The Guardian*, May 27, 2025, https://www.theguardian.com/world/2025/may/27/tuesday-briefing-first-edition-trump-putin-relationship.

38. Francis FitzGerald, *Way Out There in the Blue: Reagan, Star Wars and the End of the Cold War* (Simon & Schuster, 2000), 25.

39. FitzGerald, *Way Out There in the Blue*, 26.

40. Ronald Reagan, "Address to the National Association of Evangelicals," March 8, 1983, Ronald Reagan Presidential Library, https://www.reaganlibrary.gov/public/documents/card2.pdf.

41. Ronald Reagan, "Address to the National Association of Evangelicals."

42. FitzGerald, *Way Out There in the Blue*, 19.

43. Ronald Reagan, "Address to the Nation on Defense and National Security," March 23, 1983, Ronald Reagan Presidential Library, https://www.reaganlibrary.gov/archives/speech/address-nation-defense-and-national-security. President Trump has returned to this idea: W. J. Hennigan, "The Reality of Trump's Golden Dome," *The New York Times*, May 20, 2025, https://www.nytimes.com/2025/05/20/opinion/golden-dome-trump-iron-dome.html.

44. Ronald Reagan, "Address to the Nation on Defense and National Security."

45. FitzGerald, *Way Out There in the Blue*, 38.

46. Ronald Reagan, Second Inaugural Address of Ronald Reagan, January 21, 1985, Yale Law School, https://avalon.law.yale.edu/20th_century/reagan2.asp.

47. "Memorandum of Conversation," First Private Meeting, Reagan-Gorbachev Meetings in Geneva, November 19, 1985, Office of the Historian, Department of State, https://history.state.gov/historicaldocuments/frus1981-88v05/d155.

48. Lou Cannon, *President Reagan: The Role of a Lifetime* (Public Affairs, 2000), 673.

49. Cannon, *President Reagan*, 673; "Memorandum of Conversation," First Private Meeting, Reagan-Gorbachev Meetings in Geneva.

50. Cannon, *President Reagan*, 675.

51. "Memorandum of Conversation," Second Plenary Meeting, Reagan-Gorbachev Meetings in Geneva, November 19, 1985, National Security Archive, https://

nsarchive.gwu.edu/document/18253-national-security-archive-doc-01-
memorandum.

52. Jack F. Matlock Jr., *Reagan and Gorbachev: How the Cold War Ended* (Random House, 2004), 170, 172.

53. Matlock, *Reagan and Gorbachev*, 178.

54. Matlock, *Reagan and Gorbachev*, 179–80.

55. Matlock, *Reagan and Gorbachev*, 184, 186.

56. Matlock, *Reagan and Gorbachev*, 207, 211, 213, 218–19, 220–21, 222, 224.

57. Matlock, *Reagan and Gorbachev*, 232, 235.

58. Matlock, *Reagan and Gorbachev*, 238–39, 242, 245, 248–49, 251–53, 254.

59. Matlock, *Reagan and Gorbachev*, 259, 260, 269.

CONCLUSION

1. Bernhard Schlink's 1995 novel *The Reader* caused an international stir: Is there forgiveness for genocide? The 2008 film won an Oscar for Kate Winslet. She plays Hanna, the thirty-something-year-old Nazi worker at Auschwitz. Later, as her young lover, Michael (David Kross), a boy of fifteen reads to her. But she abruptly leaves him. He refuses to forgive her in the courtroom when she is tried for murder eight years later. As Roger Ebert says, "The enormity of her sin far outweighs his, but they are both guilty of allowing harm because they reject the choice to do good." Instead, I saw it as a story of forgiveness, both for Michael's unwillingness to speak up in her defense to prevent or soften the court's sentence. She got life in prison but was released after twenty years. Her crime, locking Jews in a burning church, certainly does not equal his. Yet there is sadness in her plight as a poor, uneducated, illiterate German worker who never learned to read and was recruited out of desperation for this brutal Nazi death camp. In prison she teaches herself to read while listening to Michael's posted literary tapes. A tender moment is his sole visit, offering her an apartment and a job and holding her hand. When Michael presents Hanna's prison savings after her suicide to that church's only Jewess survivor, it is unforgivingly refused. He forgives, turns Hanna's savings over to a Jewish organization, and has Hanna properly buried. Schlink teaches us forgiveness, not forgetting, however difficult; Roger Ebert, "How Your Own Secret Shame Can Create All-Devouring Evil," RogerEbert.com, December 23, 2008, https://www.rogerebert.com/reviews/the-reader-2008.

2. Isabel Kershner, "Nazi Tapes Provide a Chilling Sequel to the Eichmann Trial," *The New York Times*, July 4, 2022, https://www.nytimes.com/2022/07/04/world/middleeast/adolf-eichmann-documentary-israel.html.

3. William J. Broad and David E. Sanger, "Putin's Threats Highlight the Dangers of a New, Riskier Nuclear Era," *The New York Times*, June 1, 2022, https://www.nytimes.com/2022/06/01/us/politics/nuclear-arms-treaties.html.

4. Kenneth Clark, *Civilisation*, 321; Benjamín Labatut, *When We Cease to Understand the World*, trans. Adrian Nathan West (Anagrama, 2021), 186–88.

5. James Temperton, "'Now I Am Become Death, the Destroyer of Worlds.' The Story of Oppenheimer's Infamous Quote," *Wired*, July 21, 2023, https://www.wired.co.uk/article/manhattan-project-robert-oppenheimer; Bird and Sherwin suggest Oppenheimer became a new kind of hero, a scientific one. However, when Edward

Teller took his place, Oppenheimer could be, it seems, cast as an antihero: Bird and Sherwin, *American Prometheus*, 464–65, 556.

6. Bird and Sherwin, *American Prometheus*, 465: "The National Nuclear Security Administration maintains, refurbishes, and keeps safe the United States' more than 3,000 nuclear warheads. It also supervises the production of new nuclear warheads. It has a $25 billion annual budget and more than 57,000 employees"; Minho Kim, "Trump Fired, Then Unfired, National Nuclear Security Administration Employees. What Were Their Jobs?" *The New York Times*, February 16, 2025, https://www.nytimes.com/2025/02/16/us/politics/trump-national-nuclear-security-administration-employees-firings.html.

7. Jacqueline Rose, "Fascism Plucking the Strings," *The New York Review*, May 11, 2023, https://www.nybooks.com/articles/2023/05/11/fascism-plucking-the-strings-good-c-p-taylor/, 42. As to Biden's reactions to Putin's intimidation: "What I am talking about, I am talking to Putin. He, in fact, cannot continue with impunity to talk about the use of a tactical nuclear weapon as if that's a rational thing to do," Biden said, "before warning of dangerous consequences of such a move. The mistakes get made, the miscalculation could occur, no one could be sure what would happen, and it could end in Armageddon," he said, again stressing that a nuclear blast that kills thousands of people could lead to events barreling way out of control; Stephen Collinson, "Biden Sends a Careful But Chilling New Nuclear Message to Putin in CNN Interview," *CNN*, October 12, 2022, https://www.cnn.com/2022/10/12/politics/joe-biden-nuclear-message-putin-cnntv-analysis/index.html#:~:text=; William J. Broad, "U.S. Wires Ukraine with Radiation Sensors to Detect Nuclear Blasts," *The New York Times*, April 28, 2023, https://www.nytimes.com/2023/04/28/science/ukraine-nuclear-radiation-sensors.html; Keir A. Lieber and Daryl G. Press, "The Return of Nuclear Escalation: How America's Adversaries Have Hijacked Its Old Deterrence Strategy," October 24, 2023, *Foreign Affairs*, https://www.foreignaffairs.com/united-states/return-nuclear-escalation. They say, "The risk of nuclear escalation during a conventional war is much greater than is generally appreciated." Nuclear development continues: Aaron Mehta, "US to Introduce New Nuclear Gravity Bomb Design: B61-13," *Breaking Defense*, October 27, 2023, https://breakingdefense.com/2023/10/us-to-introduce-new-nuclear-gravity-bomb-design-b61-13/; David Szondy, "US to Build New Nuclear Gravity Bomb," *New Atlas*, October 30, 2023, https://newatlas.com/military/us-to-build-new-nuclear-gravity-bomb/.

8. François Diaz-Maurin, "Nowhere to Hide: How a Nuclear War Would Kill You—and Almost Everyone Else," *Bulletin of the Atomic Scientists*, https://thebulletin.org/2022/10/nowhere-to-hide-how-a-nuclear-war-would-kill-you-and-almost-everyone-else/; Annie M. Jacobsen, *Nuclear War: A Scenario*, "Prelude: Hell on Earth" (Dutton, 2024), xvii–xxiv. Check the diagram on xix, where a one megaton thermonuclear bomb is dropped on the Pentagon. "[Its] light superheats the surrounding air to millions of degrees, creating a massive fireball that expands at millions of miles per hour. [It] increases to a diameter of a little more than a mile (5,700 feet across), its light and heat so intense that concrete surfaces explode, metal objects melt or evaporate, stone shatters, humans instantaneously convert into combusting carbon."

9. Anton Troianovsky, "Putin Says West Risks Nuclear Conflict If It Intervenes More

in Ukraine," *The New York Times*, February 29, 2024, https://www.nytimes.com/2024/02/29/world/europe/putin-speech-ukraine-nuclear-conflict.html.

10. "Vera Lynn We'll Meet Again: Nuclear Montage," Mauser Bear, March 14, 2013, accessed August 22, 2025, YouTube, https://youtu.be/caAZ5Vm9ZtM. As of 1993, "there have been 2,121 tests done since the first in July 1945, involving 2,476 nuclear devices": "List of Nuclear Weapons Tests," Wikipedia, accessed August 22, 2025, https://en.wikipedia.org/wiki/List_of_nuclear_weapons_tests.

POSTSCRIPT

1. **Postscript**
     Edward Teller, *Memoirs: A Twentieth-Century Journey in Science and Politics* (Cambridge University Press, 2001), 190.

2. Richard Rhodes, *Dark Sun: The Making of the Hydrogen Bomb* (Simon & Schuster, 1995), 382; Richard Garwin actually designed the H-bomb: William J. Broad, "A Scientist Fighting Nuclear Armageddon Hid a 50-Year Secret," *The New York Times*, May 19, 2025, https://www.nytimes.com/2025/05/19/science/richard-garwin-hydrogen-bomb.html.

3. Rhodes, *Dark Sun*, 387–92.

4. Rhodes, *Dark Sun*, 394.

5. Sarah Scoles, "Behind the Scenes at a U.S. Factory Building: New Nuclear Bombs," *Scientific American*, December 1, 2023, https://www.scientificamerican.com/article/behind-the-scenes-at-a-u-s-factory-building-new-nuclear-bombs/.

6. Rhodes, *Dark Sun*, 395, 397, 399–400, discussing the "Main Report" of October 1949.

7. Rhodes, *Dark Sun*, 407. Two physicists of the Manhattan Project, Enrico Fermi and Israel "Isidor" Rabi, disagreed with the Super's supporters. They wrote Truman and declared the hydrogen bomb was "an evil thing." They went on to say, "The fact that [there are] no limits to the destructiveness of this weapon makes its very existence and the knowledge of its construction a danger to humanity as a whole. It is necessarily an evil thing considered in any light"; Annie Jacobsen, *Nuclear Warfare*, 17.

8. Joseph Cirincione, *Bomb Scare: The History & Future of Nuclear Weapons* (Columbia University Press, 2007), 197.

ABBREVIATIONS

ABM (Anti-Ballistic Missile)
AEC (Atomic Energy Commission)
AF (After Ford)
AI (Artificial Intelligence)
AWOL (Absent Without Leave)
BBC (British Broadcasting Corporation)
B-52 Bombers
DEF (Deutsche Emailwarenfabrik)
CC (Central Committee)
CE (Common Era)
CPSU (Communist Party of the Soviet Union)
FDR (Franklin Delano Roosevelt)
FRUS (Foreign Relations of the United States)
GAC (General Advisory Committee)
GDR (German Democratic Republic)
GENSEK (General Secretary of the Communist Party)
GRC (Government of the Republic of China)
Gulag (State Administered Camps)
INF (Intermediate-Range Nuclear Forces)
IOC (International Olympic Committee)
MAD (Mutual Assured Destruction)
NSA (National Security Agency)
NATO (North Atlantic Treaty Organization)
NCO (Non-Commissioned Officer)
NDRC (National Defense Research Committee)
NSA (National Security Agency)
NSDAP (National Socialist Workers' Party)
NSC-68 (National Security Council Paper NSC-68)
OGPU (Joint State Political Directorate)
PLA (People's Liberation Army)
PLO (Palestine Liberation Organization)
PM (Prime Minister)
PRC (People's Republic of China)
RAF (Royal Air Force)
RUR (Rossum's Universal Robots)
SA (Sturmabteilung)
SAC (Strategic Air Command)

SALT (Strategic Arms Limitation Treaty)
SS (Schutzstaffel)
SDI (Space Defense Initiative)
US (United States)
USSR (Union of Soviet Socialist Republics)

BIBLIOGRAPHY

Web References, Archival Sources, and Films: Please check the relevant chapters' footnotes. Web citations were accessed between 2020 and 2025. Films obtained from Amazon. The Henry Kissinger Papers are at the National Archives (NARA); Paul Nitze's Papers are at the Library of Congress (LC); Ronald Reagan's Papers are at the Ronald Reagan Presidential Library, Simi Valley, California.

BOOKS AND ARTICLES

Acheson, Dean. *Present at the Creation: My Years in the State Department.* W. W. Norton & Co., 1969.

Allday, Elizabeth. *Stefan Zweig: A Critical Biography.* J. P. O'Hara, 1972.

Allen, Frederick Lewis. *Only Yesterday: An Informal History of the 1920s.* Bantam Books, 1959.

Alperovitz, Gar. *The Decision to Use the Atomic Bomb.* Knopf, 1995.

Alsberg, Henry G. *Stefan and Friderike Zweig: Their Correspondence, 1912-1942.* Hastings House, 1954.

Améry, Jean. *At the Mind's Limits: Contemplations by a Survivor on Auschwitz and Its Realities.* Indiana University Press, 1980.

Angier, Carole. *Speak, Silence: In Search of W. G. Sebald.* Bloomsbury Circus, 2021.

Applebaum, Anne. *Twilight of Democracy: The Seductive Lure of Authoritarianism.* Doubleday, 2020.

Arendt, Hannah. *Eichmann in Jerusalem: A Report on the Banality of Evil.* Penguin, 2006.

Arendt, Hannah. *Men in Dark Times.* Harcourt, 1995.

Arendt, Hannah. *The Jewish Writings.* Schocken Books, 2007.

Arendt, Hannah. *Totalitarianism (Origins of Totalitarianism).* Harcourt, 1962.

Bach, Steven. *Leni: The Life and Work of Leni Riefenstahl.* Vintage Books, 2008.

Baker, Carlos. *Ernest Hemingway: A Life Story.* Charles Scribner's Sons, 1969.

Baker III, James A. *The Politics of Diplomacy: Revolution, War & Peace, 1989-1992.* Putnam, 2004.

Barsam, Richard M. *Non-Fiction Film: A Critical History.* Indiana University Press, 1992.

Barsam, Richard M. *Filmguide to Triumph of the Will.* Indiana University Press, 1975.

Benda, Julien. *The Betrayal of the Intellectuals.* Beacon Press, 1955.

Bird, Kai and Martin J. Sherwin. *American Prometheus: The Triumph and Tragedy of J. Robert Oppenheimer.* Vintage, 2006.

Blight, James A. and McGeorge Bundy, "October 27, 1962: Transcript of the Meetings of the ExComm," *International Security* 12, no. 13 (Winter 1987–1988).

Blume, Lesley M. M. *Everybody Behaves Badly: The True Story Behind Hemingway's Masterpiece, The Sun Also Rises.* Mariner Books, 2016.

Blume, Lesley M. M. *Fallout: The Hiroshima Cover-Up and the Reporter Who Revealed It to the World*. Simon & Schuster, 2020.

Boell, Heinrich. *The Silent Angel*. Picador, 1995.

Bohlen, Charles E. *Witness to History, 1929-1969*. W. W. Norton & Co., 1973.

Bouverie, Tim. *Appeasement: Chamberlain, Hitler, Churchill and the Road to War*. Tim Duggan Books, 2019.

Bradbury, Ray. *Fahrenheit 451*. Simon & Schuster, 2013.

Broad, William J. "When the Soviets Set Off the Biggest Nuclear Bomb, J.F.K. Didn't Flinch," *New York Times*, October 31, 2021. https://www.nytimes.com/2021/10/30/science/tsar-bomba-60.html.

Brokaw, Tom. *The Greatest Generation*. Random House, 1998.

Brown, Calvin S., Lillian H. Hornstein, and G. D. Percy, eds. *The Reader's Companion to World Literature*. New American Library, 1956.

Brown, Clarence. "Into the Heart of Darkness: Mandelstam's Ode to Stalin," *Slavic Review* 26, no. 4 (1967): 584–604.

Browning, Christopher R. "When Did They Decide?" *New York Review of Books* (March 24, 2022): 29–31.

Browning, Christopher R. *Ordinary Men: Reserve Police Battalion 101 and the Final Solution in Poland*. Harper Perennial, 1992.

Briggs, Kate, Tom Briggs, and Phil Clarke, *Extreme Evil: Taking Crime to the Next Level*. Canary Press, 2011. Kindle.

Buntzen, Rodney. "This Is What It's Like to Witness a Nuclear Explosion," *New York Times* and *Salt Lake Tribune*, March 27, 2022, and March 29, 2022, respectively. https://www.sltrib.com/opinion/commentary/2022/03/29/rod-buntzen-this-is-what/.

Burgess, Anthony. *A Clockwork Orange*. Heinemann, 1962.

Burgess, Anthony. *Here Comes Everybody: An Introduction to James Joyce for the Ordinary Reader*. Cambridge University Press, 2019.

Bush, George and Brent Scowcroft. *A World Transformed*. Vintage Books, 1998.

Callahan, David. *Dangerous Capabilities: Paul Nitze and the Cold War*. HarperCollins, 1990.

Cannon, Lou. *President Reagan: The Role of a Lifetime*. Public Affairs, 2000.

Čapek, Karel. *R.U.R. (Rossum's Universal Robots)*. Digireads.com, 2019.

Carruthers, Bob, ed. *Hitler's Wartime Conversations: His Personal Thoughts as Recorded by Martin Bormann*. Pen and Sword Military, 2018.

Cassidy, David C. *J. Robert Oppenheimer and the American Century*. Plunkett Lake, 2017.

Chang, Iris. *The Rape of Nanking: The Forgotten Holocaust of World War II*. Basic Books, 1997.

Cirincione, Joseph. *Bomb Scare: The History & Future of Nuclear Weapons*. Colombia University Press, 2007.

Claeys, Gregory. *Dystopia: A Natural History*. Oxford University Press, 2017.

Clark, Kenneth. *Civilisation*. Harper & Row, 1969.

Conquest, Robert. *Courage of Genius: The Pasternak Affair*. Collins and Harvill Press, 1961.

Conquest, Robert. *The Great Terror: A Reassessment*. Oxford University Press, 1990.

Couvee, Petra and Peter Finn. *The Zhivago Affair: The Kremlin, the CIA, and the Battle Over a Forbidden Book*. Pantheon Books, 2014.

Cowell, Alan. "Walter Abish, Daring Writer Who Pondered Germany, Dies at 90." *New York Times*, May 31, 2022. https://www.nytimes.com/2022/05/31/books/walter-abish-dead.html.

Davis, Darien J. and Oliver Marshall, eds. *Stefan and Lotte Zweig's South American Letters.* Continuum International Publishing Group, 2010.

Davis, Donald E. and Eugene P. Trani. *Distorted Mirrors: Americans and Their Relations with Russia and China in the Twentieth Century.* University of Missouri Press, 2009.

Davis, Donald E. and Eugene P. Trani. *The Reporter Who Knew Too Much: Harrison Salisbury and the New York Times.* Rowman & Littlefield, 2012.

Department of State. *Papers Relating to the Foreign Relations of the United States, 1948: UN-General* I, part 2. Government Printing Office (GPO), 1976. Also see *1948-1949: The Far East-China* 7–9 and 1950. *National Security Affairs-Foreign Economic Policy.* Government Printing Office, 1973–1977.

Dick, Kay. *They: A Sequence of Unease.* McNally Editions, 2022.

Dines, Alberto, Kristina Michahelles, et al. *A Network of Friends: Stefan Zweig, His Last Address Book, 1940-1942*, edited by Israel Beloch. Memoria Brasil, 2014.

Eliot, T. S. *The Waste Land and Other Poems.* Harvest Books, 1962.

Evans, Richard J. *Hitler's People: The Faces of the Third Reich.* Penguin, 2024.

Ferrell, Robert H. *Harry S. Truman: A Life.* University of Missouri, 1994.

FitzGerald, Francis. *Way Out There in the Blue: Reagan, Star Wars and the End of the Cold War.* Simon & Schuster, 2000.

Frankel, Max, "Willing Executioners?" *New York Times*, June 28, 1998. https://www.nytimes.com/1998/06/28/books/willing-executioners.html.

Gaddis, John Lewis and Paul Nitze. "NSC 68 and the Soviet Threat Reconsidered." *International Security* 4, no. 4 (Spring 1980).

Gay, Peter. *Modernism: The Lure of Heresy.* W. W. Norton & Co., 2007.

Gay, Peter. *Weimar Culture: The Outsider as Insider.* Harper Torchbooks, 1968.

Gedye, G. E. R. *Fallen Bastions.* Victor Gollancz, 1939.

Gessen, Masha. *The Man Without a Face: The Unlikely Rise of Vladimir Putin.* Riverhead Books, 2012.

Goldhagen, Daniel Jonah. *Hitler's Willing Executioners: Ordinary Germans and the Holocaust.* Vintage Books, 1997.

Goldhagen, Daniel Jonah. "A Reply to My Critics: Motives, Causes, and Alibis." *The New Republic.* December 13, 1996. https://www.libraryofsocialscience.com/assets/pdf/Goldhagen-A_Reply.pdf.

Graham, Cooper C. *Leni Riefenstahl and Olympia.* Scarecrow Press, 1986.

Graves, Robert. *Good-Bye to All That.* Knopf, 2018.

Hamby, Alonzo L. *Man of the People: A Life of Harry S. Truman.* Oxford University Press, 1995.

Hansen, Randall. *Fire and Fury: The Allied Bombing of Germany, 1942-1945.* Doubleday, 2008.

Haulsee, W. M. and F. G. Howe. *Soldiers of the Great War* Vols. 1–3. Soldiers Record Publishing Association, 1920.

Heaney, Seamus. "Osip and Nadezhda Mandelstam." *London Review of Books* 3, no. 5 (August 20, 1981).

Hemingway, Ernest. *A Farewell to Arms*. Charles Scribner's Sons, 1929.

Hemingway, Ernest. *A Moveable Feast*. Charles Scribner's and Sons, 1990.

Hemingway, Ernest. *The Sun Also Rises*. Simon & Schuster, 1926.

Hennigan, W. J., et al. "At the Brink: A Series About the Threat of Nuclear Weapons in an Unstable World," *New York Times*. June 20 and August 6, 2024. https://www.nytimes.com/interactive/2024/10/10/opinion/nuclear-weapons-nytimes.html.

Hersey, John. *Hiroshima*. Vintage Books, 1989.

Hinton, David B. *The Films of Leni Riefenstahl*. Rowman & Littlefield, 2000.

Hitler, Adolf. *Mein Kampf/My Struggle*. White Wolf, 1925–1926.

Hobsbawm, Eric. *The Age of Extremes: The Short Twentieth Century, 1914-1991*. Abacus, 1994.

Hovey, Graham. "Gov. Harriman—Salty Views on SALT, Etc." *New York Times*, October 9, 1977.   https://www.nytimes.com/1977/10/09/archives/gov-harriman-salty-views-on-salt-etc-opportunity-to-improve.html.

Howie, Guy. "Dr. Strangelove Explained: The Truth Behind Stanley Kubrick's Comedy Ending." *Far Out*, May 4, 2024. https://faroutmagazine.co.uk/explaining-ending-stanley-kubrick-dr-strangelove/.

Hoyt, Edwin P. *Inferno: The Fire Bombing of Japan, March 9–August 15, 1945*. Madison Books, 2000.

Hughes, H. Stuart. *Oswald Spengler: A Critical Estimate*. Transaction Publishers, 1992.

Huttenlocher, Daniel, Henry A. Kissinger, and Eric Schmidt. *The Age of AI and Our Human Future*. Little, Brown and Company, 2021.

Huxley, Aldous. *Brave New World*. Harper Perennial, 2006.

Isaacson, Walter. *Einstein: His Life and Universe*. Simon & Shuster, 2007.

Isaacson, Walter. *Kissinger: A Biography*. Simon & Schuster, 2005.

Jacobs, Kevin. "ISU Professor Meets Gorbachev." *The Daily Vidette*, September 5, 2001.

Jacobsen, Annie M. *Nuclear War: A Scenario*. Dutton, 2024.

Jahner, Harald. *Aftermath: Life in the Fallout of the Third Reich, 1945-1955*. Borzoi Books, 2022.

Jaspers, Karl. *The Question of German Guilt*. Fordham University Press, 2001.

Johnson, Lyndon. *The Vantage Point: Perspectives of the Presidency, 1963–1969*. Holt, Rinehart and Winston, 1971.

Joyce, James. *Ulysses*. Vintage Books, 1986.

Kakutani, Michiko. *Ex-Libris:100+ Books to Read and Reread*. Clarkson Potter, 2020.

Kalb, Marvin. *Imperial Gamble: Putin, Ukraine, and the New Cold War*. Brookings Institution Press, 2015.

Keneally, Thomas. *Schindler's List*. Touchstone Books, 1982.

Kenney, George C. *Air War in the Pacific: The Journal of General George Kenney, Commander of the Fifth U.S. Air Force*. Duell, Sloan and Pearce, 1949.

Kennedy, Robert F. *Thirteen Days: A Memoir of the Cuban Missile Crisis*. W. W. Norton & Co., 1969.

Kershaw, Ian. *Hitler: A Biography*. W. W. Norton & Co., 2007.

Kissinger, Henry A. *White House Years*. Little, Brown and Company, 1979.

Kissinger, Henry A. *Years of Upheaval*. Little, Brown and Company, 1982.

Kitchen, Martin. *Speer: Hitler's Architect*. Yale University Press, 2015.

Kracauer, Siegfried. *From Caligari to Hitler: A Psychological History of the German Film*. Princeton University Press, 1947.

Lane, Anthony. "The Shocks and Aftershocks of 'The Waste Land.'" *The New Yorker*, September 26, 2022.

Langer, William L. *An Encyclopedia of World History*. Houghton Mifflin Company, 1968.

Leffler, Melvin P. *A Preponderance of Power: National Security, the Truman Administration, and the Cold War*. Stanford University Press, 1992.

Leffler, Melvin P. *The Specter of Communism: The United States and the Origins of the Cold War*. Hill and Wang, 1994.

Lemann, Nicholas. "John Hersey and the Art of the Fact." *The New Yorker*, April 22, 2019. https://www.newyorker.com/magazine/2019/04/29/john-hersey-and-the-art-of-fact.

Lipstadt, Deborah E. *The Eichmann Trial*. Schocken, 2011.

Longerich, Peter with Jeremy Noakes and Lesley Sharpe. *Wannsee: The Road to the Final Solution*. Oxford University Press, 2021.

Lynskey, Dorian. *The Ministry of Truth: The Biography of George Orwell's 1984*. Doubleday, 2019.

MacMillan, Margaret. *War: How Conflict Shaped Us*. Random House, 2020; *The New York Review*, November 29, 2020.

Mallac, Guy de. *Boris Pasternak: His Life and Art*. University of Oklahoma Press, 1981.

Mandelstam, Nadezhda. *Hope Abandoned: A Memoir*. Translated by Max Hayward. Penguin Books, 1976.

Mandelstam, Nadezhda. *Hope Against Hope: A Memoir*. Translated by Max Hayward. Penguin books, 1975.

Mann, James. *About Face: A History of America's Curious Relationship with China, from Nixon to Clinton*. Vintage Books, 1998.

Matlock, Jack F. *Reagan and Gorbachev: How the Cold War Ended*. Random House, 2004.

Matuschek, Oliver. *Three Lives: A Biography of Stefan Zweig*. Pushkin Press, 2011.

Maytum, Matt. "Grave New World." *Total Film*, no. 332 (December 15, 2022).

McCarthy, Cormac. *The Road*. Vintage International, 2006.

McCullough, David. *Truman*. Simon & Schuster, 1992.

Montefiore, Simon Sebag. *Stalin: The Court of the Red Tsar*. Knopf, 2004.

Morand, Paul. *1900 A.D.* William Farquhar Payson, 1931.

Moser, Benjamin. *Sontag: Her Life and Work*. HarperCollins, 2019.

Moyn, Samuel. "The Trouble with Comparisons." *The New York Review*, May 19, 2020. https://www.nybooks.com/online/2020/05/19/the-trouble-with-comparisons/.

Myers, Steven. *The New Tsar: The Rise and Reign of Vladimir Putin*. Knopf, 2015.

Nabokov, Vladimir. *Lectures on Literature*. Harcourt Brace Jovanovich, 1980.

Napa Daily Register, September 17, 1921.

Nazaroff, Alexander. "Fouche, Whom Napoleon Called 'The Perfect Traitor.'" *New York Times*, August 17, 1930. https://www.nytimes.com/1930/08/17/archives/fouche-whom-napoleon-called-the-perfect-traitor-stefan-zweig-blows.html.

Nitze, Paul. *From Hiroshima to Glasnost: At the Center of Decision—A Memoir.* Grove Atlantic, 1989.

Nitze, Paul. "Limited Wars or Massive Retaliation?" *The Reporter* 17, no. 3 (September 5, 1957).

Nitze, Paul. "The Development of NSC 68." *International Security* 4, no. 4 (Spring 1980).

Nixon, Richard M. *RM: The Memoirs of Richard Nixon.* Grosset & Dunlap, 1978.

O'Donnell, James. "The Devil's Architect." *New York Times,* October 26, 1969. https://www.nytimes.com/1969/10/26/archives/the-devils-architect-one-seldom-recognizes-the-devil-when-he-puts.html.

Orwell, George. *1984.* Harcourt, 2003.

Orwell, George. *Animal Farm.* Harcourt, 2003.

Pasternak, Boris. *Doctor Zhivago.* Pantheon Books, 1958.

Paxton, Robert O. *The Anatomy of Fascism.* Vintage Books, 2005.

Power, Samantha. *"A Problem from Hell:" America and the Age of Genocide.* Basic Books, 2002.

Prater, D. A. *European of Yesterday: A Biography of Stefan Zweig.* Oxford University Press, 1972.

Prochnik, George. *The Impossible Exile: Stefan Zweig at the End of the World.* Other Press, 2014.

Rearden, Steven L., and Kenneth W. Thompson. *Paul H. Nitze on National Security and Arms Control.* University Press of America, 1990.

Rhodes, Richard. *Dark Sun: The Making of the Hydrogen Bomb.* Simon & Schuster, 1995.

Rhodes, Richard. *The Making of the Atomic Bomb.* Simon & Schuster, 1986.

Riefenstahl, Leni. *Leni Riefenstahl: A Memoir.* St. Martin's Press, 1993.

Riefenstahl, Leni. *Behind the Scenes of the National Party Convention Film.* International Historic Films, 2010.

Rose, Jacqueline. "Fascism Plucking the Strings." *The New York Review* (May 11, 2023): 40–42.

Sagan, Carl. *The Demon-Haunted World: Science as a Candle in the Dark.* Ballantine Books, 1996.

Salisbury, Harrison E. *Behind the Lines-Hanoi, December 23, 1966-January 7, 1967.* Harper & Row, 1967.

Salisbury, Harrison E. "Solzhenitsyn Questions Authorship of Classic Novel by Sholokhov, A Fellow Winner of the Nobel Prize." *New York Times,* September 1, 1974. https://www.nytimes.com/1974/09/01/archives/solzhenitsyn-questions-authorsip-of-classic-novel-by-sholokhov-a.html.

Salisbury, Harrison, E. *Heroes of My Time.* Walker & Co., 1993.

Salisbury, Harrison E. *The New Emperors: China in the Era of Mao and Deng.* Little, Brown and Company, 1992.

Salisbury, Harrison E. *Tiananmen Diary: Thirteen Days in June.* Little, Brown and Company, 1989.

Salisbury, Harrison E. *To Peking-and Beyond: A Report on the New Asia.* Quadrangle, 1973.

Saunders, Francis Stonor. "The Writer and the Valet." *London Review of Books* 36, no. 18 (September 25, 2014).

Schlesinger Jr., Arthur M. *A Thousand Days: John F. Kennedy in the White House.* Houghton Mifflin, 1965.

Schlink, Bernhard. *The Reader.* Vintage International, 1997.

Sebald, W. G. *On the Natural History of Destruction.* Random House, 2003.

Seymour, Miranda. *Robert Graves: Life on the Edge.* Henry Holt & Co., 1995.

Sherwin, Martin J. *A World Destroyed: Hiroshima and Its Legacies.* Stanford University Press, 2003.

Snyder, Timothy. *Bloodlands: Europe Between Hitler and Stalin.* Basic Books, 2010.

Snyder, Timothy. *On Tyranny: Twenty Lessons from the Twentieth Century.* Tim Duggan Books, 2017.

Solzhenitsyn, Alexander. *Nobel Prize Lecture* (English and Russian Edition). Farrar, Straus and Giroux, 1972.

Sontag, Susan. "Fashionable Fascism." *The New York Review,* February 6, 1975. https://www.nybooks.com/articles/1975/02/06/fascinating-fascism/.

Sontag, Susan. *Notes on "Camp."* Picador, 2019. Kindle.

Soter, Steven. "Bombing Civilians: The World War II Lesson." *New York Times,* May 22, 1983. https://www.nytimes.com/1983/05/22/opinion/l-bombing-civilians-the-world-war-ii-lesson-182408.html.

Speer, Albert. *Inside the Third Reich.* Macmillan, 1970.

Spengler, Oswald. *The Decline of the West.* George Allen & Unwin Ltd., 1926.

Spiegelman, Art. *Maus: A Survivor's Tale.* Pantheon Books, 2011.

Stettinius Jr., Edward R. *Roosevelt and the Russians: The Yalta Conference.* Doubleday, 1949.

Strauss, Richard and Stefan Zweig. Translated by Max Knight. *A Confidential Matter: The Letters of Richard Strauss and Stefan Zweig, 1931-1935.* University of California Press, 1977.

Stuckey, W. J. "*The Sun Also Rises* on Its Own Ground." *The Journal of Narrative Technique* 6, no. 3 (Fall 1976): 224–32.

Talbott, Strobe. *The Master of the Game: Paul Nitze and the Nuclear Peace.* Knopf, 1988.

Taylor, C. P., *Good & A Nightingale Sang . . .* Bloomsbury, 1982.

Teller, Edward. *Memoirs: A Twentieth-Century Journey in Science and Politics.* Cambridge University Press, 2001.

Trimborn, Jurgen. *Leni Riefenstahl: A Life.* Farrar, Straus and Giroux, 2007.

Troianovsky, Anton. "Putin Says West Risks Nuclear Conflict If It Intervenes More in Ukraine." *New York Times,* February 29, 2024. https://www.nytimes.com/2024/02/29/world/europe/putin-speech-ukraine-nuclear-conflict.html.

Tuchman, Barbara. *The Proud Tower: A Portrait of the World Before the War: 1890–1914.* Macmillan, 1996.

Turner, Jenny. "We Must Think!" *London Review of Books* 43, no. 21 (November 4, 2021): 15–21. https://www.lrb.co.uk/the-paper/v43/n21/jenny-turner/we-must-think.

Updike, John. "Sentimental Re-Education." *The New Yorker,* February 8, 2004. https://www.newyorker.com/magazine/2004/02/16/sentimental-re-education.

"Valentin Zorin Criticizes Campaign to Poison U.S.-USSR Relations." *International Affairs.* October 21, 1978.

Wells Jr., Samuel F. "Sounding the Tocsin: NSC 68 and the Soviet Threat." *International Security* 4, no. 2 (Fall 1979).

Wertheim, Stephen. "World War III Begins with Forgetting." *New York Times*, December 2, 2022. https://www.nytimes.com/2022/12/02/opinion/america-world-war-iii.html.

Wilson, Edmund. "Doctor Life and His Guardian Angel." *The Bit Between My Teeth: A Literary Chronicle of 1950-1965*. Farrar, Straus and Giroux, 1965.

Woolf, Virginia. "Modern Fiction." *The Essays of Virginia Woolf Volume 4: 1925–1928*. The Hogarth Press, 1984.

Yergin, Daniel. "The Riga/Yalta Knot." *New York Times*, May 23, 1977. https://www.nytimes.com/1977/05/23/archives/the-rigayalta-knot.html.

Young-Bruehl, Elisabeth. *Hannah Arendt: For Love of the World*. Yale University Press, 1982.

Zamyatin, Yevgeny, *We*. Translated by S. Viatchanin Translation. New York Concept Book, 1946.

Zweig, Friderike. *Married to Stefan Zweig*. Plunkett Lake Press, 2012.

Zweig, Stefan. *The World of Yesterday*. Plunkett Lake Press, 2011.

INDEX

Note: References followed by "n" refer to endnotes.

ACKNOWLEDGMENTS

The author wishes to express his thanks to Torchflame Books for their encouragement, careful editing, and layout of this book.

ABOUT THE AUTHOR

Don Davis earned his bachelor's degree from San Francisco State University. He attended graduate school at Indiana University, where he obtained his MA and PhD, focusing on Russian history. Davis wrote his dissertation on Vladimir Lenin and theories of warfare, especially those of Clausewitz.

Davis edited, *No East or West: The Memoirs of Paul B. Anderson*. He co-authored *The First Cold War: The Legacy of Woodrow Wilson in U.S. - Soviet Relations* with Eugene P. Trani, an American diplomatic historian. Additionally, they published *Distorted Mirrors*, *The Reporter Who Knew Too Much*, and *A Bridge to Somewhere*. In 2004, Davis retired from Illinois State University after forty years of teaching courses in European, Russian, and Soviet history. He was one of the university's longest-serving faculty members in the history department. He is a member of the American Association for Slavic, East European, and Eurasian Studies (AASEEES) and has published in its journal, the Slavic Review ("The American YMCA and the Russian Revolution" vol. 33, no. 3, pp. 469–91) as well as in many other scholarly journals and anthologies. His personal archive, the "Davis Collection," is at the Hoover Institution, Stanford University.

Davis is married to Mary Davis, a retired elementary school teacher and director of SHOW BUS, a multi-county rural transport system. They have a son and a daughter.

Visit his website, newinfamy.com, or connect with him on social media.

THANK YOU!

Thank you for reading! If you enjoyed this book, please leave a review on Amazon, Goodreads, BookBub, The Story Graph, or anywhere else you like to track your recent reads. Alternatively, you could post online or tell a friend about it. This helps our authors more than you may know.

   - The Team at Torchflame Books

Follow Torchflame Books for news about our authors and upcoming new releases @TorchflameBooks.

Find your next great read at www.torchflamebooks.com.